The Best of
Beachcomber

Books by J. B. Morton

Beachcomber Selections

Mr Thake
Mr Thake Again
By The Way
Morton's Folly
The Adventures of Mr Thake
Mr Thake and the Ladies
Stuff and Nonsense
Gallimaufry
Sideways through Borneo
A Diet of Thistles
A Bonfire of Weeds
I Do Not Think So
Fool's Paradise
Captain Foulenough & Company
Here and Now
The Misadventures of Dr Strabismus
The Tibetan Venus
Merry-Go-Round

History & Biography

The Bastille Falls
The Dauphin
Saint-Just
Brumaire
Camille Desmoulins
Marshal Ney
Sobieski
Hilaire Belloc: a Memoir
St Thérèse of Lisieux

Short Stories

Springtime

Politics

The New Ireland

Essays

Enchanter's Nightshade
Penny Royai
Old Man's Beard
Vagabondage

Novels

The Barber of Putney
Skylighters
Drink up, Gentlemen
The Cow jumped over the Moon
Hag's Harvest
The Gascon
Maladetta

Travel

Pyrenean

Parodies

Gorgeous Poetry
Tally-Ho!

Comic Verse

Who's Who in the Zoo
1933, and Still Going Wrong
The Dancing Cabman

Fairy Tales

The Death of the Dragon

The Best of
Beachcomber

─────────◆─────────

J. B. MORTON

─────────◆─────────

Selected and introduced by
Michael Frayn

Mandarin

A Mandarin Paperback
THE BEST OF BEACHCOMBER

First published in Great Britain 1963
by William Heinemann Ltd
This edition published 1991
by Mandarin Paperbacks
Michelin House, 81 Fulham Road, London SW3 6RB

Mandarin is an imprint of the Octopus Publishing Group,
a division of Reed International Books Limited

Copyright © J. B. Morton 1963
Introduction © William Heinemann Ltd 1963

A CIP catalogue record for this title
is available from the British Library
ISBN 0 7493 0962 8

Printed and bound in Great Britain
by Cox & Wyman Ltd, Reading, Berks

Introduction

by Michael Frayn

BEACHCOMBER was one of the funniest modern English humorists. Some (including a number of the other humorists) would say the funniest. But his humour is dispersed majestically through eighteen volumes, many of them now out of print, and there must be a lot of people in my own generation who have never had the chance to get their hands on the stuff. It seems an unnecessary deprivation.

'Beachcomber' was the pen-name of J. B. Morton, who died in 1979, and who each day for nearly forty years wrote the 'By the Way' column in the *Daily Express*. It would be wrong to say that Morton invented the funny column. I suppose there have been funny columns in newspapers since newspapers began, and Morton always claimed that he was indebted to his lifelong friend D. B. Wyndham Lewis, who had been Beachcomber before him, and who subsequently became Timothy Shy, the humorous columnist of the *News Chronicle*. Between them, at any rate, they introduced to newspapers the superb anarchy of the English nonsense-writing tradition, the brief, devastating parody, and the permanent staff of characters. In an age when most newspapers were either cosy or pompous they used them to mount a sustained and outrageous lampoon.

Some of Beachcomber's characters have become more famous than their creator – Captain Foulenough, for example, Dr Smart-Allick of Narkover, Mr Justice Cocklecarrot, and Dr Strabismus (Whom God Preserve) of Utrecht. Like Sherlock Holmes, Svengali, Billy Bunter, Jeeves, Frankenstein, and Robinson Crusoe, they have outstripped the page and become members of that heterogeneous collection of public heroes who make up English mythology. One day some diligent pedant will search the records to discover whether the human race ever did suffer some terrible judicial cataclysm of the sort recorded in the great courtroom sagas of Mr Justice Cocklecarrot and the twelve red-bearded dwarfs who plagued him. The dull respectability of some future age will be sadly compared against the heroic lack of tone with which the outrageous Captain Foulenough pursued his campaign of cordial pillage against the rest of society. The various accounts extant of where he acquired his captaincy will be critically compared. Parallels will be drawn between the encounter of Hector and Achilles and the epic clash of cards between Foulenough and Smart-Allick, on that famous day when the two mighty rogues finally met, and the plains around Narkover rang from dusk till dawn with the thud of ace of spades upon ace of spades.

One of Morton's great advantages is his superb talent for inventing funny names. His only modern peer, to my knowledge, is Joseph Heller. When Mr Heller's *Catch-22* came out, some of the reviewers turned up their noses at the characters' names (like Milo Minderbinder, Lieutenant Scheisskopf, and Major Major Major). Perhaps one day the refined sensibility that can be jarred by 'Milo Minderbinder' will be canalised in a great purity drive to rechristen all the characters in English comic literature, from Ben Jonson to Sheridan, with names like Roscoe and J. B. To my simple mind, the world seems a nicer place since someone decorated it with a moronic drill fetishist called Scheisskopf, and since Beachcomber invented a bishop called Dr Urcher, a Wagnerian prima donna called Rustiguzzi, and two imperial potentates called the Clam of Chowdah and the M'Babwa of M'Gonkawiwi. I suspect the critics are annoyed because it looks so simple that they could do it themselves. As a matter of fact it isn't, and they couldn't. You try it.

All humorists live to some extent by cultivating their individuality. But I think Morton's individuality just grew wild, and a staggering plant it is. He really didn't care a damn what the readers thought of his opinions. I don't believe he even cared very much whether they thought he was funny (a noble detachment that every other humorist in the business would give 10 per cent of his royalties to share). He frequently stops whatever he is doing in the column to insult them, elaborately and colourfully, or to turn savagely on poor Prodnose, the plain, reasonable oaf who interrupts his creator's wilder flights because he cannot understand 'where all this is leading to'. Often he abruptly turns aside to recount an episode from the Chanson de Roland or the history of revolutionary France, or to recall, as if it were a legend from a lost heroic past, a walking tour of his youth in the Auvergne or the Pyrenees. There is something heroic, too, about the sheer scale of his literary output – not only eighteen volumes of collected pieces, culled from a column written six days a week for forty years – but *another* twenty-nine books as well (mainly novels and French history). He makes me feel rather delicate – a delicate member of a delicate generation.

His own generation was the one that came to its prime in the two decades between the wars, and his writing, scornful though it is of the times, evokes in me an odd nostalgia for that silly, shallow, bouncy, industrious, cruel age. He was born in 1893, the son of Edward Morton, journalist and dramatist. He was educated at Harrow, spent one not very successful year at Oxford, and during the First World War served in France, both in the ranks and as an officer. He was for a time in Intelligence – in M.I.7b, a department which sounds as though he had invented it. In 1920 he joined the *Sunday Express* as resident poet, adorning the paper's leader-page with slim verses and stories about fairyland, and after two years of that moved to the reporters' room of the *Daily Express*. He became Beachcomber in 1924.

Morton was a Catholic convert. He was received into the Church in 1922, and came to know Hilaire Belloc through his friendship with Belloc's son Peter. I think one would know he was a Catholic from reading him, even without any direct reference. There is an echo in his work of that tone of voice, hard to describe yet curiously distinctive, which sounds through a great many of the English Catholic writers. Perhaps it is a certain intellectual perverseness. I find it can become irritating, particularly when it takes the form, as it does, not in Morton, but in Chesterton and Graham Greene, of a galloping obsession with paradox. In Morton you can just catch a suggestion of it, like the salt in porridge, and I suppose, like the porridge, his work wouldn't be the same without it.

I greatly enjoyed reading the eighteen holy books of Beachcomber to make this selection. I even enjoyed a lot of the blurbs. There is something about a blurb-writer paying his respects to a funny book which puts one in mind of a short-sighted lord mayor raising his hat to a hippopotamus. Many of the dust-jacketeers gloss Morton as a satirist. They mean it as a compliment, in the very puritan belief that satire is the highest form of humour because it does you good. But I don't think that Morton was at his best as a satirist (though I may be prejudiced by the unbridgeable chasm between his views and mine). I think he was a cut above it. A satirist wants to make you laugh as a way of persuading you to an opinion. Morton, at his best, wanted to make you laugh just for the pleasure of laughing. The opinion is merely the means to an end; the pleasure of laughing is a good in itself.

Anyway, the important thing is that J. B. Morton was one of the great English humorists of the century, and that here in this book is a selection of some of his funniest stuff. I suppose I'm going to spend the rest of my life being complained to by people whose favourite bits of Strabismus or Cocklecarrot I have overlooked. Well, *I'm* happy; all my favourite bits are in – Big White Carstairs, the A. A. Milne parodies, the collected wit of Stultitia Cabstanleigh, 'The Thunderbolt' . . . I hope you enjoy them, too, and I hope that this collection will convey some of the flavour of the extraordinary sideshow at the literary fair that Morton sustained in his column for the greater part of half a century.

The Best of
Beachcomber

Chapter 1

The Case of the
Twelve Red-Bearded Dwarfs

MR JUSTICE COCKLECARROT began the hearing of a very curious case yesterday. A Mrs Tasker is accused of continually ringing the doorbell of a Mrs Renton, and then, when the door is opened, pushing a dozen red-bearded dwarfs into the hall and leaving them there.

For some weeks Mrs Renton had protested by letter and by telephone to Mrs Tasker, but one day she waited in the hall and caught Mrs Tasker in the act of pushing the dwarfs into the hall. Mrs Renton questioned them, and their leader said, 'We know nothing about it. It's just that this Mrs Tasker pays us a shilling each every time she pushes us into your hall.'

'But why does she do it?' asked Mrs Renton.

'That's what we don't know,' said the spokesman of the little men.

MR TINKLEBURY SNAPDRIVER *(for the plaintiff)*: Now Mrs – er – Tasker, where were you on the afternoon of 26th January? Think carefully before you answer.

MRS TASKER: Which year?

MR SNAPDRIVER: What?

MRS TASKER: Which year?

Mr Snapdriver appeared disconcerted. He consulted his notes and one or two books. Then he whispered to a clerk and consulted another barrister.

MR JUSTICE COCKLECARROT: Well, Mr Snapdriver, which year?

MR SNAPDRIVER: Am I bound to answer that question, m'lud?

COCKLECARROT: It was you who asked it, you know. *(Roars of laughter in court.)*

MRS TASKER: M'lud, I think I can tell him the year. It was 1937.

COCKLECARROT: Why, that's this year. What then?

MR SNAPDRIVER: Where were you, Mrs Tasker, on the morning of 26th January 1937?

MRS TASKER: I called at Mrs Renton's house to leave a dozen red-bearded dwarfs with her.

COCKLECARROT: Had she ordered them? *(Howls of laughter.)*

The court then rose.

This extraordinary case was continued yesterday. The first sensation came when Mrs Tasker submitted a list of over seven thousand people whom she wished to call as witnesses. Counsel for the defence, Mr Bastin Hermitage, was about to read the list when Mr Justice Cocklecarrot intervened.

MR JUSTICE COCKLECARROT: Is it necessary to call all these people?

MR HERMITAGE: I believe so, m'lud.

MR JUSTICE COCKLECARROT: But surely they cannot all be connected with the case. For instance, I see here the name of a Cabinet Minister. Also a well-known film actor. What have they to do with these dwarfs?

MR HERMITAGE: I understand that some of these dwarfs claim to be related to the Cabinet Minister.

MR JUSTICE COCKLECARROT: And that distinguished sailor Rear-Admiral Sir Ewart Hodgson?

MR HERMITAGE: I understand he knows one of the dwarfs.

(Sensation in court.)

After lunch there was a brisk passage when Mr Snapdriver, for the prosecution, threatened to call more than twelve thousand witnesses if counsel for the defence called seven thousand.

COCKLECARROT: Come, come, you two. This is becoming farcical.

HERMITAGE: It is a bluff, m'lud. He hasn't got twelve thousand witnesses.

SNAPDRIVER: Here is my list, m'lud.

COCKLECARROT: Yum. I see it includes two Cabinet Ministers and an entire football team. *(Sarcastically)*: I suppose they, too, are related to the dwarfs.

SNAPDRIVER: So I understand, m'lud.

COCKLECARROT: *(in a ringing voice)*: Who on earth are these astonishing little red-bearded gentry?

HERMITAGE: I think Admiral Sir Ewart Hodgson could tell us that.

COCKLECARROT: Very well. Call him. We are wasting our time.

Mr Snapdriver, cross-examining, said, 'Now Sir Ewart, will you, as a distinguished sailor, be good enough to tell the court what you know of these dwarfs, of whose persistent interference Mrs Renton complains?'

There was a hush of expectation as the admiral adjusted his spectacles, produced a sheaf of papers from an attaché case, and began to read the following: 'By the might of the Navy our Empire was built up. By the might of the Navy it must be protected. Britannia did not rise from out the azure main merely to sink back into it again. The salt is in our blood, and—'

By this time the court was filled with wild cheering, and several ladies waved small Union Jacks.

MR JUSTICE COCKLECARROT: Yes, yes, Sir Ewart, but what has this to do with the case?

SIR EWART: The future of our Navy – *(cheers)* – is the concern of us all *(cheers)*.

COCKLECARROT: Really, I shall have to clear the court if this goes on.

MR SNAPDRIVER: I beg leave to enter a residuum, with jaggidge.

COCKLECARROT: Don't talk rubbish.

MR SNAPDRIVER: Now, Sir Ewart, do you know these dwarfs?

SIR EWART: Dwarfs or no dwarfs, Britannia's bulwarks are her great ships. *(Cheers.)* See how they churn the farthest seas, their enormous prows cleaving—

MR SNAPDRIVER: Please, please Sir Ewart, try to confine your remarks to the matter in hand. Do you or do you not know these dwarfs?

SIR EWART: I should be sorry to allow my acquaintanceship with dwarfs, giants, or anyone else to distract my attention from Britain's need today – a stronger Fleet. (*Cheers.*) Britannia, Mother of Ships, Queen of the Deep, and—

COCKLECARROT: Mr Snapdriver, why was this witness ever called?

MR SNAPDRIVER: It was a subpoena.

COCKLECARROT: In demurrage?

MR SNAPDRIVER: Yes, and in toto.

COCKLECARROT: Oh, I shall have to grant a *mandatum sui generis.*
(*The case was then adjourned.*)

The hearing of the case was continued today. Mr Justice Cocklecarrot said: 'So far, hardly a mention has been made of these dwarfs. We have heard a long speech about the British Navy, and there has been a brawl in the canteen about the cost of coffee and sandwiches. It is not thus that the majesty of the Law is upheld.'

MR TINKLEBURY SNAPDRIVER: I apply for a writ of *tu quoque.*

MR BASTIN HERMITAGE: And I for a writ of *sine mensis.*

COCKLECARROT: Ah, that's better. That's more like the Law. I well remember in the case of the Pentagon Chemical Foodstuffs and Miss Widgeon *versus* Packbury's Weather Prophecies, Ltd, Captain Goodspeed intervening, a colleague of mine laid down that – however, let us to the matter in hand. I understand, Mr Hermitage, that you intend to call the Tellingby fire brigade. May I ask why?

MR HERMITAGE: They had been summoned to Mrs Renton's house to extricate a child's head from between her chestnut fencing on a day when Mrs Tasker arrived with the dwarfs. The chief of the brigade will tell us that Mrs Tasker pushed the little men into the hall as soon as the maid, Agatha, had opened the door.

FIRE BRIGADE CHIEF (*from back of court*): No, I won't!
(*Consternation. Laughter. Cheers. An Asiatic carpet-seller is thrown out.*)

Mrs Renton told her story yesterday. She said:

I was resting after lunch in my boudoir, when the maid, Angelica, informed me that some gentlemen were in the hall. I asked her who they were, and how many. She said she had counted twelve, but that she had never seen any of them before. I said, 'Do they want to see me?' And Angelica said, 'I don't think so.'

Very mystified, I went into the hall. My first instinct was to laugh. Imagine the effect of seeing a group of twelve red-bearded dwarfs, each fingering his little round hat nervously. I said, 'What can I do for you, gentlemen?' The spokesman answered nervously, 'Mrs Tasker pushed us in here.' 'Why?' I asked. 'We don't know,' replied the spokesman.

MR BASTIN HERMITAGE: I suggest they were an advertisement for Red Dwarf Horseradish Sauce.

MRS RENTON: I don't eat horseradish sauce.

COCKLECARROT: Perhaps they wanted to make you eat it.

(Laughter and ribaldry in court.)

After lunch Rear-Admiral Sir Ewart Hodgson was called again, by mistake. But before the mistake was discovered he told the court that the new Navy scheme to provide longer hammocks for tall sailors would be worthless unless shorter hammocks were provided for small sailors. Mr Justice Cocklecarrot suggested that all this was irrelevant. But Sir Ewart replied: 'Not at all. If these dwarfs were in the Navy they would be completely lost in the new hammocks.'

Cocklecarrot then said, 'It seems very difficult to keep this case within the realm of common sense. There are no red-bearded dwarfs in the Navy, so let us hear no more of this.'

When the hearing of this case was resumed and the court had assembled, Mr Justice Cocklecarrot expressed his dissatisfaction with the progress made with the case. He said that the business of the court, which was the administration of justice, was being continually held up by irrelevancies, and he recommended to both counsel rather more expedition. 'We must keep to the point,' he said.

And at those words a piercing scream rang through the court. A woman was seen to be standing on a bench and pointing at one of the dwarfs.

'It's my Ludwig, my own little son Ludwig,' she cried. 'Ludwig, Ludwig, don't you know your mother?'

There was no answer.

'Well, do you or don't you?' asked Cocklecarrot impatiently.

'My name is Bob,' said the dwarf with slow dignity, 'and I am an orphan. I was left on the doorstep of a house in Eaton Square. In a basket. A month later both my parents died.'

'How do you know?' asked Cocklecarrot.

'I read it in the paper.'

'You read it?' shouted the judge. 'Why, how old were you?'

'Thirty-one,' said the dwarf. 'It happened last year.'

'Do you ask the court to believe,' interrupted Mr Hermitage, 'that at the age of thirty-one you were put into a basket and left on the doorstep of a house in Eaton Square? Who carried the basket?'

'Two friends of my mother,' said the dwarf.

'Were you covered up in any way?'

'Oh yes,' said the dwarf, 'with an old travelling-rug.'

'And what happened when you were found?'

'The lady of the house fell over the basket when she came out to go to a dance. She thought it was the washing, and had me carried in by the back entrance. The maids had hysterics when I got out of the basket, and, of course, I had to clear out. So I went to Nuneaton to seek employment; and it was while working there for a haulage contractor that I met the lady who afterwards became my wife, and a dearer, sweeter creature—'

'All this,' interrupted Cocklecarrot, 'has nothing whatever to do with the case. Mr Hermitage, please try to confine yourself to the matter in hand. The whole thing is becoming impossible.'

A scene occurred after lunch, when the dwarf was asked whether he had ever served in the Navy. He burst into tears and said, between sobs, 'Ever since I was a little fellow – well, I mean, ever since I was even smaller than I am now, I longed to be a sailor. I always wore a sailor suit. But my eyesight made my dream impossible of fulfilment. And now, of course, it is too late. There has always seemed to me to be something wonderful in the surge of the waves and the roar of the wind. Then there is the comradeship. I tell you, after such ambitions, it is difficult to resign myself to being pushed through doors by ladies like Mrs Tasker, for no apparent reason.'

At this point Cocklecarrot intervened impatiently, and the dwarf left the witness-box, still sobbing. A lady who shouted, 'I'll adopt the little dear' was asked to leave the court.

Another ludicrous scene occurred while Mr Tinklebury Snapdriver, for the prosecution, was cross-examining Mrs Tasker.

MR SNAPDRIVER: Your name is Rhoda Tasker?

MRS TASKER: Obviously, or I wouldn't be here.

MR SNAPDRIVER: I put it to you that you were once known as Rough-House Rhoda?

MR HERMITAGE: No, no m'lud, Rough-House Rhoda is another lady, whom I propose to call – a Mrs Rhoda Mortiboy.

COCKLECARROT: What a queer name.

A DWARF: You are speaking of my mother.

(Sensation.)

COCKLECARROT: Is your name Mortiboy?

THE DWARF: No. Towler's my name.

COCKLECARROT *(burying his head in his hands)*: I suppose she married again.

THE DWARF: What do you mean – again? Her name has always been Towler.

COCKLECARROT *(groaning)*: Mr Hermitage, what is all this about?

MR HERMITAGE: M'lud, there is a third Rhoda, a Mrs Rhoda Clandon.

COCKLECARROT *(to the dwarf, sarcastically)*: Is she your mother, too?

THE DWARF: Yes. My name's Clandon.

COCKLECARROT: I think, Mr Snapdriver, we had better proceed without this Rhoda business. My nerves won't stand it.

MR SNAPDRIVER: My next witness is the artiste known as Lucinda – a Mrs Whiting.

(Everybody looks at the dwarf.)

COCKLECARROT *(with heavy sarcasm)*: And, of course—

THE DWARF: Yes, she is my mother.

COCKLECARROT *(roaring)*: Then what is your name, you oaf?

THE DWARF: Charlie Bread.

(Laughter and jeers.)

COCKLECARROT: Clear the court! This foolery is intolerable. It will ruin my political career.

MR SNAPDRIVER: Now, Mrs Tasker, you do not deny that on several occasions you drove these dwarfs, a dozen of them, into Mrs Renton's hall.

MRS TASKER: That is so.

MR SNAPDRIVER: What was your motive?

MRS TASKER: I wanted to drive the dwarfs into her hall.

MR SNAPDRIVER: But why? Can you give me any reason? You will admit it is an unusual occupation.

MRS TASKER: Not for me. I've done it all my life.

MR SNAPDRIVER: You have driven dwarfs into other ladies' houses?

MRS TASKER: Certainly.

COCKLECARROT: Where do you get your supply of dwarfs?

MRS TASKER: From an agency. Fudlow and Trivett.

COCKLECARROT: Extraordinary. Most extraordinary.

MR HERMITAGE: Now, Dr Spunton, is there, to your knowledge, any disease which would account for Mrs Tasker's strange habits?

DR SPUNTON: There is. It is called rufo-nanitis. The spymptoms—

MR HERMITAGE: Symptoms.

DR SPUNTON: Yes, spymptoms, but I always put a 'p' before a 'y'.

COCKLECARROT: With what object, might we ask?

DR SPUNTON: I can't help it, m'lud.

COCKLECARROT: Do you say pyesterday?

DR SPUNTON: Pyes, unfortunatelpy. It's hereditarpy. Mpy familpy all do it.

COCKLECARROT: But why 'p'?

DR SPUNTON: No, py, m'lud.

COCKLECARROT: This case is the most preposterous I ever heard. We get nowhere. The evidence is drivel, the whole thing is a travesty of justice. In two weeks we have done nothing but listen to a lot of nonsense. The case will be adjourned until we can clear things up a bit.

DR SPUNTON: But I was brought all the wapy from Pyelverton.

COCKLECARROT: Well, go pyack to Pyelverton. Goodpye, and a phappy pjournepy. Pshaw!

The hearing was held up for a long time today, when the Deputy Puisne Serjeant-at-Arraigns discovered that, owing to an error of the Chief Usher of the Wardrobe, Mr Justice Cocklecarrot had emerged from the Robing Room with his wig on back to front. According to an old statute of Canute (Op. II. C. in dom: reg: circ.: 37. Cap. 9 pp.: gh: od: ba: ha: 26, per Hohum 46: 98 (e). Tan: 64 by 36: zh: vos: H. Mid: sub rosa 49) the wig must be changed round by the Bailiff of the Wards. So they sent a messenger to bring him from Gregson's Dive. When he arrived he had forgotten the words of the prescribed ritual, and instead of taking Cocklecarrot's left foot in his right hand, he took his right foot in his left hand, thus invalidating the whole tomfoolery.

Meanwhile, a brawl was taking place outside the court. A lady bearing a banner which said, 'Litigate, Don't Arbitrate', was accidentally pushed off the pavement by the dwarfs, who had come in a large motor-car.

When Mrs Tasker arrived, she held a newspaper in front of her face, thus enabling the unwary Press photographers to advertise the *Hunstanton Daily Courier*.

The dwarfs were cross-examined today. At least, one of them was cross-examined.

MR HERMITAGE: Your name is Howard Brassington?
THE DWARF *(in a deep, loud voice)*: It is no such thing.
MR HERMITAGE *(consulting his notes)*: What is your name, then?
THE DWARF: Stanislas George Romney Barlow Barlow Orchmeynders.
MR HERMITAGE: Two Barlows?
THE DWARF: Why not?
MR HERMITAGE: You are a night watchman.
THE DWARF: Why not?
COCKLECARROT: Mr Porchminder, you will please answer yes or no.
THE DWARF: No.

MR HERMITAGE: Where were you on the night of 10th April?

THE DWARF: No.

COCKLECARROT (*to counsel*): Apart from retaining fees, would it not be better to speed up this case a bit?

THE DWARF: Yes.

COCKLECARROT: Send him away. Call Mrs Renton.

MR HERMITAGE: Speak your mind, Mrs Renton, speak your mind.

MRS RENTON: I will. I accused Mrs Tasker of driving a dozen red-bearded dwarfs into my hall. She admits she did it. The dwarfs say she did it. Well, what more is there to be said? What are we waiting for?

COCKLECARROT: Mrs Renton, you do not understand that certain formalities – er – the Law has its own way of doing things.

MRS RENTON: And that is why I have to come here day after day to listen to all this irrelevant foolery – speeches about the Navy, arguments about a dwarf's mother, fuss about dates, and so on.

COCKLECARROT: I am the first to admit that there have been irregularities and delays in this case, but—

(*A dwarf shouts loudly, 'M'lud! M'lud!' Cocklecarrot and Mrs Renton exchange glances.*)

MR HERMITAGE: Well?

THE DWARF: I think I'm going to be sick.

MRS RENTON: That is about the only thing that hasn't happened in this case so far.

COCKLECARROT: Usher! Remove that dwarf.

The time has, I think, come for you, ladies and gentlemen of the jury, to consider this case on its merits.

FOREMAN OF JURY: And what, sir, would you say were its merits?

COCKLECARROT: What would you?

FOREMAN: We have not so far understood one word of the proceedings.

COCKLECARROT: I must say there have been moments when I myself seemed to have lost touch with the real world. Nevertheless, certain facts stand out.

FOREMAN: For instance?

COCKLECARROT: I will not be cross-examined by my own jury. You are here to deliver a verdict, not to question me. You have heard the evidence.

FOREMAN: Was that the evidence? All that horseplay?

COCKLECARROT: If this continues I shall discharge the jury, and the case will be heard all over again with a new jury. Stop those dwarfs singing! This is not a music hall.

When Mr Justice Cocklecarrot continued his attempts to address the jury, interruption came even sooner than before.

COCKLECARROT: Now these red-bearded dwarfs—

CHORUS OF DWARFS: M'lud! M'lud! M'lud!

COCKLECARROT (*testily*): Well? What is it *now*?

A DWARF: We object to being called red-bearded. Our beards are not red.

(*Sensation in court. The dwarfs, standing up in line, are seen to have dyed their beards bright yellow. Laughter breaks out.*)

COCKLECARROT: This is a very foolish trick. There is no law to prevent a man dyeing his beard any colour he pleases, but the question arises whether a beard of bright yellow is not perilously near contempt of court.

MR HERMITAGE: But, m'lud, surely the colour of the beards of these gentlemen is not material to the case.

COCKLECARROT: I will not be led off into another idiotic argument. If they come in on stilts it is not material to the case, but it is contempt of court. 'Now then,' continued the learned judge, 'let us hope that there will be no more of these interruptions. For though the law must be impartially administered, and everybody given an equal chance, yet there are certain restrictions which must be imposed upon merely irresponsible behaviour. These dwarfs—'

A DWARF: Small gentlemen is a more polite description of us. It is not our fault that nature has been niggardly in the matter of inches. Why should a dwarf be funnier than a giant?

ANOTHER DWARF: Yes, why?

COCKLECARROT: If you two small gentlemen have finished your conversation perhaps I might be permitted to proceed. (*Sarcastically*) Have you any objection?

A THIRD DWARF: Some of us haven't said a word all through this case.

A FOURTH DWARF: There is a tendency everywhere to bully the undersized. Yet in the eyes of the law we are citizens like everybody else.

A FIFTH DWARF: And proud of it.

(The other dwarfs cry, 'Hear, hear!' Uproar breaks out. Cocklecarrot sighs heavily and shrugs his shoulders.)

COCKLECARROT *(to the jury)*: Perhaps I may be able to continue my address tomorrow.

Next day Mr Justice Cocklecarrot endeavoured once more to deliver his summing up in this remarkable case. 'What the jury has to decide,' he said, 'is whether Mrs Tasker deliberately drove those dwarfs into Mrs Renton's house, or rather into the hall of her house; whether the maid Célestine—'

MRS RENTON: Angelica.

COCKLECARROT: What?

MRS RENTON: Angelica.

COCKLECARROT: What do you mean, Angelica? Why do you keep on saying Angelica?

MRS RENTON: It is my maid's name.

MR HERMITAGE: It is her maid's name, m'lud.

COCKLECARROT *(angrily, but with a show of patience)*: All right, then, Angelica. Now—

MR SNAPDRIVER: Perhaps there is another maid, called Célestine, m'lud.

MRS RENTON: No. The other is Minnie.

(Roars of laughter.)

COCKLECARROT: There may be forty maids. I am speaking of Angelica.

Now what the jury has to decide is whether this maid – er – Min – er – Angel – er – Cél— Whether this maid Célestine—

MRS RENTON: Angelica.

COCKLECARROT *(dropping his head in his hands and speaking wearily)*: Mrs Renton, will you please allow me to say what I have to say? The name of the maid is immaterial.

MR SNAPDRIVER: But, m'lud, Célestine was on holiday at Bournemouth at the time.

MR HERMITAGE: My learned friend means Eastbourne, m'lud.

MR SNAPDRIVER: My learned friend is right. Eastbourne.

COCKLECARROT *(satirically)*: Well, now that this very important
matter has been settled, perhaps we can continue, unless someone
would like to tell me that Minnie was at Blackpool.

A DWARF: If it comes to that, I myself have been to Blackpool.

(Howls of laughter.)

COCKLECARROT *(regarding the dwarf with rage)*: That is most
interesting and most relevant.

(The court rises for lunch.)

'I intend,' said Mr Justice Cocklecarrot, 'to make a supreme and
almost despairing attempt to sum up this most curious case. Therefore, if anybody has any questions to ask, let them be asked at once,
so that I may be released for my next case, that of Hungarian Lighthouses, Ltd, *versus* Miss Myra Keekie.'

SEVERAL DWARFS: We're in that, too.

COCKLECARROT *(with heavy sarcasm)*: I cannot tell you how
delighted I am at the prospect of having you with me again. May
I ask how you small gentry come to be involved in such a case?

A DWARF: We are Miss Myra Keekie. It is we who wrote the famous
letter cancelling an order for twelve hundred and thirty lighthouses.

COCKLECARROT: All this seems to be quite clear and straightforward. It looks as though I am in for another month of tomfoolery. Hungarian lighthouses, indeed! Why, Hungary—

MRS RENTON: May I implore your lordship not to start this case
before mine is disposed of?

COCKLECARROT: Oh, certainly, certainly. Now, where were we?
Hum. *(With sudden anger.)* It is these damnable small gentlemen
who keep on confusing the issue.

*Sun streaming through a water-bottle and glass on the judge's
desk set alight to papers.*

(News item)

Mr Justice Cocklecarrot, informed of this accident, saw an excellent way to deal with the case. He cunningly set alight to all the papers relevant to the case – if anything can be called relevant to such a case – by manipulating the water-bottle and the glass. He then fed the flames with his wig and various bits of wood which he kept in his pocket. Within an hour the court was burnt down.

The following letter speaks for itself:

Dear Sir,

As you are aware, I recently played a small but not unsensational part in the Dwarf case. I flatter myself that I conducted myself more as an ardent supporter of a strong Navy than as a witness for or against anything in particular. I now learn that the case is to be tried again, owing to some technical flapdoodle or other. May I take this opportunity of stating as publicly as possible that, if I am called again, I shall to the best of my ability once more defend the Navy? What these dwarfs did or did not do is no affair of mine. To-day we are concerned with more important matters. For there can be no safeguard for the peace of Europe until our British-built warships lie keel to keel across every knot of the seven seas, and until every port of the habitable globe harbours a British submarine.

Yours faithfully,
Ewart Hodgson (Rear-Adml.)

Chapter 2

The Intrusions of Captain Foulenough

AT DRAINWATER HOUSE

CAPTAIN FOULENOUGH, who is causing so much disturbance in Scotland, made his appearance at lunch-time yesterday at Drainwater House, the residence of Colonel and Mrs McGawke.

The McGawkes were entertaining a large house-party, and luncheon was about to be served when the hostess heard voices in the entrance hall.

She heard her butler say, 'What name did you say, sir?' and then a loud voice replied, 'A Foulenough by any name would smell as sweet. He droppeth as the gentle dew from Heaven. Go hence, my man, and tell them that their old Uncle Fred waits without. Say their Aunt Emma has returned from sea. Say that I am the little waif you found abandoned in a linen-basket on the doorstep. Say anything you please.'

Mrs McGawke then came to the great oaken door, and the captain flung his arms round her, crying, 'My dear old godmother! Have you forgotten the old days? Is there anything to drink in this doss-house?'

The colonel joined his wife and endeavoured to rescue her from the embrace of the noisy intruder. He said, 'If you do not go at once, I shall ring up the police. We have been warned about you.'

'For the honour of your old regiment give me a meal,' said the captain.

Then, picking up a bust of Joseph Chamberlain, he said, 'What'll you give me on this? What am I bid?'

The colonel, edging the captain towards the door, said, 'Here's five shillings.'

'The bust's yours,' replied Foulenough, handing it to Mrs Mc-Gawke with a bow.

They watched him go down the drive, and as he went he sang in a deep, thunderous voice, 'Flossie Is The Girl For Me.'

AT TINWHISTLE LODGE

Captain Foulenough turned up yesterday evening at Tinwhistle Lodge, near Cailzie, where Lord Lochstock and Barrel was entertaining heavily for the shooting. The captain, with that candour which disdains subterfuge, swung up the drive in full view of the guests gathered on the lawn, crying, 'Any empties?'

Lady Lochstock and Barrel (before her marriage a Whussett), said haughtily:

'We have no empties, whatever they may be. You will find the tradesmen's entrance at the back.'

'No empties?' replied Foulenough.

'Not one,' said Lord Lochstock and Barrel.

'Any fulls, then?' asked the captain. 'In other words – have you the wherewithal to wet my tyrannous whistle?'

At a sign from the master of the house Foulenough was taken to the servants' quarters and refreshed.

IMPASSE

The thud of hoofs is far from welcome on Clackwhidden Moor at this season of the year. The shoot was entirely ruined yesterday by a mysterious horseman who cantered up and down in front of the butts, waving a sword and crying, 'Don't hold your fire! Charge!' One or two sportsmen recognized Captain Foulenough, who has made such a nuisance of himself in the district.

Colonel Grampound shouted to him, 'I say! You are masking our fire. Can't you see you're in the way, there's a good fellow, I mean.'

To which the irrepressible captain replied. 'Fear nothing. Follow me. I will lead you against those birds. Don't cower in those trenches. Grouse don't bite. After them, boys!' And he raised himself in his stirrups and waved them on. 'Take cover,' he added, 'when I blow two blasts on my bottle.' So saying, he raised a pint bottle of stout to his lips and drank heartily.

Nobody knows quite what to do about it all.

London's Upper Thirty-seven, the cream of the *haut monde*, the life-above-stairs gang, are organizing a committee to concert measures for the ending, once and for all, of the Foulenough menace.

Several dowagers and other hostesses complain that the captain's name has crept into the accounts of their social activities which their secretaries have sent to the gossip writers. The general opinion is that the captain must be either a lunatic or a determined climber. The prospect of his attendance at dances and dinners and cocktail-parties during the coming season is too much for most people to contemplate.

As an instance of what is happening, Lady Cabstanleigh read the following at the first committee meeting. It was taken from 'Lobelia's' column of chatter in the *Evening Scream*:

Witty and intelligent Lady Cabstanleigh is giving a send-off cocktail-party for the Trowser girls, who are off on one of their intrepid dashes to Scotland. The Bopples will be there, and Lady Urging and Mr 'Dirt' Cobblestone, and, of course, the handsome and popular Captain Foulenough.

I append a few more extracts from various columns of social chatter, which have given great offence to Lady Cabstanleigh's committee, formed to combat Captain Foulenough's attempts to get into Society:

It is understood that the best man at the Garkington–Thwackhurst wedding will be Captain Foulenough who describes himself as 'an old friend of the groom, and of all other grooms'. When informed of this news the groom, Mr Ernest ('Stink') Garkington said, 'I've never even heard of the chap.'

. . . Among those who will bring parties to the dance given by Lady Vowpe for her daughter Celery is the popular Captain Foulenough. He will probably bring the Kempton Park gang.

Captain Foulenough, whose address, according to him, is the Cavalry Club, calls every day for letters. He has been told that he is not a member, and has been asked not to call at the club. His invari-

able reply is, 'I have to come here to get my letters. It's not my fault if everyone writes to me at this address. When I marry Babs, it will be different.'

This last remark has thrown many hostesses into a frenzy. Nobody knows whether the Babs in question is:

> (a) Mrs Simeon Grout's daughter;
> (b) Lady Barger's niece;
> (c) Sir Arthur Cutaway's widow;
> (d) Lady Thistleburn's daughter;
> (e) Lady 'Connie' Clatter's daughter;
> (f) The divorced Mrs Rowdgett;
> (g) The orphan Babs Watercress;
> (h) A barmaid at the Horse and Hounds;
> (i) One of the Farragut twins;
> (j) Lady Nausea ('Babs') Bottledown.

Many hostesses have decided to employ detectives to scrutinize their guests on arrival. In this way it is hoped to keep Captain Foulenough away from houses where he is neither known nor wanted.

But this is a dangerous way of dealing with the menace, as is shown by the complaints of a Mr Cowparsleigh, who has already been refused admission to two houses, owing to his resemblance to the captain. The fact of this resemblance is making people even more nervous, since none of them can afford to offend a banker's nephew of Mr Cowparsleigh's status.

News has just come in of the appearance of Captain Foulenough at Lady Drain's cocktail-party. He is said to have entered by the tradesmen's entrance. Suspicions were aroused when he seized the arm of Aurora Bagstone, and holding it to his lips, in the manner of a flute-player, kissed it up and down the scale, from wrist to elbow. Aurora remarked afterwards, 'One does like to know who is kissing one, after all.'

Meanwhile Mr Cowparsleigh had been flung down the steps of Mrs Woodle's house in Crabapple Mews, and has threatened to make his uncle call in her overdraft.

A COMEDY OF ERRORS

A ridiculous scene marred Lady Hounde's party the other night. 'All one has to do,' said the hostess, 'to stop this man Foulenough from interfering with our social engagements is to search any suspect. The so-called captain always carries a bottle of strong drink in his pocket.'

The arrival of the unfortunate Mr Augustus Cowparsleigh, who is Foulenough's double, was the signal for an outbreak of suspicion that you could have cut with a knife. Cowparsleigh's recent misadventures have, of course, made him very timid, and he entered Lady Hounde's room blushing and looking guilty.

Lady Hounde pounced like a starving jaguar. 'Have you a bottle on you?' she demanded sternly, while plunging her hand into his side pocket.

'I didn't know we were supposed to bring our own drink,' retorted Cowparsleigh.

'Don't quibble,' roared the hostess, 'where's your bottle? I know you've got one.'

'If you are as thirsty as all that,' replied the victim testily, 'why don't you get one of your own drinks?'

Taken aback, the hostess faltered. 'I do believe it's really Augustus,' she said. And everybody breathed freely.

The only other odd incident occurred half an hour later. Boubou Flaring crossed the room to speak to Cowparsleigh as he was leaving.

'I hear you were mistaken for Captain Foulenough,' she said. The reply was a wicked wink, and Boubou was surprised to see him leave with a little box full of caviare sandwiches and a bottle in each pocket, and without saying good-bye to anybody.

Ten minutes later she was amazed to see him again. She said, 'Where have you dumped the sandwiches and the booze?' Augustus Cowparsleigh flushed angrily. 'I think you're all mad here,' he said. Boubou pondered in silence.

At 7.15 the supply of drink failed – an unknown occurrence in that house. It was only then that Lady Hounde heard Boubou's story, and realized that the dreaded warrior had indeed slipped through her fingers.

Mr Augustus Cowparsleigh, who has the misfortune to be Captain

Foulenough's double, was refused admittance yesterday to the divorce reception given by Lady Doublecross to celebrate the divorce of her daughter Goatie from Sir Stanley Biskett. In vain did poor Augustus produce his card. In vain did he show the monogram on his shirt.

To make matters worse this mildest of men has been asked to resign from one of his clubs, because he came into the smoking-room with his shirt outside his waistcoat, placed a funnel down the back of old General Dunderhead's neck, and poured Sir Raymond Funbelow's whisky down the funnel.

Needless to say, one suspects Foulenough once more.

MR COWPARSLEIGH AND FLORA SCREAMING

I learn that the timid but worthy Mr Augustus Cowparsleigh is on the point of announcing his engagement to Flora, the lovely daughter of Mrs Screaming.

Or should I say, 'was on the point'?

Yesterday the fond suitor for the largest hand in Upper Beauclerque Mews had arranged to meet his lady in the cocktail bar at that most exclusive of pigsties, 'Chez Nussbaum'. She arrived punctually and seated herself on one of the red glass rocking-horses ranged round the bar. A moment later she was astounded to see her fiancé in animated conversation with a Creature. If ever there was a hussy this was one. Approaching cautiously, Flora saw the man who had always been so courtly and so reserved with her pinch the Creature's ear and smack her cheek playfully. He called her 'Carrots'. Feeling as though she had been slogged over the head with a steel hammer the poor girl called feebly for brandy.

When she came to, Augustus was bending over her tenderly, and saying repeatedly, 'So sorry I was late.'

Coldly she pushed him away and rose to her feet, then she left the premises in comparatively high dudgeon.

Mr Cowparsleigh was dining quietly with Flora Screaming and her mother the other night, when their butler, Mason, uttered a loud cry in the kitchen. A moment or two later he brought in the fish, and Mrs Screaming was about to ask him what had happened when he suddenly executed a dance step and whipped off a wig, revealing the red hair of Foulenough. Tongue-tied, they shrank from him. He said,

'Cowparsleigh, old soak, I just wanted to thank you in person for settling that little matter for me. Flora, my love, I will not attempt to screen my identity. I am Foulenough, and proud of it. We came over with King Alfred. However, as I see violence in your lady mother's eye, I will do a scarper.' And he left the room.

MR COWPARSLEIGH DEVISES A SCHEME

'There is only one way out of this,' said poor Mr Cowparsleigh to Flora Screaming. 'There is an infallible sign by which you can always distinguish me from Captain Foulenough. You see, fortunately, I have a birth-mark about the size of a florin on my chest.'

'Very nice,' said Flora sarcastically. 'And I am supposed to go about at parties asking to see people's chests?'

'Certainly not, my dear,' said Mr Cowparsleigh. 'But when you are in doubt about me, I will—'

'Remove your shirt, I suppose?'

'Oh no. The birth-mark is high up, near the throat. I need only take my collar and tie off, and unbutton the top button of my shirt.'

'Splendid,' sneered Flora. 'Nobody would think it odd. And if I know the captain, he's quite capable of buying a sham birth-mark and sticking it on. Then we should have the pair of you behaving like lunatics.'

AND CARRIES IT OUT

Next day the Fauconbridge-Fauconbridge-Fauconbridges gave a little sherry-party, and asked Flora and her fiancé to look in. Flora arrived late, and when she saw Mr Cowparsleigh beaming at her with more than his customary gaiety, thankful to have forestalled his double, she at once suspected that he was the dreaded captain, and turned her back on him. Whereupon the well-meaning Augustus shouldered his way towards her, but was intercepted by a voluble lady, who could not understand why he was fiddling with his tie and collar so nervously. When he whipped off his collar and undid his shirt at the neck she uttered a scream. People crowded round, and above the din the voice of the hostess was heard bawling, 'Mason, show Captain Foulenough to the door!'

So Mr Cowparsleigh's little scheme miscarried.

THE CAPTAIN AT LARGE

A paragraph in a local paper informs me that:

Captain de Courcy Foulenough, the well-known clubman, has succeeded, by using the names of prominent London hostesses, in obtaining credit at some of the more shady whelk-stalls at Brighton. It is difficult to imagine that the proprietors of the stalls can have had business dealings with any of these ladies, and it can only be assumed that they are sufficiently impressed by the captain's manner to believe that their bills will be settled by his rich friends.

Lady Cabstanleigh commented on this paragraph yesterday. She said, 'I, for one, have no intention of standing him whelks.'

Mr Cowparsleigh, who has received a bill for four dozen whelks, has sent the money, 'Merely because I prefer to hush the matter up.' Other well-known people who have received bills are consulting their solicitors.

Mrs Taswill-Fogstone has received this letter:

Dear Madam,
I enclose a bill for whelks inkurred by a gent what come ere with a lady and eat three doz. bitween them. I was give to understan you was his mother, so I enclose the bill for the whelks they eat. Any other custumiers you are cortious enough to send to my stall will be assuared the best intenteons of the house not counting credit and the sky being the limmitt. A post order by return will oblige.

Your obedien servant,
Ted Rigger

The unfortunate Mr Cowparsleigh was dumbfounded yesterday when he looked in at Dibbler's Club in Ryder Street for his letters, and found this:

Dear Sir,—I enclose as requested the bill for the jamboree at my stall last Wednesday. The breakages come rather heavy, but you will remember that Violet had words with Connie and threw a cup at her. When the fun was over I found Aggie's hat under the counter, and am forwarding it to you as I don't know her address. I've slipped in Tom's outstanding account as you told me to, and am giving Mabel and her friend tick. Hoping this is all right.

Yrs. respectfully,
Alfred Birago

'What monstrous nonsense is this?' exclaimed poor Cowparsleigh as he rang up his solicitors.

*   *   *   *   *

BEDSIDE READING

'So you dare to criticize the Captain of the School!'

The voice of the headmistress was ice-cold and as sharp as a scimitar.

Joyce hung her head.

Then the Captain, a frank smile lighting up her young face, advanced and held out her hand.

At this gesture of friendliness the whole school began to bawl its eyes out. As for Joyce, she took the proffered hand and drenched it with her tears.

The headmistress turned aside. She, too, was human.

(*From* The Beastliest Girl at St Bede's.)

A NEAT INVENTION

Dr Strabismus (Whom God Preserve) of Utrecht has invented a series of mousetraps whose aim is 'to wear the mouse out psychologically'.

The mouse sees a bit of cheese and suspects a trap. But it is dummy cheese, and the mouse says to itself, 'Nobody would set a trap with sham cheese, because no mouse would risk its life for such a thing. Therefore there is no trap.'

In walks the mouse, brushing aside the sham cheese, and bumps against a bit of real cheese. 'This must be the trap,' says he, and at once retreats and saves himself.

He finds, all around him, other traps, some baited with real and some with sham cheese, and he grows tired and nervous, until finally he takes a bite at a bit of sham cheese which has been smeared with poison.

SONG OF A PLEASURE CRUISER

I shall always remember Venice . . .
For wasn't that the place
Where Mrs Mason hurt her foot,
And mother bought the lace?

'PING-PU'

Let us get on with *Ping-Pu*, that great story (see publisher's puff) of a man's vast love for a woman, and of how a local tyrant tried to make the Chinese smoke cork-tipped cigarettes instead of opium. Read on, faithful heart, nor falter by the way.

'Dawn, that daily miracle, was breaking.

' "Fung-go," said Ah Fi.

' "Fung-gi," said Ah Fo.

'Nothing was heard in the Concession but the gentle boiling of opium in a large changfu, made of beaten zinc and embroidered with crystallized fruit in eighteen colours.

' "Hoo foo," said Ah Hi.

' "Hoo fi," said Ah Hoo.

'Together they laughed the saturnine laugh of the inscrutable East.

' "Poo-poo," said a laundress, entering suddenly from the settlement, her pigtail shining in the Eastern sun.

' "Kwang-ko," commented another laundress, entering suddenly from another settlement.

' "Flu," concluded a third laundress, entering suddenly from yet another settlement.

'Slowly the hills faded from aquamarine to burnt sienna. Suddenly a scream rent the night air.'

There will be more of this.

YOUR BUTT

I hardly know what to say. It is most fearfully good of you all to sit there, waiting to read me. I – er – I am most frightfully bucked about the whole thing. I – er – I hope that I shall not disappoint you, and if you have any sense at all I certainly shall not. You are nothing but a crowd of urchins, in any case. Accustomed, as I am, to public writing, I must now insist on the importance of whatever-it-is. Here, as the last light falls on field and mart, I sit, pen in hand. This tiny instrument, crammed with ink, is capable of the finest flights of prose, but today has a cold in its nib. And I have grown painfully self-conscious. I cannot bear the idea of being laughed at by a lot of people to whom I have never had the pleasure of being introduced.

I think, if you don't mind, we will pass on to some general topic, as I have a feeling that I am merely your butt. Therefore, good people, go and boil your great heads.

NARKOVER NEWS

Dr Smart-Allick was playing bridge with three of the masters the other day. It became obvious that something was wrong when a simple sum in addition revealed the fact that, in the first rubber, no fewer than thirty-one aces had made their appearance. The Doctor said, 'Since I only had seven myself you men must have been rather overdoing things.' The incident passed off in laughter. Mr Relf lost eighteen pounds and a cuff-link, Mr Sprott a silver cigar-cutter, Mr Shoggs a counterfeit ten-pound note, and Dr Smart-Allick three valuable letters.

The claims of the science master, Mr Alf Spoddoes, to be able to make gold are not questioned for a moment. As Dr Smart-Allick said yesterday: 'A science master at Narkover gets the ordinary salary and the usual extras, but Spoddoes has a house in Chester Terrace, a flat in Paris, an estate in Dorsetshire, and, I understand, a grouse moor in Wigtownshire. All these things, taken in conjunction with his five cars and his yacht, point to considerable private means. I should not be surprised to hear that he can make paper money as easily as he can make gold.'

An uncensored letter, written home to his parents by a Narkover boy, runs as follows:

Dear Dad,
I am glad to say I won the cup for the most goles scored up to October the fifteenth, but here's a funny thing dad, it's a fine silver cup and I'm to have my name ingraved on it, but there's a bit of ingraving orlready

*and I can just red it, it says something about the Dawlish golf challenge
cup and a man called Fittlestone won it, so how did it get to me I
wonder, eh, and it says 1928 so what eh, this is a rum school I can tell
you dad, and when I had my fingerprints taken it reminded me of what
you told me about your early days I must leaf off now dad.*

Yore son,
Billy

RUSTIGUZZI'S ISOLDE

It is now almost certain that Rustiguzzi will play Isolde to Ravioli's
Tristan. There will be a specially augmented orchestra – 334 instru-
ments more than the usual ration, and mostly trombones. This will
probably be the first occasion on which the untrained voices of the
rich women in the audience will have had to take second place.
Musical critics are beginning to ask themselves whether quality is
not after all better than quantity. Further, Rustiguzzi has developed
a tiresome habit. When she has emitted a resounding yell, and draws
in her breath with a noise like the November tide receding over the
shingle at Kemp Town, she is apt to whistle through her teeth. And
as everything she does is on a huge scale, this bitter east wind between
her teeth takes the listeners' attention from the yelling and summons
expectant cabmen from all streets within a mile of the Strand.

Rash conductors who put up umbrellas while she is singing will
only have them blown inside out.

(Tomorrow: Scampi in 'Maraschino'.)

DR STRABISMUS IS BUSY

Dr Strabismus (Whom God Preserve) of Utrecht is working hard at
about fourteen thousand and fifty more inventions. These include a
collapsible salt-bag, a bottle with its neck in the middle, a rice-sifter,
a stanchion to prop up other stanchions, a suet-container, a foghorn
key, a leather grape, a new method of stencilling on ivory, basalt
cubes for roofing swimming-baths, a fox-trap, a dummy jellyfish,
waterproof onions, false teeth for swordfish, a method of freezing
meat-skewers, a hand-woven esparto grass egg-cosy which plays
'Thora' when released from the egg, a glass stilt, a revolving wheel-
barrow, an iron thumb for postmen, a hash-pricker, a beer-swivel

with blunt flanges and a red go-by, a fish-detector, a screw for screwing screws into other screws, hot pliers, a plush sausage-sharpener, a rope-soled skate for using in mountain quarries, an oiled cork for holes in rabbit-hutches, a cheese-anchor and a chivet for smearing radishes.

TAIL-PIECE

One disadvantage of being a hog is that at any moment some blundering fool may try to make a silk purse out of your wife's ear.

Chapter 3

The Giddy Girlhood of Mrs Wretch

THE LOVELY CIRCUS GIRL

IT IS NOT generally known that in her wild youth Mrs Wretch was the girl who stood on the elephant's back in Wugwell's Mammoth Circus. Her brother Ted was the Corsican brigand who was fired out of a cannon's mouth.

It was while standing on the elephant's back that Mrs Wretch, then Miss Whackaway, was introduced to Colonel Wretch, the big-game hunter, who died in Putumayo after swallowing forty leather thongs for a bet made at a rum-rally.

The lovely creature in her spangled tights entranced the warrior. He lifted her down and proposed. She, having no prospect but a possible promotion on the death of the old woman who held the whisky and soda for the great ape, accepted his offer.

The rest belongs to history.

Mrs Wretch has been prevailed upon to give me some more details of her girlhood in Wugwell's Mammoth Circus before she met Colonel Wretch.

My readers will not be surprised to learn that the Bearded Afghan Lady whom Mrs Wretch (then Miss Whackaway) understudied for a year is now a famous society hostess. The beard was on show at the recent Exhibition of Sporting Trophies.

One day the man who fired the Corsican from the cannon's mouth (a Mr Bill Armitage from Cricklewood) persuaded the beautiful Miss Whackaway to climb inside the muzzle for a lark. The young lady was propelled through the opening of a tent, and landed with a thud on the fortune-teller's drum, just as that Arabian seer (a Mrs Cox) was saying, 'A fair young lady is coming over the sea.'

Miss Whackaway and the gunner were not on speaking terms after that.

I have described the evening when Colonel Wretch first set eyes on his future bride, the lovely Miss Whackaway. After lifting her from the elephant, the Colonel could not keep away from Wugwell's Mammoth Circus.

He was an Englishman by nature, and was considerably disturbed when, on his second visit, he saw her buttering a slice of bread for the tallest of the Twelve West African Head-Hunters of Zimbobo.

The Colonel led her aside, and pointed out that she was losing caste, and that no white girl should perform a menial task for a black man.

He was considerably relieved when Miss Whackaway revealed to him the fact that the black men were out-of-work bill-posters hired by Wugwell at a shilling a night.

Night after night the gallant Colonel was to be seen in his seat at Wugwell's Mammoth Circus.

Being a man with a strong sense of the fitness of things, he was horrified one night to find that the lovely Miss Whackaway was not in her usual place on the elephant's back.

On making inquiries he learned that the girl who waltzed with the small Siberian bear had sprained her ankle, and that his beloved had stepped into the curious breach.

'My love,' said the Colonel. 'I do not think you should waltz with bears.'

'Anthony,' replied Miss Whackaway, 'if I never do anything worse than that, you need not complain. Anyhow, is it any more derogatory than standing on an elephant's back?'

'Sweet blossom,' said the warrior, 'an elephant is a beast of Empire, a noble beast, not unconnected with Rajahs, but the Siberian bear is an impossible outsider.'

One night, the Colonel, when the show was over, was introduced to Wugwell himself.

'Ha!' said Wugwell, 'so you're the josser that's going to rob us of our little Sweeticums.'

'I beg your pardon,' said the Colonel coldly.

'We all call 'er that,' said Wugwell, 'ever since the day the lion-tamer kissed 'er behind a beer-barrel.'

Later the Colonel said to Miss Whackaway, 'What's all this about kisses given to lion-tamers behind barrels? Remember you are to be the chatelaine of Sodgecross Manor. You must give up these low friendships.'

Miss Whackaway pouted.

'I only kissed him,' she said, 'because he threatened to put me into the barrel if I didn't.'

The Colonel made a wry grimace of disgust, and sulked for twenty minutes.

One evening, the beautiful Miss Whackaway deputized for the Equestrian Belle. While she was standing with one leg on Diamond and one on Saucy Boy, balancing a dummy bottle of port on her nose, and holding in her left hand the paper hoop through which Monty the seal was to jump – she slipped and fell to the ground.

Immediately the gallant Colonel rushed into the arena, tripped over a recumbent clown named Tandley, got his legs entangled in Wild Walter's lasso, and was hit on the head with an umbrella by a woman who shouted, 'My little boy can't see the seals!'

So grieved was the Colonel when the audience laughed at his misadventure that he sulked for three days, and did not come near the circus. On the fourth night he turned up again with a large box of crystallized fruit for Miss Whackaway.

The sweets were eaten by the Arabian fortune-teller, and the Singing Ostrich laid an egg in the Colonel's hat.

One day the Colonel hinted to Miss Whackaway that the time had come for the future chatelaine of Sodgecross Manor to abandon the tights and the spangles for the more staid dress of a county hostess.

Wugwell himself was angry.

Said he to the warrior: 'Mark my words, guv'nor' – the Colonel winced at this familiar form of address – 'Mark my words. This filly o' yours has a future, but only if she sticks to 'er art. I never yet knew a married woman that put 'er 'ole 'eart into the helephant business. You're robbing 'er of a great chance, cully. I don't mind tellin' you. I 'ad 'er marked down for the Egyptian queen, to balance on top of a plaster pyramid with a serpent round 'er neck. Marriage can't 'elp but muck up 'er spirit of adventure.'

The Colonel, who protested that Wugwell's conversation reeked of the pothouse, said that he would take care of her future, and that he had other plans for her, more becoming to a lady than any amount of balancing on pyramids. So it was arranged that, after a gala performance, Miss Whackaway should shake the sawdust from her feet and become Mrs Wretch.

How she developed into the horrible welfare-worker we all know is another story.

FAREWELL TO THE CIRCUS

There was not a dry eye in the two-and-fourpennies when the beautiful Miss Whackaway, standing on the elephant, kissed her hands to the public for the last time. When she drove away with the Colonel, she was overcome with emotion, and on her lap was Monty the Seal, a present from Wugwell himself.

'My dear – the seal – do you quite think . . . ?' said the Colonel.

Whereat the seal barked at the warrior, and Miss Whackaway fumbled in a paper bag for a tasty fish with which to pacify the animal.

'My dear,' said the Colonel, 'we really cannot carry fish about with us when we are married.'

'You don't love me,' she replied, 'or you wouldn't be so terribly unkind about Monty.'

'Nonsense, delightful blossom,' averred the warrior, 'you come first, naturally.'

'And Monty second?' wheedled the circus-queen.

'And Monty second,' vouchsafed the reluctant bridegroom-to-be.

'There, Monty,' cooed Miss Whackaway, 'we all love you.'

And the seal shoved its slimy snout into the Colonel's coat pocket and bit his pipe in two.

A LOVERS' QUARREL

The courtship of the beautiful Miss Whackaway by the gallant Colonel Wretch did not always go smoothly.

When Miss Whackaway announced that, her father being deceased, she would like to be given away by the knife-thrower, Eddie Swipe, the Colonel objected.

Swipe joined the two of them one night at the Coin des Juifs. 'I won't 'arf give 'er away,' he said to the Colonel, with a wink. Then he picked up six knives from neighbouring tables and flung them at the wall. Miss Whackaway laughed, but Colonel Wretch was indignant.

Finally, when his lovely blossom wept, the Colonel agreed to compromise, and Wugwell himself was asked to give her away. He was forbidden to bring any of the animals, and was given to understand that the lavish scale of the subsequent entertainment would render it unnecessary for him to carry his usual quart bottle in his coat pocket.

So the happy day drew near, and the presents began to arrive; not the least embarrassing being a performing parrot, with a label round its neck bearing the words, 'Souvenir from Wugwell's'.

When the Colonel said, 'Pretty Poll!' the bird replied, 'Don't be a damned fool!'

After the marriage Colonel and Mrs Wretch (née Whackaway) settled at Sodgecross Manor, the seat of the Rutland Wretches.

At the first meet of the season the ex-Circus Queen caused a mild sensation by planting one leg on the back of her own mount and the other on that of her neighbour's mount. For a few moments she stood erect, blowing kisses to Captain Screaming, the Master.

Her neighbour was a certain Lady Tongue, who at once lodged a complaint.

Later on Mrs Wretch tried to induce the hounds to leap through a paper hoop which she had brought with her. The Colonel rode up and remonstrated.

That night, excited by the day's sport, the young bride balanced a bottle of sherry on her forehead, went slowly down on her hands and knees, raised her left leg backwards, and scratched the back of her neck with her left foot.

The Colonel, though proud of her versatility, deplored such unconventional behaviour.

The old air of the circus which still clung to the lovely Mrs Wretch marred many a social occasion, until the gallant Colonel was forced to consider the advisability of taking her away.

One night, for instance, at a dinner party the conversation turned on elephants, and the guests were astounded to hear the bride tell a story about Wugwell's Bearded Lady, who threw a bun at the elephant and hit one of the West African Head-Hunters. She explained that she, at the time, was standing on the elephant's back.

The guests coughed nervously, and the Colonel hastily explained that it was done for a wager.

About this time the Colonel was asked to join an expedition to study the flora and fauna of the Lower Woogli River. He accepted with alacrity, and Mrs Wretch prepared to accompany him.

It was this expedition which proved to be the second turning-point in her life. For it was among the natives of this remote spot that she learned all those bestial ideals of service, meddling, uplift, and hugaboo which have made her name a byword during the last ten years.

* * * * *

THE EMANCIPATION OF ELEPHANTS

Dear Mr Beachcomber,

May one who has for many years worked to improve and brighten the lives of elephants, speak a word? I have the honour to be the secretary of a society whose object is to get elephants interested in their cages, and to counteract the modern tendency to regard life as a wild round of irresponsible gaiety.

The elephant's memory is proverbial, and part of our work centres round the establishment of school-treats. Each elephant is encouraged to try to remember the faces of the children. A measure of success has attended our efforts, but it is felt that the children might help by wearing masks. This would not only make the task more interesting and more difficult, but would veil some of the repulsive faces, upon which greed, sloth and cruelty have already set their ugly marks.

May I add that my elephant-workers are always glad of any old biscuits or buns. These may be sent to the Elephants' Improvement League, or to little Mr Aubrey Hammond.

I am, sir,
Yours truly,
(MRS) JUMBO

A TOUCHING SCENE

A scene was caused yesterday in the Strand when a young man wearing a B.F. (Buchmanite Fellowship) badge on the front of his hat stood in the middle of the road and held up the traffic.

He said he wanted to confess to all the great big world that in August 1927, at about 4.15 p.m., he had lied to his aunt about the number of lumps of sugar in his warm milk.

NOVELIST FOUND IN PUDDING

It is not generally known that when the annual Pudding was opened at the famous Fleet Street hostelry, where Americans write their names on Dr Johnson's sun-hat, kiss his boots, gape at his saucer, and collect small phials of the actual sawdust he trod – when I say, the Pudding was opened, the astonished assembly, led by Sir John ('Fighting Jack') Simon, saw that it contained not only the usual ingredients, but also Mr Hugh Walpole.

What is *not* generally known is how he got into the Pudding.

Mr Walpole's jealous rivals say that the whole thing was a publicity stunt. His friends say that he fell asleep while choosing the Greatest Novel Of The Century, and was hastily bundled into the Pudding by a hysterical mob of women novel-readers.

In any case, it was great fun, and when the awakened author said, 'Where am I?' and received the reply, 'In the Pudding,' he hastily scrambled out, brushed his clothes and, blushing a good deal, left the hostelry amid cries of 'God bless you, Mr Walpole. Pick us a good book, sir!'

FILTHY PICTURES

'I say, Professor, why do all the cultured people avoid that dark man in the corner? Who is he?'

'Haven't you heard? That's the great art collector, Brushforth, and he's got a dirty Van Dyck. It hasn't been washed for years.'

'Why doesn't he try Snibbo?'

'By Jove! That's an idea. I'll tell him.'

(*One week later.*) 'I say, they *do* crowd round old Brushforth, don't they?'

'No wonder! He's tried Snibbo on his Van Dyck, and it's as good as new.'

Hear what Professor Crowell says:

For three years I was a martyr to dirty pictures. Then one day a friend told me about Snibbo. I applied it to my pictures, with the most amazing results. Now I tell all my artistic friends about it.
(Signed) ARTHUR CROWELL

INTERLUDE

PRODNOSE: I really think the time is ripe for a spring song.

MYSELF: What, dog? You call for twiddly Mendelssohn stuff?

PRODNOSE: No. Verse will do. You need not worry about the music.

MYSELF: Well, there is an old verse, and a very beautiful one, I will sing it once more for you:

> Let poets praise the softer winds of spring,
>   The cleaner skies, the magic-laden air;
> I mark the season by a greater thing—
>   Lady Cabstanleigh's back in Berkeley-square.

PRODNOSE: Is that all of it?

MYSELF: I'm afraid there is no more, as—

PRODNOSE: Then heaven be praised, that makes one's agonies to cease before they become intolerable. I never heard such a rubbishy song in my life.

MYSELF: Could you do better?

PRODNOSE: If I had a mind to, but, as you know very well, I do not sing in Lent.

MYSELF: Then go and put your dismal head in a thick bag, and keep it there.

THE GREAT PUDDING SCANDAL

The disgraceful affair of the Pudding has been complicated by the assertion of a waiter that when Mr Hugh Walpole was about to get into it he discovered that another writer had forestalled him. With a trick learnt from a Cumberland wrestling champion the angry *littérateur* ejected his rival, and himself took his place in the Pudding.

Everybody in the clubs is asking who the presumptuous writer was.

VETS SWEAR BY THEM

The leopard leads a healthy life,
But cannot lose his spots.
He has not tried those magic pills
They sell in little pots.

(Advt.)

SCENES AT BOURNEMOUTH

Dr Strabismus (Whom God Preserve) of Utrecht, addressing the Premature Urn Burial Society at Bournemouth, confined himself to booing and hissing the audience. The moment the chairman began to introduce him the Doctor threw an egg at him, which, at such close range, spattered two ladies who were also on the platform. The Doctor then heckled the audience whenever any one of them tried to ask why he did not begin. Finally he was removed by the police for creating a disturbance. He said afterwards, 'I seem to have got things the wrong way round.'

THE GREAT PUDDING SCANDAL

I am asked by the Great Western Railway Company to deny categorically an absurd report current yesterday that when the Pudding was opened, disclosing Mr Walpole, there was a lady with him. It is true that a lady's handkerchief was found afterwards embedded in the north-west crust, but I am assured by one of our leading engineering firms that it belonged to a Mrs Wodger, who had looked in for an hour or two to write an Outline. She and Mr Walpole never addressed a single word to each other.

DIPLOMATIC COURSE

Quoting a recent dictum that 'There should no longer be any room for gentlemen in the diplomatic service', Dr Smart-Allick has decided to prepare some of his more promising pupils for a diplomatic career.

A recent examination paper is worth quoting. One of the questions was:

How would you, as an Ambassador in a foreign capital, set about procuring an interview with the Minister for Foreign Affairs of the country to which you are accredited?

One of the answers was: 'I wood send a beutiferl wumman to elure him into my clutches.'

Here are one or two more answers:

'Sanbag him in a loanley ally.'

'Get old uv some inkeriminating letters and blackmale im.'

'Brake in to his ministery and hold him up at the point of the ruvvolver.'

'Get him into a game of whist behind locked dores.'

'Pertend to be his long lorst unkil.'

'Dissgise meself as a gass inspekter cum to read his metre.'

THE GREAT PUDDING SCANDAL

It has now transpired that the writer who got into the Pudding before Mr Hugh Walpole was a comparatively unimportant novelist sent on ahead to reserve the place. It had come to the ears – and what ears! – of the authorities that an attempt was to be made by some women writers to introduce Miss Rebecca West into the pudding by stealth.

Mr Walpole's strategic move foiled the conspiracy, and both literature and the Pudding were the gainers.

BLAME THE FOG

Dr Strabismus (Whom God Preserve) of Utrecht was a victim of the thick fog the other night. He was due to address the St Agnes Study Circle on the skull of the Peking Man (*Sinanthropus Pekinensis*), but went to the wrong place. He entered a crowded hall, dashed on to the platform, and began: 'When we remember that this remarkable thing is about a million years old—' A menacing roar greeted the words, and he was informed by the chairman that he had interrupted the presentation of a rose-bowl to a lady physical-drill instructor.

WINE IS A MOCKER

The new Paris Police Commissioner has ordered that wine may be obtained by the police free of charge whenever the weather is cold.

I cannot tell you precisely how the order operates – in fact, I am as ignorant in this matter as any framer of an Act of Parliament – but I have my imagination, and I remember how French people talked when I was at school. It would be like this:

POLICEMAN: Where is the wine?

CAFÉ KEEPER: The wine is in the bottle.

POLICEMAN: It is extremely cold today.

CAFÉ KEEPER: That is a matter of opinion.

POLICEMAN: My nose is blue.

CAFÉ KEEPER: The nose of my wife is not blue.

POLICEMAN: I do not care for the nose of your wife. Where is the wine? I am a policeman. It is not pleasant to be arrested by a policeman. Let your wife bring the wine.

WIFE: Here is some wine.

POLICEMAN (*suddenly*): I do not feel well. You must excuse me. I must depart.

CAFÉ KEEPER: He did not like our wine.

WIFE: He did not like my nose.

CAFÉ KEEPER: What was wrong with the wine?

WIFE: It was not wine. It was the red ink of the bookkeeper.

They say that drink gets more and more fiery in America, and they tell the story of a fisherman who couldn't get a bite. Up came a bootlegger, and, seeing his disconsolate expression, poured some drops from a bottle over the worm. The fisherman lowered his line again, and in a few moments there was a commotion that nearly dragged the man into the water. When the line was drawn up it was observed that the worm had an enormous fish in its grip, and was lashing it with its tail and making warlike noises.

THE GREAT PUDDING SCANDAL

The finding of Mr Hugh Walpole in the Pudding has led to a sharp encounter between his supporters and the supporters of the women candidates.

I am glad to be able to publish the following letter, which throws some light on the controversy. I got a copy of this letter by threatening to tell the lady's publisher that she had boomed a book published by another firm.

Here is the document, addressed to the editor of a weekly paper that has a well-earned reputation for airing such grievances:

'Sir. – While unable to deny that Mr Hugh Walpole succeeded in getting into the Pudding at the Cheshire Cheese, at the same time the public should know that as long ago as last July a small committee of the Lady Novelists' Club decided that if a lady writer could be introduced into the Pudding, it would be a good stroke of publicity. That Mr Walpole should have, as it were, elbowed us aside, is regrettable in the extreme. But that he should flaunt his victory in our faces is monstrous. I venture to assert that Miss Rebecca West, Miss Sackville-West, or even Mrs Woolf have as much right to be found in a Pudding as Mr Walpole.

'Yours indignantly,
'MERIEL HOOPOE.'

Chapter 4

Trousers Over Africa

BIG WHITE CARSTAIRS has been spending a few days at the Residency in Jaboola. Imagine, then, his chagrin on discovering that his fool of a native servant has not packed his dress clothes. Being too humiliated to admit this, and too decent by far to pollute the dinner table by appearing in day clothes, he stayed in his room last night, pleading a headache. His hostess herself brought him up some dirti-beeste soup, but he had locked his door, and dared not open it, lest she should note the absence of the ritual uniform. He pleaded giddi-ness. Whereupon the Resident sent Dr Gilmartin up a ladder to break into the room. Poor Carstairs, half-starved and mortified with shame, unlatched the window, and confessed the whole truth to the kindly physician, who promised to keep the secret, and later brought him a cupful of cold curry. But what, oh what, will tomorrow bring forth? The native tailor, perhaps, may come to the rescue.

Meanwhile the hostess tried once more to bring Carstairs some comfort, this time with light literature. The Resident found her, at 10 p.m., whispering outside his door, 'Let me in. I have a *Life of Livingstone* for you.' 'My dear,' said the Resident, 'don't you think? I mean to say – the natives – this time of night – better come away.' Amazed at the scurviness of her husband's mind, she flounced away from the door, leaving Carstairs to his martyrdom.

Poor Carstairs! Having feigned illness rather than admit that he had no dress clothes with him, he has had to keep up the pretence, and cannot even appear during the day. His hostess, with diabolical persistence, sends him dull books by the ton. Yesterday he determined to confess the truth, and when the Resident called from the veranda, 'How are you today?' Carstairs began, 'The fact is I—' But he got no further. The words stuck in his throat like shark-bones. How could a fellow admit that he hadn't got any dress clothes with him? He would be the laughing-stock of Africa. So he kept his guilty secret, and remained in his room until – oh joy – a trader who happened to look in for a drink brought word of a dress suit left in his hut long ago by a political officer. Carstairs confessed his predicament, and the Resident at once sent a native to fetch the suit. But Carstairs, fuming in his room, said to himself, 'It'll be years out of date. Wrong pockets. Stripe down trousers too narrow. What a position to be in!'

A pretty kettle of fish! A beautiful cauldron of mackerel! A fine saucepan of turbot! The dress suit arrived at the Residency yesterday, and Carstairs unpacked it with feverish fingers. Ha! No trousers!

A fellow in the middle of Africa without dress trousers! A tiny cog in the great machine of Empire! A ball-bearing in the skates of the Raj! And no dress trousers!

Poor Carstairs! When the Resident banged on his door and asked if he was dressed, he had to pretend he had had a relapse, and couldn't appear at dinner. The Resident then informed him that on the next night there was a large party, and that it was most important for him to meet a new political officer and various high officials.

On rejoining his wife, the Resident said, 'He may be big, he may be white, and his name may be Carstairs, but he's a queer bird. Seems to be always ill.'

In his room Carstairs paced to and fro, almost tempted to envy those backward and superstitious foreigners who dine in ordinary clothes. And that foul thought, against which so many Englishmen have battled successfully, remained with him until he fell asleep.

Once more, last night, Carstairs had his evening meal alone in his bedroom. The Resident, having been once more informed of the truth, feels that the whole situation is becoming rather absurd, and is hinting that the visit has lasted long enough. After dinner both he and his wife talked to their guest through the half-open door of his room, for, of course, he could not appear in day clothes, even after dinner was over. The conversation was stilted and dull, and all three were soon yawning.

'I suppose,' said the Resident's wife, loudly enough for Carstairs to hear, 'I suppose, my dear, he couldn't just wear his dinner jacket and stiff shirt and so on, with ordinary lounge suit or flannel trousers.'

'Impossible!' snapped the Resident. 'Nor would he consent to do so.'

'Not for a moment!' said Carstairs indignantly.

For decent men always stick together in a crisis.

So it is stalemate still. All day long Carstairs takes part in the normal life of the Residency, but the moment it is time to dress for dinner he retires and is seen no more.

The Resident sat at his desk writing a confidential report to the Colonial Secretary on the subject of a grant for a local fire brigade in Jamalawoo. A faint hum in the air made him raise his head. Far above the Residency a single air machine was circling. It came lower and lower. Carstairs, sunning himself on the veranda, shaded his eyes to watch it. The machine descended to about 200 feet above the ground, and the pilot, leaning out, threw a small object overboard. This object floated down until it got caught on the flagstaff. The Resident dashed out. 'Saved!' cried Carstairs excitedly, as he waved to the departing machine.

'What do you mean – "saved"?' asked the Resident peevishly.

Carstairs pointed to the flagstaff. 'My dress trousers,' he said simply, and he added: 'I hope you will include in your next report to the Colonial Office, sir, a strong recommendation for the fellow who brought them.'

'That's a personal matter,' said the Resident touchily. 'Your trousers are not a State affair. And, damn it, we can't have dress trousers up there when the flag is hoisted at sundown. We must get 'em down.'

They got the trousers down from the flagstaff, and everybody was happy. Even the natives whistled at their work. The Resident said, 'Now we can dine together like civilized people.' Old Umtifooti grinned broadly as he sounded the dressing gong. The household was at peace.

But what is this, dirty reader? In his room Carstairs almost weeps with rage. For the dress trousers are not his own, and are apparently intended for a man the size of a house. He tries them on. They are monstrous. And at that moment the cheery voice of the Resident cries, 'Are you ready, old boy? Get a move on.' Desperately the empire-builder tries expedients. The trousers are so big round the waist that he has to wear four shirts, one on top of the other. They are so long that when he has finished tightening his braces the trouser-top shows above the bulging waistcoat. They are bell-bottomed, like a sailor's, and still so long that his dress shoes are muffled in them. And the Resident is shouting impatiently. With beads of perspiration twinkling on his forehead like fairy lights, the miserable Carstairs stumbles and shuffles towards the drawing-room. His paunch of shirt is so fat that he cannot see the trailing trousers. But he sets his teeth and enters the room with as jaunty an air as he can manage.

The appearance of Carstairs in the doorway of the drawing-room was followed by a ghastly hush. The Resident's eyes grew round with horror. His wife wanted to laugh. For Carstairs looked like a circus clown in his enormous billowing trousers and with his padded stomach bulging. He himself, as though conscious of all this, paused on the threshold in some anxiety.

'What – on – earth—?' gasped the Resident. 'Look here, old man, I don't want to be personal, but why don't you wear braces?'

'I am wearing braces, sir,' said Carstairs, flushing angrily.

'Well, what the devil is the matter with your trousers? And why have you padded yourself out? This is not a circus, after all.'

The Resident's wife, shaking with mirth, moved away to a window.

'I must apologize, sir,' said Carstairs with ridiculous dignity. 'These trousers aren't mine. They don't fit.'

'So I observe,' remarked the Resident, with an angry glance at the floor, where several inches of trouser obscured each of the empire-builder's feet.

Shrugging his shoulders, the Resident called to his wife to lead the way into dinner.

Stumbling and shuffling, and with one of his four shirts over-flowing outside his waistcoat, Carstairs followed.

Dinner was a dreadful meal. Carstairs, owing to the four shirts which he wore to make the enormous trousers fit round his waist, had to sit back from the table, and as he leaned forward to his food the trouser-tops appeared above the straining waistcoat. The Resident affecting not to notice these things, clicked his teeth impatiently. When finally the waistcoat burst with a report like a small airgun, one button hit him on the cheek, another fell into his wife's glass, and a third rebounded from the ceiling on to the head of the native waiter, who fled screaming from the room. 'I'm really most terribly sorry,' said Carstairs.

'Deuced awkward,' said the Resident. And then, very loudly, 'Of course, we can't go on like this. We must get you some proper dress clothes somehow, damn it. Look here, can't you, I mean, tighten up your confounded braces?'

'They're as tight as they'll go,' said Carstairs. 'If they burst—'

'If *they* burst,' roared the Resident, 'the whole show will come tumbling down, and a nice pack of savages we'll all look. Why four shirts should be necessary to hold your trousers up is beyond me. However, things have changed since my young days.'

'I think I'll leave you men to your fun,' said the Resident's wife with a tolerant smile.

The manly conduct of Carstairs at the Residency, while enhancing his popularity, has done nothing to solve the immediate problem. *He has no dress trousers.* The Resident's wife, a kindly lady, said yesterday to her lord and master, 'Look here, old divot, tonight there'll be only a few at dinner. No guests. Couldn't we kind of stretch a point for Carstairs?' 'You mean,' thundered the Resident, 'you mean, *let him dine in day clothes*?'

'Why not?' said the châtelaine.

For a moment the Resident seemed to be about to burst in pieces. His neck swelled. His face turned magenta under its chemical sunburn. Then he shouted:

'Have you gone mad? *What on earth would the natives think*?'

'Ah, I had not thought of that,' said she.

'One must never cease to think of that,' roared the Resident. 'Better he should starve than give a lot of agitators in England a chance to say that Greater England is represented by fellows who can't even dress decently.'

'Yes, dear,' said his wife soothingly.

'Time to dress.'

The voice of the Resident broke in on the despair of our hero. Hot African twilight, guests about to arrive, and he trouserless. Suddenly he shot to his feet. He had thought of a way out. 'Oh, sir,' he shouted, 'I wonder if you'd mind if I wore my kilt tonight. It's the gathering of our clan, back in Busby, tonight, and the old customs, you know. . . .' 'Delighted, old boy,' said the Resident.

In his bedroom he said to his wife, 'That fellow Carstairs is an odd customer. Wants to wear a kilt. Some damned local Scottish nonsense or other.'

Carstairs, meanwhile, was rigging up a bath towel with safety-pins.

The guests were arriving – traders, political officers, agents, *dibris*, a doctor, a missionary, and so on. The entry of Carstairs, in evening dress, save for what looked like a bath towel, caused a stir. 'His clan,' explained the Resident. 'What clan?' queried one of the ladies. 'The Clan Lochjaugh,' said the Resident, on the spur of the moment. 'They have the right to wear a white kilt.' Carstairs hung his head in shame, and when the Resident's wife said loudly, 'The white kilt of the Lochjaughs looks very like the white bath towel of the Resident,' the empire-builder flushed and stammered. There was a ghastly silence.

All were silent at the dining-table, while Carstairs, with rare courage, explained what had occurred.

'My kilt,' he said, 'is a bath towel. I am not a Lochjaugh. I deceived you all. But what was the alternative? I had no dress trousers.'

A murmur of admiration greeted this manly confession, made so simply and quietly.

'Anybody,' said the doctor, rather churlishly, 'could have lent you a spare pair.'

Carstairs lowered his eyes. 'I didn't dare to admit I needed them,' he said.

Here the Resident came to his aid. 'Knew a chap down-country, at Papawatta, who came to dinner in ordinary togs. Sheer ignorance, I suppose. Or damned Bolshevism. He was sent home. Damned good cricketer. Outsider, though. Grammar school or something. Knew another chap, up-country, at Wappapoopa. All right. Top drawer. But *made-up* tie. Tied by some infernal machine. Came off at dance. Picked up by his poor wife. She tried to hide it. No good. Sent home. Plucky little woman. Met 'em last year after Henley. Tie still made-up. Hopeless.'

'A man like that would murder his own grandmother,' said a young political agent.

'Probably did,' said the Resident.

'Look here, sir,' said Carstairs, 'we must settle this. Either I must come in to dinner tonight in ordinary clothes, or else we must go through this farce again, with four shirts and those awful trousers.'

The Resident looked at him icily.

'Are you suggesting,' he asked, 'that I should encourage you not to dress for dinner?'

'Certainly not, sir,' said Carstairs. 'You know what my choice would be. I'm only thinking of you and your wife.'

'Then don't,' said the Resident with a bark. 'Think only of the Raj.'

Carstairs was about to leave the room when the Resident added, 'But, damn it, try to be presentable. Can't you *cut* off the ends of the trousers?'

'By Jove, sir,' said Carstairs, his eyes alight. 'That's the idea.'

That night, happily and carelessly, the scissors were wielded – too carelessly. The trousers became shorts. There was nothing for it but to go in to dinner. The Resident hated unpunctuality. In the doorway appeared Carstairs, still with four shirts to fill up the waistline, and with dress-trousers which ended at the knee. The Resident's wife went into screaming hysterics. The Resident said in his parade voice, 'Major Carstairs, are you a political officer or a – a – some damned kind of fat Boy Scout in mourning?'

And then – oh, joy! a parcel arrived from up-country, addressed to Carstairs. His dress clothes. At last everything was going to be all right again. The Resident, when he heard the news, smiled broadly. 'Now,' he said, 'we can get back to normal decent living.' An American lady explorer was asked to dinner, and Carstairs regained his self-confidence. During the day he inspected the native cricket team, and gave a short lecture on the team spirit. When he went to his room to dress for dinner, he found the dear, well-remembered clothes laid out on the bed. He could have hugged them. He fingered the coat, the waistcoat – and then horror caught him by the throat. There were no trousers! Feverishly he examined every corner of the room. He summoned the native servants. No.

No trousers. In a rage he paced his room, ignoring the dressing gong. And when the Resident knocked on the door and shouted cheerfully, 'Get a move on, old man!' he gritted his teeth.

The dinner gong went. The Resident knocked and shouted again. 'What's keeping you?' he cried. 'That parcel,' answered Carstairs in a voice of despair, 'contained everything but my trousers.' Outside the door there was a short, sharp gasp, and then the bellow of a creature mortally wounded. 'Damnation!' shouted the Resident, 'this is more than I can stand!'

It cannot be said that any tears were shed when Carstairs left the Residency at the end of his visit. It has been a nerve-racking time for everybody. The Resident, with bluff good humour, said, 'Next time you come, old boy, I suggest you bring your dress clothes.'

Hardly had he left when the post arrived. Bale after bale of parcels addressed to Carstairs, and all marked, 'Dress Clothes. Handle With Care.' They were offerings from well-wishers all over the Empire, but, alas, they arrived too late.

'One more day,' said the Resident, 'and he'd have had enough trousers to make a sleeping-bag for an elephant.'

'One more day,' said his wife, 'and I should have forgotten my Position and begged him to dine in day clothes.' The Resident glared at her as though she had plunged a dagger into his chest. 'I know you don't mean that, little woman,' he said uncomfortably.

To the Editor,
The Daily Express

Dear Sir,
I am sure many of your readers will fail to see anything excruciatingly funny in the idea of a gentleman habitually dressing for dinner. 'Beachcomber', like all subversive snobs, probably has no notion of the meaning of self-respect and prestige. I consider the whole Carstairs episode as not only bad manners, but disgracefully bad taste. And it is not the Empire-builders who are made to look absurd, but 'Beachcomber' himself. Of course, the idea of a man without trousers will always raise a cheap laugh from certain types of people, but I am sure it is not on the taste of such as these that your great newspaper has built up its popularity.

Yours faithfully,
'Not Amused.'

I enclose my card.

Chapter 5

Bracerot

THE DOCTOR is said to have invented an extraordinary weapon which will make war less brutal. It is described as a very powerful liquid which rots braces at a distance of a mile.

This liquid, which is sprayed out of a sprayer, has no ill effect. It smells like a spring morning. But it is deadly to the material from which braces are made.

Within an hour of an attack by this liquid – which is heavier than air – the braces begin to rot; and finally disintegrate. The air becomes full of the rustle and plop of falling breeches, and the hapless infantrymen find that their movements are impeded by the descended garments.

Also, the idly flapping shirts give them a sense of inferiority.

An experiment was tried in a field near Aldershot, but the wind changed, and a group of interested Staff Officers had to waddle hastily to cover behind a lorry, where they remained until spare braces had been brought from Aldershot.

A certain major, whose trousers had fallen over his horse's head, was thrown into a garbage heap. He is now seconded to a Highland regiment.

Several foreign Governments have become interested in the new Strabismus invention for rotting the braces of an army in the field. The story of how the invention, called Bracerot, was introduced into Germany is not without interest.

A very beautiful spy, as blonde as an egg and Nordic to the fingertips, dropped her handbag in front of one of the uniformed Storm

Milkmen. He retrieved the fallen gewgaw, and she at once told him a ghastly story of the oppression of the Nazis who were being prevented from seizing power in Pomorze, that Ancient Prussian territory.

He took the story to the Great High Shock-Council of the Weldgeführengebundgeschluchtverein.

A special parade was announced in Berlin, to demand the return of Pomorze to the Reich. The Führer himself mounted a rostrum to address the assembled troops.

But what is this? His sensitive nostrils twitch. The air is full of a sweet aroma, and at his first barbarian shriek all hands are raised in the Nazi salute.

Imagine his mortification on hearing a crash of falling trousers, and finding himself confronted with rank upon rank of bony knees.

Holding up his own trousers, he took refuge in his car and drove away, but the troops, being Prussian, did not budge. They remained at the salute, with their breeches about their ankles, because their officers were too confused to give any word of command.

Not a smile illumined those wooden faces.

And who, you ask, was the spy? Reader, it was – but, no! That is a State secret.

The Prussian Reich is now considering a new kind of steel braces, which would resist the inroads of Bracerot.

Professor Grossvolk has already produced a pamphlet in which he proves that ordinary braces are effeminate and un-Aryan. 'The braces of a Prussian should be of the finest, hardest steel, to match his indomitable soul.'

Mr Eden is to go to Peking to ask representatives of the Chinese Admiralty whether steel braces ought to be considered as protective armour, if they exceed a certain width. After that he will go to North Borneo to ask the Albanian Foreign Secretary who started the European war, and why.

And then he will go to Carlstad to ask representatives of the

Swedish Women's Co-operative Industrial Federation why Prussia has torn up another treaty. A representative of Bracerot, Ltd will accompany him.

The Great High Prussian Storm-and-Shock Commander has issued an order that during the present epidemic of Bracerot every Nordic man is to wear two pairs of braces, and to carry a third pair of Emergency Braces in his knapsack.

When he feels his braces disintegrating he is to sing a patriotic air, salute with one hand, and adjust the Emergency Braces with the other.

General Goering said yesterday:

There are weaker Non-Aryan races who may imagine that an Aryan can be made to look undignified if you deprive him of braces. Our reply is that the old Norse gods never knew what braces were, and if necessary we will dress like them, in monstrous nightshirts. The Latins, softened by luxury, think that no man can go into battle with his trousers down. Trousers or no trousers, it is our mission to save Europe from Shintoism, and I—

PHWOOSH! Down fell his Nordic breeches.

The spy who succeeded in introducing Bracerot into Prussia seems to have discovered how easy it is to make the pompous and foolish Boche look even sillier than he is.

At a mammoth meeting in Berlin to protest against the existence of the Polish Army, the principal speakers suddenly felt their trousers loosening, and had to disappear hurriedly. At another meeting to protest against the existence of the French Army, three very high officials were subject to the same humiliating experience.

Later in the day a march-past of Storm Troops, held on the occasion of the protest against the continued occupation of Switzerland by the Swiss, had to be discontinued. As each battalion drew level with the saluting base its breeches fell with a rush.

But as for me, would that I were in Perpignan, at the Sign of the Golden Lion.

A long memorandum, drawn up by some of the most prominent men in Prussia, suggests that belts should be substituted for braces.

These belts would be coated with a certain chemical capable of resisting Bracerot, and nullifying its effects.

At the first test, in a field outside Berlin, the trousers of the savants fell with the customary crash.

The same thing occurred at a mass demonstration in favour of the return of the French Channel ports to the Reich.

I learn that Prussia will on no account join any conference unless a guarantee is given that disarmament shall apply first and foremost to Bracerot, which saps the fighting spirit of even Nordic fools. The English reply will be that the manufacture of large quantities of Bracerot stimulates the braces industry, and does not necessarily make a nation bloodthirsty.

Prussia maintains that the deliberate rotting of braces constitutes an act of aggression. She refuses to be encircled by the brace-rotting nations.

* * * * *

HOGWASCH

Hogwasch is planning a big spectacular film about the Charge of the Light Brigade. He said yesterday: I shall send a whole outfit to the Cashmea, and there will be a scene taken on the actual field of Omdurman, the idea being that Jenny Wrenn, the Swedish night-ingale with the lamp, is in love with a Moorish chieftain. She gets shut up in the fortress of Calbava, and to emancipate her Lord Nolan orders his army to charge. We aim to have far more than six hundred on in that scene, and we shall show the Persians being driven into the harbour at St Bastipool. Jenny is rescued, and in the final scene we show Gladstone being best man at her wedding in the crip of the House of Commons.

WHEN WE WERE VERY SILLY

There is a great vogue for what is called the Woogie-Poogie-Boo kind of children's book, and I am doing my best to get one ready. I don't know what it will be called, but I rather fancy *Songs Through My Hat*, or perhaps *When We Were Very Silly*. Here is a poem called 'Theobald James'.

I've got a silk-worm,
A teeny-tiny silk-worm;
I call *my* silk-worm
Theobald James.
But nursie says it's cruel,
Nursie says it's wicked
To call a teeny-tiny little
        Silk-
            Worm
        NAMES

I said to *my* silk-worm
    'Oh, Mr Silk-worm,
I'd rather be a silk-worm
Than anything far!'
And nursie says he answered,
Nursie says he shouted,
'You wish you were a silk-worm?
You little
        Prig,
        You
    ARE!'

*   *   *   *   *

As I strode through London, brushing aside the crowds like flies, and pausing now and then to kick or cuff a man whose face displeased me, I came to the fountains in Trafalgar Square, and they were playing. And as I gazed at them, I began to think of other fountains; of the stillness of old gardens, and the sunlight on the falling water.

What fun it must have been for the first man who discovered that these tricks can be played with water! Whoever he was, he is dishonoured in every place where an ornamental fountain has been allowed to decay and moulder.

I never come upon a maimed Triton or a nereid whose face is chipped and discoloured by time and weather without mourning for a world that is gone. For who today cares twopence about fountains?

There is, upon the great road that runs through the Jura from

Poligny to Geneva, a thing which is marked on the maps as the Fontaine de Napoléon. The name drew me, and in spite of the fact that I had found a little track that would take me from the Faucille down to Gex, I took to the main road to see this fountain of Napoleon. And what do you think I found? Why, a miserable drinking-trough with an old tap dribbling into it.

On the road over the Col des Goules in Auvergne the map speaks of a Fontaine du Berger. I hunted for it in the woods, picturing to myself something of Fragonard come to life. I never found it, but two days later, on the edge of the Corrèze, I was drinking rough wine in a broken-down house when, raising my eyes, I saw standing in the doorway a girl of great beauty, with a shepherd's crook in her hand, and on her head a wide-brimmed hat in the style of a time long gone by.

Thus was I consoled for the unsuccessful search for the fountain in the woods.

PRODNOSE: Are we to have any other subject today?

MYSELF: Certainly not. I've been got at by the Big Five in the Fountain World.

PRODNOSE: Promise not to become mawkish about your old friend the Fountain of Perpetual Youth.

MYSELF: I promise.

PRODNOSE: And you won't mention Bandusia or Bellerie?

MYSELF: No.

PRODNOSE: Then you may continue.

AT THE EISTEDDFOD

The Eisteddfod was in full swing. A choir of 28,364 Welsh voices was roaring 'Softly Awake, O Rose of Llanpwchlleth'. A particularly arch druid with his bardic crown at a jaunty angle was massing the shock-druids in their white nightgowns. A second choir of 32,841 Welsh voices was howling 'Sweet and Low'. A poet was bawling a long poem about King's Cross Station. A third choir of 47,298 Welsh voices was screaming 'Hush, My Little Baby, Sleep, My Pretty Dear'. A fourth choir of 937,110 Welsh voices was bellowing 'Silent is the Night'. All this was going on, when a lonely voice rose during a

lull in the hullabaloo. 'Flossie,' sang the interloper, 'is the Girl for
Me,' and there stood Foulenough in a huge nightgown embroidered
with stars, and on his head a straw hat. On the band of the hat was
written: 'The Ancient Order of Welsh Rabbits.' He was requested to
leave.

SEESAW

*We three have noticed in your column, if such may we call it, we
hope, a number of letters about phenomena in restaurants. Sir, we are
the three Persian gentlemen who played seesaw in the lounge of the
restaurant. It was upon the belly of the fattest of us, Risamughan, that
the plank (from a sugar-melon tree of Kermanshah) was gently but
firmly laid. Then Ashura and I, Kazbulagh, sat one at each end of the
plank, and the sport, as you English call it, began. Sir, we beg to state
that we did not do this to advertise anything except our own extreme
happiness. For, sir, we were going home to our own families in Filthistan, the gramophone company for which we had the honour to act as
night-watchers having gone burst. So, sir, we played seesaw for fun in
the nearest place we could find. And, sir, one day, if we ever return
from Persia, we hope to play seesaw again in that most hospitable
restaurant. And, sir, P.S., it does not at all hurt Rizamughan's belly,
since he wears a thick cork bathmat, with 'Welcome' written on it,
under his shirt – a souvenir from our boarding-house, sir, in the Crom-
well Road. Astonishing good luck, sir, and remember us as*

The Filthistan Trio.

MOONLINESS

By Roland Milk

(I)

The moon and I
   Came face to face
In a sequestered
   Country place.

(II)

I thought the moon
   Was heavenly;
I wonder what
   It thought of me.

THE CLAM OF CHOWDAH

I found the Clam of Chowdah stuck to his chair. His mouth was so full that I could not hear a word he said, and if I had heard anything it would have been meaningless, since he spoke in his own language, beast that he was, and there was no interpreter present, as that is against the etiquette of the Clam. I cursed him to his face in good round English, but in the tone usually employed for fulsome compliments. 'Can it be,' I said softly, bowing and smirking, 'can it be that there is in the world such a filthy reptile as you? How hideous you are, and how abominable is your nature.' He grinned and nodded his head, and said something – probably a curse-word, as he clearly detested my intrusion. 'Good-bye and good riddance, you horror,' I said, sweeping the ground with my cap. And thus we parted. He was still eating when I left.

The impending visit of the Clam of Chowdah has been postponed, owing to what spokesmen in touch with preposterous circles call a technical hitch.

It was hoped that the Clam would inundate this country with foreign currency, but all he understands is barter. Owners of billiard saloons who expected to sell him quantities of tables now find that they are asked to swop them for liquorice, which the Clam hates. And there are no forms on which the big billiard operators can apply for a licence to own liquorice. The Clam's Prime Minister, vital, human, dynamic Jaja Hopu Homf, said yesterday, according to an agency message, 'It is of democracy that one cares.'

WHEN WE WERE VERY SILLY

There are Communists and Socialists and Conservatives and things,
There are cranks, and dupes, and forgers and their slimy underlings,
There's a roaring man with a ruddy face, and another as quiet as a
  mouse—
But *I* gave a bun to the Premier when *I* went down to the House.

There's a man who brays 'Protection', and a lady who curses drink,
And at least three hundred and forty-six who never knew how to
  think,

There's one who cries the Millennium, and one with a permanent
   grouse,
But *I* gave a bun to the Premier when *I* went down to the House.

There's a wretched, lonely Liberal, with a face as long as a flute,
And a man who spends his leisure hours in making a corner in jute,
There's every shade of incompetence, and all humbug under the sun,
But whenever *I* go down to the House the *Premier* takes the bun.

THE TOASTMASTER

The eating part of the annual banquet of the Incorporated Society of
Usurers was drawing to a close. The toast of the King had been given,
the ladies had lit their cigarettes and the gentlemen their cigars. 'Twas
speechtime. Behind the chairman stood the toastmaster, resplendent
in red and gold, and ready to yell.

Here it comes!

'Ladies and gentlemen, pray silence for your toastmaster!'

There was an intake of breath all over the room, then gasping and
tittering. The chairman waited nervously for the correction to be
made. But as he turned in his chair the toastmaster shouted, 'With
your toastmaster's love!' and began to throw pieces of toast, which
he produced from a sack, to the diners.

'Foulenough!'

The word went up from a hundred throats.

ANODYNE

One of my contemporaries is very fond of a little wodge of humour,
tucked away into a corner. After careful study I have decided that
it generally goes something like this:

'Carol of Rumania has not given up hope of attaining his ambition.'
Christmas Carol?

'I like a man with a will.' (*A woman at Marylebone Police Court.*)
– It depends in whose favour it is.

'Accused said he was smoking a cigarette.' – Lighting-up time?

'The ninth man fell to the floor.' – One over the eight?

EPITAPH

Tread softly; bid a solemn music sound;
Here in a little plot of English ground
Lies Smudge, who sold us medicated beer,
And double-crossed his friends, and died a peer.

WHEN WE WERE VERY SILLY

Here is part of another poem from my book:

John Percy
Said to his nursy,
  'Nursy,' he said, said he,
'Tell father
I'd much rather
  He didn't write books about me.'
'Lawkamercy!'
Shouted nursy,
  'John Percy,' said she,
'If dad stopped it,
If dad dropped it,
  We shouldn't have honey for tea!'

CORRESPONDENCE

Dear Sir,
  In reference to the waggling of ears practised by those who have more aural dexterity than sense, the other night I was at a big dinner-party, attended by several members of the Diplomatic Corps. The gentleman next to me had very large ears, and when he leaned towards me the tip of his left ear caressed my cheek and made me giggle. I felt very foolish, especially as he mistook my laughter for genuine mirth and enjoyment, and began to flap the ear noisily; it was like the crack of a small whip, and the gust of air it set up untidied my hair. The gentleman on the other side of me complained of draught, but I could only giggle, because in between the flapping the gentleman with the big ears continued the caressing motion. I heard an ambassador say, 'That little lady can't carry her Burgundy.' I wanted to be angry, but

could not stop giggling. What should I have done? I prefer to remain anonymous.

P.S. – I heard afterwards that he blew out all the candles with his ears after the ladies had withdrawn. He is some sort of attaché.

SOL HOGWASCH

Referring to a new film about Velasquez, now being made, Mr Sol Hogwasch said yesterday: 'We're having the largest palate ever built for Verlaskus to paint from. It's held by four Moorish obelisks, daughters of a Sheik from the Guadalarama mountains. By an arrangement of electricity and a magnificator, when Verlaskus paints he paints forty-three times larger than any painting ever seen. He puts the pickments on a foot thick with a chromium trawl bigger than a spade. And every time he paints, the music plays "My Spanish Orange Lady", the theme song. For background we've got factual reconstitutions of scenes in Andalasturia and Arandora.'

The following letter, signed 'Sol Hogwasch', appeared in the morning paper today:

Dear Sir,

As one who is making a fillum about the life and loves of the painter Verlaskus, when I read about the cleaning of the varnish on Philip XIV I want to say that the star who plays Philip is going to play it in dirty clothing so as to get the putina of an old master. I don't think liberties ought to be taken with works of art, and even when Philip appears in the cabaret scene as a young man, he is stained and dirty like the picture, because the public wants reelism. It may interest the chairman of the British Museum to know that in the picture Philip smears oil in his face to get it more like the aboriginal, and his boots are glazed.

TWENTY YEARS OF UPROAR

At a concert in the *Conservatoire Royal de Musique* in Brussels, Sprautz had just begun to conduct Dvořák's New World Symphony when a kindly thought occurred to him. Turning to the audience, while still waving his baton, he shouted: 'Stop me if you've heard this one!'

AMONG THE NEW BOOKS

Brittle Galaxy. By Barbara Snorte.

A colourful and courageous attempt to put the point of view of the artist misunderstood in a world of wars and rumours of wars. Dalton Sparleigh is the eternal figure of the hero who is the centre of his world, and regards his own personality as the most important thing in life. 1,578 pages of undiluted enthralment.

Groaning Carcase. By Frederick Duddle.
A very delicate and tactfully written plea for old horses, against a background of country-house life. It is fiction made more compelling than fact by one who seems to be right inside the horse's mind.

Splendid Sorrow. By Walter Fallow.
Was Ernst Hörenwurst, adventurer and rake, the Margrave Friedrich Meiningen of Hohefurstenau-Lebensbletter? Mr Fallow, in his new historical romance, has no hesitation in leaving the question unanswered.

Tricks With Cheese. By 'Cheesophile' (of the *Cheese World*).
The author appears to be able to make everything, from a model of the Palace of Justice in Brussels to a bust of his aunt, out of cheese. A good book for the fireside.

Fain Had I Thus Loved. By Freda Trowte.
Miss Trowte has been called by the *Outcry* the Anatole France of Herefordshire. There is an indescribable quality of something evocative yet elusively incomprehensible about her work. The character of Nydda is burningly etched by as corrosive a pen as is now being wielded anywhere.

No Second Churning. By Arthur Clawes.
An almost unbearably vital study of a gas-inspector who puts gas-inspecting before love. Awarded the Prix de Seattle, this book should enhance the author's growing reputation as an interpreter of life's passionate bypaths.

Pursuant To What Shame. By Goola Drain.
All those who enjoyed Miss Drain's romantic handling of a love-story in *Better Thine Endeavour* and *Immediate Beasts* will welcome this trenchant tale of an irresponsible girl who poisons her uncle.

A famous tennis player said, before he had even seen the book, 'In my opinion Miss Drain is unique and unchallengeable. Her command of words is a delight.'

A STORY

A witness was being examined in an assault case.

'Did you see this man assaulted?' asked counsel.

'No, but I heard him cry for help,' was the answer.

'That is not satisfactory evidence,' said counsel.

As he left the witness-box the witness laughed loudly.

The judge rebuked him, and reminded him that he was showing contempt of court.

'What?' said the witness, in surprise. 'Did you see me laugh, while I had my back to you?'

'No, but I heard you,' said the judge.

'That is not satisfactory evidence,' answered the witness.

NOW WE ARE SICK

Hush, hush,
Nobody cares!
Christopher Robin
Has
     Fallen
         Down-
             Stairs.

Chapter 6

Life at Boulton Wynfevers

WHEN I WAS head aquarium keeper at Boulton Wynfevers, the commodious Tudor residence of the seventeenth Baron Shortcake, we had goldfish in every room. 'Travers,' my master would say to me, 'have you changed the fish-water in Lady Katharine's room?' or 'Travers,' he would call from the minstrels' gallery, 'are the fish in the Hon. Guy Clobbock's room eating well?' or, 'Travers,' he would yell from the gunroom, 'the fish in Lady Muriel's boudoir are making so much damned noise I can't hear myself eat.'

We had one fish that snored, and we always put it in Lord Thwacker's room, and told him it was the ghost of the ninth baron.

It was my duty as head aquarium keeper to keep an eye on all the different kinds of fish in our aquarium, and every night, before retiring to bed, Baron Shortcake expected me to report that all was well. The men under me had to count the fish, and then I would hand a slip of paper to my master, with the figure written on it. He always feared that some might escape – an impossible contingency, since the fish were in tanks and were watched night and day. I once ventured to ask the Baron where the fish could go to if they escaped. He answered: 'Travers, fish are queer customers. They might break out. I wish to run no risks.' One night he roused the household saying he had dreamed that a China Sea pterolotl had escaped, and was not satisfied until I had shown him the little beast asleep among weeds in his tank.

Towards his eightieth year my dear old master became an even greater goldfish-addict than before. He filled the house and grounds with goldfish, and I, as head aquarium keeper, was often called to flick the fish off people's clothes, or to drive them from the dining-hall table.

One evening, when sprats Melba were on the menu, Lady Thrashurst ate six sleeping goldfish by mistake. They had crept on to her plate. The consciousness of her error brought her to her feet with a roar of shame and anguish, and so energetically did she wriggle and squirm as the rudely awakened fish struggled in her throat that my master, recalling the Eastern dances of his youth, shouted an Oriental oath and clapped his hands.

On the morning after my old master had lost £73,000 in IOU's to a guest, we sold the entire Boulton Wynfevers collection of goldfish to a lonely old lady who had just cut her niece out of her will. From that day the Baron changed. He would wander listlessly from room to room, calling the absent fish by name and starting guiltily if he thought he saw a movement in the empty bowls.

He would sit late at his dinner, and would often call for me to repeat some story of the fish, saying, 'Travers, tell them about that time when two Burmese Rovers got down the back of Lady Felspar's dress,' or, 'Travers, do you recall how that little devil Silver Slipper drank a glass of my Meursault on the night of the fire?' or, 'Travers, I do not think Sir Arthur knows the story of how Tiny and his gang got into the Bishop's hot-water bottle and tickled his feet.' And he would sigh and say, 'Those were the days.'

They were, indeed, the days. Once a year the grounds were thrown open to the villagers and their friends, and the London papers would send photographers and reporters. The Baron was usually photographed standing between two of the biggest bowls, and little girls dressed as goldfish would curtsey to him and present him with an album in which to stick snapshots of his favourites and prizewinners.

Twelve years running we won the Shires Cup for the smartest turn-out, and the fish always got fresh water and an extra meal – not to mention a playful flip on the back from the beaming owner.

I still treasure the photograph of myself standing between my master and Lady Mockett and holding up Jellaby Wonder II by the tail.

Deafness troubled my old master considerably towards the end of his life. I remember an occasion on which he was entertaining the Lord Lieutenant of the County to dinner. He, also, was deaf. He suggested to Lord Shortcake that the craze for tropical fish was dying out.

'By topical,' said my master, 'I presume you mean fashionable.' 'I don't agree,' rejoined the Lord Lieutenant. 'I think they are unfashionable. They are aliens in any aquarium.' 'Who are aliens?' asked my master. 'No, no,' said the Lord Lieutenant. 'Not us. I said the fish.' 'Damn it,' hotly retorted Shortcake, 'what fish are you talking of?' 'No, no,' said the Lord Lieutenant, 'not us. I said the fish.' 'What?' roared my master. 'Do you mean *all* fish?' 'Well, they *are* all fish, aren't they?' said the Lord Lieutenant angrily.

As the evening wore on and the port in the decanter sank lower and lower, the two deaf men groped for an understanding. When the Lord Lieutenant spoke of flying fish, my master thought he had said 'frying fish'. He grew enraged at the idea of frying valuable specimens of his collection. 'But surely,' said the Lord Lieutenant, 'you keep flying fish?' 'I do no such thing,' replied Shortcake, 'and if I did I should do it in the kitchen, not in the aquarium.' 'That's the first time,' said the Lord Lieutenant, 'I ever heard of anybody with an aquarium in his kitchen.' 'Besides,' said my master, 'you couldn't eat most of them, even if you fried them.' 'There you are!' said the Lord Lieutenant, 'what's the good of flying fish?'

Nothing annoyed Lord Shortcake more than an obvious indifference to his goldfish. He would say to a guest before retiring: 'You will find your bowl in your room. Don't disturb the fish more than is necessary.'

The tactless guest would sometimes grin and say nothing or even show surprise, as though he were unused to such a thing. But what my dear master liked was to get some such reply as: 'Oh, but how very thoughtful of you! What breed are they? How many? What age? Certainly I will not disturb them.'

On one occasion a young lady of title, on receiving the parting information and admonition went into screaming hysterics, which infuriated my master. 'Does she think they are mice?' he asked me several times.

On another occasion a stupid dowager cried: 'What! Real goldfish?' 'Have you ever seen goldfish that weren't real?' snapped my master. 'But, do you mean *real* goldfish, like the ones in bowls?' she continued. 'Damn it all, madam,' said my master, 'I don't know what kind of goldfish you have been used to, but there's no nonsense about mine.'

'But why in the bedroom?' asked the dowager. 'Why on earth not?' countered Lord Shortcake. 'What odds is it to them what room they are in?' 'Well, I shall put them outside the door,' said the dowager. 'You can do that with your boots, but not with my fish,' said my master. 'Why not,' he added, 'fill your boots with water and put them in the bowl with the fish instead?' The dowager considered this for a while, and then left the room in high dudgeon.

I would not like my readers to have the idea that life at Boulton Wynfevers was all goldfish. There were days when my master became profoundly dissatisfied with his hobby. 'Travers,' he would say to me, 'these damned fish never *do* anything. They roam round their bowls, but anybody can do that.'

It was my task on such occasions to comfort him by referring to the sheen on their coats, or their efforts to look intelligent when shouted at, or their value as ornaments. 'Bah,' he would say, 'I prefer a good bloater. You can, at any rate, *eat* a bloater.' I would then point out that you can't keep bloaters in bowls all over a house. 'Quite right, Travers,' he would say, 'one must make allowances.' And he would add: 'It takes all sorts to make a world.'

Curiously enough, my old master was always afraid of fire destroying his fish. An Indian law student had once told him that goldfish are terrified of fire. That is why, during the winter, their bowls were always placed as far from the fires as possible. And he even asked the chief of the local fire brigade to submit a plan for dealing with an outbreak of fire among the fish. This gentleman said: 'Oh, but they're safe enough. They're in water.' 'So are ships,' said the Baron, 'but they catch fire.' There was a fire-alarm in every room, and I, as head aquarium keeper, had to wear a fireman's helmet and carry an axe on windy days.

My dear old master, in spite of the immense wealth which enabled him to own the largest private acquarium in the shires, was a simple gentleman at heart.

Though he had a first-class chef he would never eat fish. He said to me one day: 'If I collected cows, and kept on eating beef, I should feel like a murderer. Same with fish. That is why I never shoot pheasants.'

But he was very fond of a plain boiled egg, and always kept the shells. Out of these he would make what he jestingly called 'Small porcelain bric-à-brac'. These were so fragile that no maid was allowed to dust them. They were kept on a mantelshelf in his dressing-room. And if he broke one, he would glue the pieces together again. I remember one ornament which he called a frigate in full sail. He used matches for the masts and calico for the sails. One day it disintegrated in the bath and disappeared with the bath water, to his chagrin.

Lord Shortcake collected stamps as well as goldfish – but only English twopenny stamps. He had no interest in foreign stamps, which, he said, should be left to foreigners. He had many albums filled with twopenny stamps, for he said that no two stamps were the same. Often a bored guest would be forced to admire the contents of these albums, and if he said: 'But they all look the same to me,' my dear old master would reply, 'That is because you don't study them enough. All Chinamen look the same to many Westerners, but they are really all different.'

It was the duty of my master's secretary, Aubyn Spicecraft, to keep every twopenny stamp which arrived with each day's post. Lord Shortcake showed no interest in the contents of his letters. He would ask, at breakfast, 'How many of our well-known twopennies today, Spicecraft?' And, according to the answer, he would smile or frown. Sometimes Spicecraft would venture to remark that there was a letter from a relative or a dear friend. My master would then reply, 'Well, what odds, so long as it's got the jolly old twopenny stuck to it, eh? Give me the stamp, I always say, and anybody can have the letter, eh?'

My dear old master was of so kindly a nature that he was easily victimised. He was asked once to stand for Parliament, the member for the constituency having died. On his inquiring what they would like him to stand as, a go-ahead member of the local football club said, 'Why not the Goldfish candidate? Better treatment for our dumb friends, and all that. Good publicity value.'

My old master replied that goldfish were not dumb. He said they mewed very faintly, at certain seasons. Otherwise, he said, he was prepared to present the case for better treatment for all fish to the representatives of the nation.

Lord Shortcake was actually preparing his election literature when a friend told him that if he got up in the House and talked about goldfish he would be laughed at. 'Through me, then,' he said, 'they would be laughing at the fish. I will not do it, eh?'

The newspapers, of course, ran the Goldfish candidate for all they were worth, but my dear old master could be stubborn when he wanted to be. In a final interview he said, 'I think I can best serve the interests of fish by abstaining from the rostrum of public life, eh?'

Among my duties at Boulton Wynfevers, as I have stated, was the counting of the goldfish. Every night, before the household retired to bed, I had to hand to my dear old master a slip of paper with the total figure written on it.

The figure was always 13,874, since every dead fish was replaced at once, from a reserve tank, by a living one. But Shortcake always took the thing seriously. He would say, 'Hum! 13,874. Not bad, Travers, not at all bad, eh?'; or 'By George, Travers, 13,874, did you say? Pretty sound figure, eh?'; or 'Bravo, Travers, we're keeping it up, eh?'

Once I wrote 13,847 by mistake, and my dear old master made me count them all over again. 'Slippery little devils,' he kept on saying. 'Can't be too careful.'

When the house was full of guests the counting had to be done while they were out of their rooms. I had to hang about the corridors and seize my chance. And I well remember going into the Queen Elizabeth room in the east wing to tot up the denizens of that particular bowl and hearing a scream. A young lady was arranging her hair at a mirror, and when I had explained my intrusion she said, 'It doesn't ring true, my man,' and, turning to her maid, she said, 'Germaine, lock up my jewels and give me the key.' Such base talk made me hang my head in shame, and under my breath I cursed the day those goldfish were born.

What struck me as so silly was that I had no need to count them. I knew the figure by heart, as the shrewd reader will have guessed.

My master's own personal bowl, in his bedroom, was stocked with the best of the fish, and I shall not be likely to forget the night when the lights fused and a certain bishop blundered into the room, mistaking it for his own, and plunged his right foot into the bowl. Candles were brought, but one big beauty was missing. My master surprised the bishop by saying, 'I think Wonder of Arden is hiding in your gaiter.' The bishop had to remove his gaiter, and out jumped the fish and slithered into a corner of the room. Lord Shortcake and I rounded it up and replaced it in the bowl. But it was an anxious night, and at two a.m. my dear old master beat on my door, shouting, 'I think I hear a stray fish in Sir Arthur's room.' It was a false alarm.

During the summer months it was Lord Shortcake's custom to entertain on a large scale. But the younger among his guests resented the lack of swimming pools, since every possible piece of water, ornamental or otherwise, was reserved for the goldfish.

One cocksure young lady said one day, 'Shorty, old hog, why not clear out these fish and give us a break?' My dear old master flushed with anger. 'Those fish,' he said, 'can do nothing but swim. You, my dear Poppy, have other accomplishments – or haven't you?'

I had strict orders to see that nobody dived into the main pond, and a large notice warned human beings to respect the privacy of the fish.

I remember the ghastly silence when, at dinner one night, a jovial young peer said, 'Any fishing down here, Shorty?' After a moment my dear old master replied, 'What would you say, Flinge, if, while you were lying in your bath, a beast came and fixed a hook in your throat and hauled you out?' Young Mr Flinge gaped. 'Don't sort of get the idea,' he said. 'What are you talking about?' 'A parable,' said Lord Shortcake, 'a mere parable. If the cap fits shove it on.' 'What cap?' asked Mr Flinge. 'I say, I don't know what you're talking about.' But my master had summoned me from my place next to the third butler, and now shouted loudly, 'Keep him from the fish, eh?'

When I announced to my dear old master that Polly Cragge, one of the parlourmaids at Chealvercote Grange, the residence of Lord and Lady Hoopoe, had promised to marry me, he at once asked, 'Does she understand about goldfish?' I said that we had not discussed that subject much. To which he replied that marriage with a head aquarium keeper meant something more than a passive interest in his work.

He even sent Lord Hoopoe a bowl of fish, in the hope that Polly might become fond of them. He received in return a note from Lord Hoopoe which said, 'I take it that the present of goldfish was meant for someone else. I return them herewith.' They were at once sent back to Chealvercote, where a groom fed them to an Irish wolfhound.

Our engagement dragged on, because Polly took a violent dislike to the goldfish at Boulton Wynfevers. Every time we were together, my dear old master would track us down and get us into the aquarium. He kept on asking us to guess what he was going to give us for a wedding present. We would pretend not to know, and he would chuckle and say, 'Why, six dozen spankin' fine goldfish, eh?' And one day he gave Polly one of his Golden Marvels. To humour him she took it back to Chealvercote, where it escaped and was found half-dead in Lord Hoopoe's tobacco pouch, which he had offered to the rural dean. Polly was sacked and broke off our engagement. For a while I found it difficult not to hate the fish.

Among frequent visitors was a cunning lady in straitened circumstances, the handsome widow of a ne'er-do-well. How she wheedled my dear old master in order to get into his will! She who did not know a whale from a lobster, would simulate a deep interest in goldfish, crooning over them, stroking them, and pretending to recognize each individual fish. It was only when she mistook an Orange Wonder for a Tawny Perfection that Lord Shortcake smelt a rat. But she even went so far as to crowd her bedside table with books about goldfish and once wrote a poem about King Sam, one of our prize specimens, which began: 'Round and round and round and round, he swims without a human sound, sparkling here and sparkling there, what does he know of carking care?' My old master had this framed and hung in the aquarium.

My late lamented mistress, Lady Shortcake, who died in 1938, had often been accused of feigning interest in goldfish in order to keep my old master in good humour. But is it likely that any lady of her attainments could have stooped for sixty-one years to such deceit? The only member of the family who actively disliked the fish was the third son, Stanley. 'There must be some bad streak in the boy,' my old master would say. 'It isn't natural. He's not a Shortcake.' His own excuse, that he was bitten by a Yellow Peril in boyhood was never taken seriously at Boulton Wynfevers. 'Pah,' my master said once. 'If they were only bigger I'd put my head in their mouths without a tremor.'

The thought of Lord Shortcake with his head in a goldfish's mouth was too much for one of the young butlers. His chest heaved with inward laughter, and an entire dish of peas, about to be offered to Lord Hoopoe, slithered down the ear-trumpet of the Dowager Lady Garment, who had just placed the instrument in position in anticipation of some outrageous compliment from her neighbour. The cascade of peas against her leathery old ear drew from her an eldritch shriek. 'She might have awakened the fish,' said my master calmly, when it was all over, and she had apologized to Lord Hoopoe for smacking his face.

Aubyn Spicecraft, my dear old master's secretary, was one of those secretaries who must fold a newspaper before handing it to anybody, so that it has to be unfolded again before being read. This, he said, gives an employer the idea that he is independent and can look after himself. That is why, he would say, employers always unfold newspapers so pompously.

Lord Shortcake was interested only in stories about goldfish. If there were none in the papers, he sent them out to the servants' hall. It was Mr Spicecraft's task to mark with a blue pencil any such stories, and then to cut them out and file them after my master had read them. In addition to this, we subscribed to a press-cutting agency, which sent us all references to goldfish.

It was Spicecraft, of course, who took down at dictation and typed my dear old master's monumental work, *A History of Japanese Crossbreeds,* in eight volumes, with coloured plates of every kind of odd goldfish known to mankind. I cannot resist quoting its closing words, which hang above my Aquarium-Keeper's Diploma as I write. 'And so, reader, we say farewell to goldfish. May everybody find such constant companions upon life's thoroughfare as I have found. For this world is but a bowl, where we poor mortals blunder round and round until our brief day is done. Nor, with all man's boasted brains, can he rival in beauty the little fish which has been the subject of my humble work. Gentlemen, I give you the toast: Goldfish!'

Here is another anecdote which shows the lovable simplicity of my master's character. One Christmas there was a party for all the children of the neighbourhood at Boulton Wynfevers. A Chinese conjurer (a Mr Sam Thickett) was engaged. His first trick was to make a bowl of goldfish disappear. This so annoyed Lord Shortcake that he stopped the performance, crying, 'Find them at once.' The conjurer began to produce the missing fish from the ears and pockets of the children. My master beckoned me from the room and said, 'Travers, this must be stopped.' So the magic lantern was brought in, and we had 'Glimpses of Jamaica' (Miss Grabbing at the piano).

It was for some time my dear old master's ambition to have a film made about the life of a goldfish. But he always fell out with the film people over the question of a plot. He said that no plot was needed, and that no human beings should appear.

He told one producer, 'I know what you mean by human interest, eh? Thousands of Hawaiian dancing girls.' 'What's wrong with Hawaiian dancing girls?' asked the producer. 'I want an English picture of animal life,' replied my master, 'and no jungle stuff, with mad escapes.' He insisted that the title should be 'Goldfish', and not 'Little Wonders of the Deep', which, he said, suggested a lot of dwarfs diving for pearls. Nor would he have any incidental music. 'The picture itself must hold the attention,' he said.

Finally the film was made by a week-end guest at Boulton Wynfevers, and was always shown after dinner. It was simple and beautiful. It showed the fish swimming round and round in the bowl, without any commentary. There was one tense moment when it looked as though the fish might turn and swim round in the opposite direction. At this point my master would grip the arms of his chair until his knuckles were white. But the fish, after a moment's hesitation, decided to go on as before. Then Lord Shortcake would give a contented sigh, and say loudly to the guests, 'You see? The little beggar didn't reverse after all, eh?'

My dear old master was very forthright in his views on art. When a famous portrait-painter came to Boulton Wynfevers to paint him, he said bluntly, in my hearing, 'Mark this, sir, none of your confounded cubist portraits. I'm not a three-cornered tomato on a yellow banjo, even if I look like that to you.'

The artist, who painted the conventional glossy portraits at £2,000 a go, was taken aback. 'And,' continued Lord Shortcake, 'I want a background of goldfish in bowls. Bring the fish out strong. Idealize 'em, if you like. But don't call the thing "Sunset on a Dead Horse".'

Once a year Lord Shortcake's team of house-party guests played a cricket match against the village. My master himself captained his side, and showed those qualities of gay absent-mindedness and *laissez-faire* which were the despair of his friends. While fielding, he could not resist talking to the ladies, and often sat down among them, or took the arm of one of them and paced up and down with her. When he bowled, he never would admit that he had had a complete over. 'Now, Umpire,' he would say, 'can't you *count,* eh?' And he never yielded up the ball without a laughing protest. 'Oh, well,' he would say loudly, 'if *that's* your idea of six balls, eh?' One young and timid umpire once let him have his fling. He bowled fourteen balls, and then said, 'Come, Umpire, I've had my six balls. You may call "Over", eh?'

Lady Shortcake, though not sharing her husband's passion for goldfish, was a handsome and stately lady of the old world. Her main interest was her rose garden.

But there came a clash when a rose was called after her. Her lord and master had already called a goldfish after her, and though she assured him that nobody could ever mistake the one for the other, he implored her, for the sake of appearances, to write to the authorities and get the name of the rose changed. This was done, and the bloom in question is now Mrs Hufnagle.

My mistress also liked to play the harp, which instrument she never mastered sufficiently to play a melody. But very beautiful she looked as she allowed her fingers to roam at will over the golden wires, humming an air the while.

Lord Shortcake was nothing if not unmusical. But that did not prevent him from singing 'Asleep in the Deep', in a very loud and raucous baritone, whenever he was bored. Sometimes, in his absent-minded way, he would commence this lugubrious ditty at the crowded dinner-table, without warning. It was then his helpmeet's task to recall him to reality by making some such observation as 'Ernest, your tie is very nearly back to front', or 'My dear, no Albert Hall stuff, I beg', or 'Shorty, don't break out yet'.

Once, when he was a young man, he went to a concert. A lady had just begun to sing when my master shouted, 'We don't want any coal today.' He always referred to that as his best joke.

Lord Shortcake's widowed sister, Lady Bursting, was a frequent visitor. She had a singing mouse given to her by a friend and we had to be very careful of it. It was fed on the choicest morsels of cheese, which so amused my master that one night he gave it some port. That night the singing was distinctly husky and out of tune, and when put out for its run before being shut up for the night, the mouse staggered along the terrace and finally fell down the steps into the rose garden. There a stray cat got it.

To console his sister, my master wrote an epitaph for the mouse.

> *Alas for Henrietta's mouse!*
> *It was the pet of everyone in the house.*
> *But the cat pounced like a couple of retrievers,*
> *And that was the end of the pride of Boulton Wynfevers.*

Lady Bursting's attitude to the ubiquitous goldfish was very peculiar. She affected to be unaware of their presence in the house. When her attention was called to them, she would say, non-committally, 'Oh, *those*. Yes.' Nothing would induce her to talk about them, or even to look at them. My master used to say, 'That woman goes through life with her eyes shut. Anybody would think there were no fish in the place.' As aquarium-keeper I felt myself included in her lack of interest, and once, when she found my peaked hat on a table, she picked it up between finger and thumb as though it had been a putrid rat. Doubtless she had some deep-seated hatred of goldfish which she cloaked with a veneer of apathy.

Lady Shortcake was deeply interested in folk-dancing, and we always had a village team in her lifetime. The only time my master became aware of this was when, returning one early spring morning from bird-watching on the banks of the Bottlemere, and about to let himself in by the back door, he ran into Angelica, one of the parlourmaids. She was dressed up as Queen of the May. He asked for an explanation. On being told that she was on her way to the Maypole, he thought she was referring to a local inn. 'How long have you had this dreadful habit?' he asked. 'I only began it last year,' said Angelica, 'to please her ladyship.' 'What on earth do you mean?' roared my master, so loudly that one of the guests, a Miss Fowler, opened her bedroom window, and cried, 'Can't you two make less noise?'

At breakfast, Lord Shortcake said to my mistress, 'My dear, I met Angelica going to the Maypole. She had the impudence to say she did it to please you.' 'Of course,' said Lady Shortcake. 'She's one of my most promising pupils.' 'Pupils?' bellowed my master. 'Am I mad? Since when have you been giving lessons in drinking?' Lady Shortcake drew herself up frigidly. 'Who said anything about drinking?' she asked. 'What else is there to do at the Maypole?' asked my master. 'They dance round it, you oaf,' was the reply. Lord Shortcake blinked unhappily, and murmured, 'I give it up.'

Ah, the old days at Boulton Wynfevers!

In a can of freshwater fleas intended as food for our fish, my master found one large flea, which he kept in a matchbox. He called it Polyphemus, because he said it had one large eye in the middle of its forehead. Nobody ever verified this, as the box was kept in a cupboard in the gun-room.

The flea died there, and Lord Shortcake said, somewhat inconsequently, that if only people would mind their own business these things would not keep on happening. Pressed by her ladyship for an explanation of so strange a saying, he replied, 'Shut up there in its box in the gun-room, it stood no chance.' 'Well, who shut it up?' asked Lady Shortcake. 'Somebody had to,' answered my master, 'to stop everybody peering and fussing.'

'I believe,' said Lady Shortcake, 'that it was just an ordinary flea.' 'I trust, my love,' replied her husband, with an old-world inclination of the head, 'I trust that my Lady Shortcake's experience of ordinary fleas is so negligible as to preclude the possibility of her being a competent arbiter in the matter.'

'Vulgarity,' retorted my lady, 'cannot be cloaked by a spate of words.'

On one occasion a facetious young man, when the salmon was being served at dinner, said loudly to Lady Trowell, 'What next? Ho! Goldfish and chips.' Lord Shortcake gave him a look in which pain and anger fought for mastery. 'I was only joking, sir,' said the young fool. 'Had I believed you to be speaking seriously,' replied my master, 'I should have shown you the door.' An awkward silence fell, and then silly old Mrs Fotherick-Dowler said heartily, 'And a very fine door it is, Shorty, if I may say so.' 'Jolly good show!' said a man's voice lower down the table. For everybody was trying to tide things over. 'Did you see Hobbs at the Oval in 1924?' came from a gaunt man. 'That was the year Myra married that gadget Helmsley,' screamed a woman's voice. But Shortcake sat glumly listening to jokes about his fish.

When the house was empty of guests, my master and mistress would often play a game of billiards after dinner. If the fish were quiet, I generally acted as marker. And a gloomy occasion it was. Lord Shortcake's bad eyesight and lack of skill prevented him from scoring any points, save by an occasional fluke. Lady Shortcake's eyesight was good, but she was an even worse player. And nothing less than a hundred up would suit them. Most of the scoring was done by misses, and towards the end of the game the cloth was nearly always torn by some savage and despairing stroke of my master's. What made things worse was that my master would tender advice to her ladyship before each stroke. After the stroke he would rebuke her, and outline her faults. And always, when the game ended he would say, 'I wasn't on top of my game tonight, Henrietta.'

I seem to hear their voices now. . . . Travers, the jigger for her ladyship. . . . Travers, I'll trouble you to chalk this damnable cue. . . . Shorty, keep quiet while I aim. . . . Henrietta, my love, can't you manage a bit more spin? . . . You aimed at the wrong ball, Henrietta. . . . Travers, kindly read out the score as it stands at the moment. . . . There, Henrietta, I've left you a perfect sitter, all you have to do . . . My dear girl, you're playing putridly tonight. . . . Take your hands off the table, Shorty. I can't see the pocket. . . . Travers, you aren't chalking my cue enough. . . . Women are no good at billiards . . . RRRRRP. . . . Curse the cloth, it's always tearing!

Chapter 7

Cocklecarrot's Next Case

IT WAS LEARNED late last night that the case of Miss Ruby Staggage *v.* Broxholm Hydraulic Laundries and Others will come up shortly for hearing before Mr Justice Cocklecarrot. Miss Staggage is said to be the trade name of a firm of rocking-horse makers, who are suing the B. H. Laundries for the complete ruination of sixteen yards of washable twill used in making coverings for the tails of the horses. Pending dead-freight, demurrage, charter-party, copyhold, and aznalworratry, Mr Chowdersleigh Poss will appear for the plaintiff, and Mr Charles Honey-Gander for the defendants. The case will be heard in court number 19 of the Probate, Agriculture and Fisheries Division. Miss Boubou Flaring, the famous actress, will be on the jury, and is asked not to start the autograph business while the case is being heard.

COCKLECARROT: Having regard to the curious nature of this case, I think there should be an appeal under article 6 of the Statute of Giminy and Bocage.

MR POSS: Under Statute Law, m'lud, refraction must be proven.

COCKLECARROT: Aye, an' it be not proven, there is always the right of multiple cozenage.

MR HONEY-GANDER: Ultra vires?

COCKLECARROT: Of course. *Sine die.* Tutamen being implicit, with or without barratry, responderia and plonth, except in municipal law.

MR POSS: And wivenage, in lieu of direct mandibility?

COCKLECARROT: Not concurrently with external vapimenta. Merely in plenary copyhold.

MR HONEY-GANDER: M'lud, a tort being the source of a private right of action, in common law, as distinct from equity, matrimonial, Admiralty, agriculture or piscatorial jurisdiction, *alterum non laedere*, I suggest that classification, *per se*, under the Employers' Liability Act of 1897, as in Wivenhoe *v.* Spott (1903 A.C. 274) becomes a matter of malicious nuisance, *sic utere tuo ut alienum laedas*, in which case follopy is self-evident. For instance, a turtle's egg in the Galapagos Islands—

COCKLECARROT: Quite, quite, Mr Honey-Gander. Let someone else develop the thing for a bit now. Now, my office being *jus dicere*, if not *jus dare* (see Hopkins *v.* Tollemache, it would be some considerable advantage to me to know what this case is about. Nobody, so far, has thought of mentioning such a thing.

MR HONEY-GANDER: M'lud, we have first to decide whether common usage or commercial usage is the more convenient instrument for developing and expanding a statute law.

COCKLECARROT: I don't see why we have to go into that now.

MR POSS: M'lud, if a contract is unenforceable, as in Miss Fancy Fimple *v.* The Gaiety Theatre, Buttery-on-the-Vile, then, and not till then, the interchangeable nature of judicial procedure becomes, morally speaking, paramount. Now by the Bills of Exchange Act (1876) twill was included in the category of perishable goods. But if perishable goods are used to wrap the tails of rocking-horses they become, by mansuetude, imperishable, because the tail of a rocking-horse, of which the wrapping is an integral part, is a structure and not a moving fixture.

COCKLECARROT: How can a thing be both perishable and imperishable?

MR POSS: Only the Law can tell us that, m'lud.

The second day of the hearing of the Rocking-Horse case quickly produced a sensation. Cocklecarrot asked Mr Honey-Gander, counsel for the defendants, what the twelve red-bearded dwarfs could possibly have to do with the Broxholm Hydraulic Laundries, and how they came into the case. Mr Honey-Gander made the sensational reply, 'M'lud, I understand that these gentlemen have a controlling interest in these laundries. In fact, they are Broxholm Hydraulic Laundries.'

COCKLECARROT: Then why do they call themselves 'Others'?

MR HONEY-GANDER: I believe, m'lud, that there are others connected with the laundries.

COCKLECARROT: Red-bearded dwarfs, too, I will wager.

MR HONEY-GANDER: So I understand, m'lud.

COCKLECARROT: How many?

MR HONEY-GANDER: Forty-one, m'lud.

COCKLECARROT: Merciful heavens! Call Miss Staggage.

MR HONEY-GANDER: Your name is Elvira Staggage?

MISS STAGGAGE: No, sir. It is Amy Clowte.

MR HONEY-GANDER: But—

MISS STAGGAGE: Elvira Staggage is my trade name.

MR HONEY-GANDER: I see. You own a rocking-horse factory?

MISS STAGGAGE: No, sir. I act for the real owners.

MR HONEY-GANDER: And who are they?

MISS STAGGAGE: A number of red-bearded dwarfs, sir. I see them over there.

(Sensation in court)

COCKLECARROT: This is quite intolerable. These dwarfs are plaintiffs and defendants in the same case. The thing is without precedent. What on earth are they up to, suing themselves?

MR POSS *(for the plaintiff)*: They maintain, m'lud, that in their capacity as hydraulic launderers they have swindled themselves in their capacity as rocking-horse manufacturers.

COCKLECARROT: This is really insane. I must adjourn the case for a day or two. It is without precedent, I repeat.

An attempt was made to resume this case on the next day, but since the twelve red-bearded dwarfs are both plaintiffs and defendants, Cocklecarrot was rather at a loss as to how to proceed. He had, however, discovered a precedent in volume XVIII of Blitherstone, the case of a Miss Frack, who brought an action for libel against herself. Miss Frack was a novelist who, to obtain publicity, wrote a novel under the pen-name of Miles Euston, in which she said that Miss Frack, one of the characters, was a thief and a forger. She was awarded damages against herself, and was in the papers for three days, which sent her sales bounding up.

Matters were complicated, however, by the dwarfs entering a plea of Cujusmòdo. Nobody had ever heard of this plea, until one of the counsel unearthed it in the third year of the reign of Henry II. There the matter rests at present.

'The present position,' said Mr Justice Cocklecarrot, 'would appear to be this: A body of twelve red-bearded dwarfs, in its capacity as a firm of rocking-horse makers, is bringing an action against itself, in its capacity as a hydraulic laundry, alleging that a twill covering for the tail of a rocking-horse was destroyed by the said laundry. But the position is complicated by the fact that the horse in question has no tail. It is, therefore, difficult to see how any case arises. Nor is the matter clarified by regrettable horseplay.'

A DWARF: Rocking-horseplay, I submit, your reverence.
COCKLECARROT: You will kindly address me properly or not at all.
DWARF: Not at all what?
COCKLECARROT: What do you mean, 'what'?
DWARF: No. What do *you* mean, 'what'?
COCKLECARROT: What I said was— Oh, go to the devil!

'The time of this court is valuable,' said Cocklecarrot, as four of the dwarfs carried in a large canvas cake, opened it, and released an actress who began a slow dance in the well of the court.

'Valuable to whom?' queried a dwarf.

'To the public,' replied Cocklecarrot.

'The public,' answered the dwarf, 'would far rather have all this foolery than the usual dull nonsense of cross-examinations and long speeches. See how they are all laughing.'

And, indeed, the packed court was shaking with laughter.

'Take that actress away,' shouted Cocklecarrot, and the girl flinched back in mock alarm. And at that moment paper snow fell from the ceiling, and a dwarf cried, 'Ah, do not turn our little sister out without a roof to her mouth. Have mercy, Daddy.'

Cocklecarrot laid his head in his hands and groaned audibly.

The court had to be cleared owing to the roars of ribald laughter which greeted the appearance in the witness-box of the twelve red-bearded dwarfs all in a heap. Their names were read out amid growing uproar. The names appeared to be: Sophus Barkayo-Tong, Amaninter Axling, Farjole Merrybody, Guttergorm Guttergormpton, Badly Oronparser, Churm Rincewind, Cleveland Zackhouse, Molonay Tubilderborst, Edeledel Edel, Scorpion de Rooftrouser, Listenis Youghaupt, Frums Gillygottle.

COCKLECARROT: Are these genuine names?
A DWARF: No, m'worship.
COCKLECARROT: Then what's your name?
DWARF: Bogus, m'ludship.
COCKLECARROT: No, your real name.
DWARF: My real name is Bogus, your excellency.
(At this point the court had to be cleared)

The case was held up again after lunch while the twelve red-bearded dwarfs were photographed, some riding the rocking-horse, which they had brought with them, others stroking it, and yet others crawling beneath its mottled belly and crying 'Peep-bo!'

COCKLECARROT: But this horse has no tail. I thought the whole case was about a length of twill to cover the tail?
FIRST DWARF: M'worship, it is a guinea-horse.
SECOND DWARF: Yes, your grace. If you hold it up by its tail, its head drops off.
THIRD DWARF: With a bang, your ludship.
FOURTH DWARF: We have a bicycle, too. And that has no tail, either.
FIFTH DWARF: It's a guinea-bicycle.
SIXTH DWARF: The handlebars are made of lard, as a precaution.
COCKLECARROT *(savagely)*: Against what?
CHORUS OF DWARFS: Burglary, sire.
COCKLECARROT *(groaning)*: What in Heaven's name is all this nonsense about?
MR HONEY-GANDER: I confess, m'lud, the case is developing along unexpected lines.

Cocklecarrot then suggested that this ludicrous case, which need never have come into court, could easily be settled if the dwarfs (in the person of the hydraulic laundry) would apologize to themselves (in the person of the rocking-horse firm) for having destroyed a twill covering for a non-existent tail. The dwarfs lined up, six a side, and apologized in chorus. They then left the court singing 'Moonlight and Mrs Mason'.

Cocklecarrot said afterwards, 'I am hoping that my next case will not include these tiresome little gentlemen. I think I am about due for a bit of straightforward stuff, without all these distractions and fooleries.'

* * * * *

BIG WHITE CARSTAIRS

One day at sunset, when the Union Jack was being hoisted, Carstairs was standing at attention a little too near the flagpole. The ropes got entangled in his shirt, which was torn from his body, and run up the pole in place of the flag.

With admirable sang-froid and presence of mind Carstairs lowered his hand and stood at ease.

'One does not salute one's own shirt,' he said.

On another occasion, while he was inspecting the native porters, his belt broke and his trousers fell about his feet. Carstairs waddled along as though nothing had happened, and finished the inspection before pulling up the recalcitrant garment.

Carstairs would never hit a rhinoceros when it was down.

It was his great ambition to breed these beasts for brains, and not merely for beauty. He dreamed of a day when the rhinoceros would be a faithful friend, like the dog, and man's helper, like the horse.

Whenever he captured a rhinoceros he would put it in a stable, and ride it every morning. And, although the beast remained heavy-witted, he never despaired.

To the jests of his bearers, beaters and porters he would reply:

'M'Boola was not built in a day.'

As a matter of fact, M'Boola, that small collection of bamboo and mud huts, was built in seven hours. But the saying was repeated, and all men loved Carstairs, the friend of the rhinoceros.

AFTERNOON TEA AND KISSES

Still going through life as though it were a charade, Captain Foulenough embarrassed Vita Brevis yesterday by getting himself announced as 'M. Hotspot from the Korean Embassy'. Vita was at tea with her mother, who exclaimed, 'How thrilling!' and chattered so much that her daughter could not explain. The Captain wore a long dressing-gown of black silk. When introduced to Lady Brevis he clicked his heels, kissed her hand with a loud smack, and said: 'Too charming, no, too charming, yes?' He then produced a little mouse from a brown bag, and offered it to Vita. 'Comblimunks off da Korean Ombossy,' he said. Vita gave a little scream, and the next moment the Captain had her tight in his arms, and was crowing into her ear. 'But, no, ma leetle swotheart. I, Hotspot, shall defond you oggainst this wild mouzes, no?' And before the astonished eyes of the mother, he kissed her heartily and repeatedly.

ORANGES

By Barbara Waveling

. . . Little spheres that seem to hold cloistered in their depths all the bright sunshine of Spain, all the stored colour of that *laissez-faire* land of señors and señoritas, bulls, guitars and priests. . . . As one walks beneath the swaying orange trees of Seville, hearing on all sides the lazy Spanish tongue, one cannot help being struck by the thought that all these acres of fruit will one day be marmalade in our gloomier northern homes. . . .

The child who spreads this delicious condiment on his or her bread does not dream that he or she is about to absorb the sunny south, land of passion and romance, land of hot tempers, hasty words, and knives suddenly produced from stockings . . . land of . . . land of . . . Thus are Spain and England for ever linked in a common bond of friendship . . . and . . . and . . . and . . . so that. . . for ever . . . heritage . . . friendship . . . Then there are the great pipless oranges so dear to those who find pips a deterrent to the enjoyment of this . . . fruit.

A great man once called oranges the solace of jaded palates. And indeed . . . Oranges are a reminder that the fruits of earth were given to man for his delectation. . . . I never look at one without seeing the white-walled towns of that land of . . . land of . . . and hearing the mule bells in that land of . . . land of . . .

I think I have kept the sense of the thing, without sacrificing too much of the really beautiful prose. I was forced to omit the long passage about using orange skins to clean oak panelling, and the still longer one about orangeade at Henley.

BIG WHITE CARSTAIRS

Carstairs was the victim of a mishap not long ago. He became entangled in the flag which was hoisted at sunset over the Residency at Umpupi, and was hauled, with it, to the top of the pole. Arrived there, he saluted with the utmost sang-froid, and insisted on remaining at his post, or rather pole, until the next morning when the flag was lowered. 'My only regret is,' he said, afterwards, 'that it was too windy to shave up there.'

FOULENOUGH AND VITA BREVIS

Psychologists have often said that the apparent dislike of Captain Foulenough shown by Miss Vita Brevis masks a kind of involuntary admiration.

He is certainly a persistent wooer, and on his return to England he has once more begun to lay siege to her. He said yesterday: 'If I don't marry her, I won't marry anyone – at least, hardly anyone.' Miss Brevis said yesterday: 'It's his practical jokes I can't stand. He called the other day while my brother the Dean was with me. The maid announced "Mr Claude Thirst", and he bounded in, seized a decanter of sherry, shouting, "Thirst come, Thirst served", drained it, and handed it to my brother, saying: "Give me twopence on this empty." My brother was nonplussed.'

It appears that the Dean, in order not to appear priggish, handed the Captain twopence and took the decanter. 'Fill it up,' said Foulenough, 'and here's another twopence for you.' And he handed the Dean one of his own pennies. 'Are you on the stage, Mr Thirst?' inquired the Dean courteously. 'Didn't you see my Macbeth at Ashby-de-la-Zouch?' asked the Captain. 'I did not have that pleasure,' replied the Dean. 'The pleasure,' said Foulenough, 'according to the audience, was all mine. My next appearance, old boy, is as Romeo.' 'Indeed, and where?' asked the astonished cleric. 'In this very room, when dusk falls,' said the Captain, ogling Vita Brevis. The Dean coughed, and took his leave with a puzzled expression.

CARSTAIRS COMES TO BHOO

Controversy still rages round Mr Peter Fleming. Some say he should have dragged a six-inch howitzer from China to India. Others think that a knuckleduster would have been sufficient protection.

When Carstairs – Big White Carstairs – crossed the unspeakable Wudgi desert that lies between Seringapahaha and Klang-Klang he took with him nothing but a dozen Union Jacks, a dress suit, and a water-pistol.

'And why,' lisps the sub-human reader, 'why a water-pistol?'

Because there are no wells in that desert, ghoulish lout.

'But,' continues the idiot reader, 'a water-pistol holds very little water.'

That is true enough, but there are times when very little water will save a man's life, as the bailiff said to the actress when she poured him out a stiff whisky and bade him, with old-world courtesy, say when.

Carstairs allowed himself one drop of water a day from the pistol.

'But,' clamours the footling reader, 'did he meet no wild animals or nomads?'

Of course he did. Filthistan and Stin-King are infested with frightful creatures. His method with wild beasts was to choke them to death with bits of Union Jack; for the flags were made of specially stout and coarse material, suitable for hoisting in all weathers, or for making into warm waistcoats. As for the nomads, when they saw him in evening dress they knew that the Empire was upon them, and they brought him gifts of yak's liver, black rice, and camel's-milk cheese.

'And where,' asks the long-eared reader, 'did he finally end up?'

Why, in the walled city of Bhoo, where they worship their dead aunts. And the water-pistol is now in the Museum of Folk-lore at Wembley, between a letter from Mr Gladstone to the Golden Vale Laundry and half the hoof of a dirtibeeste captured by Cecil Rhodes in Matabeleland, on the occasion when the natives sang, 'Oh, dear, what can the Matabele, Cecil's so long in the kraal.'

SHORT INTERVAL FOR FUN

'Fancy that,' said the man who handed a rhinoceros to the pigeon fancier.

Chapter 8

Drama at Badger's Earth

IN THE early hours of this morning a fire broke out at Badger's Earth, Lady Cabstanleigh's charmingly appointed country residence. A maid noticed smoke issuing from the stables. Making her way thither, the interfering little hussy found a tall, gaunt stranger bent over a fire of birch twigs. He appeared to be eating the flames.

It was afterwards ascertained, and/or it afterwards transpired, that the interloper was an unemployed fire-swallower who had not had a square meal of fire for two days. The maid asked him if he could swallow swords, too, but he shook his head sadly, and replied, 'Only fire, my dear, only fire.' She watched him take another hearty mouthful of flame, and then went slowly and pensively back to her work. Faintly, in some sequestered nook of her simple heart, marriage bells had begun to peal. An hour later the stranger was sitting at his ease in the kitchen, devouring a roaring fire, while the little maiden threw coal on with the energy of a ship's stoker. 'Nothing is too good for him,' she murmured, when the chimney caught fire.

ENTER WELF

We left the maid at Badger's Earth stoking up the fire for the gaunt fire-swallower, until flames began to pour from the chimney. Then up he rose and tore along a corridor, and so came, by the back stairs, to the roof. Leaning over the spouting chimney-stack he ate his fill, while from below the maid sighed with unselfish satisfaction.

By this time the household was awake. Lady Cabstanleigh herself, looking like a moribund carthorse in the early light, questioned the butler, who had fetched his rook-rifle. As he raised the rifle to shoot, the maid flung herself at his feet, and cried in shrill accents, 'Spare him! Spare him! He is but eating fire!' At these words a shudder ran through the assembled maids, cooks, gardeners and odd-job men.

But who is this who pushes his way to the fore? It is Welf, the dear old family solicitor, Welf of Welf, Welf, Frogmarch, Dickery, Flitt and again Welf, Commissioners of Oaths, Engrossers of Deeds (at £17 4s. 9d. a paragraph), Initiallers of Parchments, Affixers of 5s. Stamps, Transferers of Transferences, Mortgage Middle-men, Public Jurisconsults and Conveyors of Conveyances.

THE LEGAL ASPECT OF IT

The man of law wetted his lips with his furry tongue, and began to read in a monotonous voice from a heavy book. He read: Whereas and whereinunder, as, to and pursuant from whichever or whatever, for, by and under, which said person or persons being or having been about to be, in or with, hereinafter called the purchasee, shall be entitled, unless otherwise injuncted, disjuncted, rejuncted or double-juncted, the aforesaid minor having, without foreknowledge, and in malice prepense, whosoever or whatsoever, shall be or shall not be declared to be or not to be the sole accessor, recessor or retrocessor, acting for and by the vendor for the vendee, by law of scriven and scroven, the which not being proven, is declared and shall be declared null and void. Oyez. Oyez. Oyez. Haro. ON ME FAIT TORT. SELIM.

All present heartily concurring, the entire company moved across the stately lawns to a tinned breakfast, supplemented by sundry bird-foods, leaving the fire-swallower writhing on the roof with indigestion after his guzzle.

No sooner were the guests, helots, and hangers-on of Badger's Earth seated at the groaning board, with Lady Cabstanleigh pouring tea from a two-quart silver pot, when all present began loudly to debate the legal position. Some contended that a flame which emerges from a chimney is part of the atmosphere and not the property of the owner of the chimney. Others hotly denied this, and pointed out that if every roof was crowded with professional fire-swallowers, all fires would gradually die down. Then did Welf, the dirty old family lawyer, settle the matter to his own satisfaction by declaring that Badger's Earth was held in entail and fantail, with copyhold and freehold tenure, by its present châtelaine, and that there was no clause in the deeds assigning to any person or persons but the assignee the right or rights to eat or devour flames proceeding from the roof of the said demesne.

To clinch the matter Welf said roundly: 'The promisor has further given pulliance to a negotiable instrument for conveyance to the conveyor of the thing to be conveyed. There can be no civil contract of sale without an absence of disability. Further, a professional fire-swallower, being a vagrant, has no legal rights (see Ellen Terry *v.* the Grand Theatre, Tavistock).'

A MAN OF LAW AT BREAKFAST

Little Welf then made a hearty breakfast of grass-seed, molten chips of bronze (for the sake of his liver), oats (for the sake of his lights), meal (for the sake of his marrow), and cold ashes (for the sake of his pineal gland). He took no milk in his tea, but instead poured in three drops of wild honey as a specific against premature baldness. To make his brain cunning and active, he rubbed a patent bread-extract into his neck just below Carter's artery, and to fortify his ganglions he inhaled a tablespoonful of sour lard mixed with the juice of four dandelions, three pomegranates and a baby quince. While digesting this hearty meal he repeatedly touched his toes, stretched his nostrils outwards, held his breath, pulled his ears downwards, smacked his knees, rubbed his ankles and murmured a magical formula against hiccoughs.

The little maid looked on, and thanked the Press astrologers that her own true love was a simple fire-swallower and not this laboratorical lunatic.

ERSKINE MOCKPUDDING

Mr Welf, the kindly old family solicitor, is apparently not to have things all his own way at Badger's Earth. The fire-eater, cajoled by the maid, decided to hire a most disreputable lawyer, on the instalment system. This gentleman, Erskine Mockpudding, arrived with his brief-case, and at once quoted an old statute of Ed. IV, by which a fire-eater without visible means of subsistence was allowed to eat fire anywhere within a fifty-mile radius of London. Badger's Earth being exactly fifty miles from London, little Welf sought to prove that the fire-eater's left leg and left shoulder, while he was on the roof, were four inches outside that fifty-mile radius. To which Mockpudding retorted that, for the purposes of fire-eating on roofs, the body must be assumed to be a complete entity, and not subject to any subdivision. 'If,' said he, 'any part of the *corpus* or body is within the said radius, then the whole *corpus* or body may, must and should be said to be or to have been within the aforementioned radius thereinunder.'

In the opinion of the Law Lords – always a jolly opinion to have – the intervention of the Sieur Mockpudding has considerably messed things up. (See Faggot's 'Law of Purchase'.)

APPROXIMATE CHARGES

Meanwhile Lady Cabstanleigh has been presented already with the following bill by the kindly old family solicitor:

	£	s.	d.
To assessing conveyance	16	3	8
To engrossing conveyance	8	1	10
Five-shilling stamp	1	4	8
Stamp duty on stamp	13	3	2
Stamp duty on stamp duty	4	6	4
Petty disbursements (various)	72	3	9
Contract stamps	3	1	3
Registration fee (say)	10	10	0
	£364	2	9½

Her ladyship has replied: 'Dear Welfie, having had nothing conveyed, I am enclosing my cheque for, say, £2.'

*   *   *   *   *

CAPTAIN FOULENOUGH, M.P.

The Tiddlehampton and South Mince by-election has been further complicated by the extraordinary news that Captain de Courcy Foulenough, D.T., has decided to stand as an Independent Progressive Liberal, that being the only interest not represented up to this moment.

The constituency has always been considered a safe seat for the first comer, partly because hardly any one of the 26,484 voters ever troubles to vote, and partly because it is difficult to get anybody to stand for such a place. But recent international affairs have ended this apathy, and there are heaps of candidates.

They include Mrs Wickstram (Independent Progressive Communist), Mr Edward Spackford (National Independent), two Siamese Twins, Mr Bargo and Mr Raego Rishfether (Progressive Nationalist), Mr Billy Fagan Thius, a clown (Conservative), Lady Thelma Snatch (National Labour), Miss Boubou Flaring, the actress (National Liberal), and several hitherto unidentified candidates.

From the Captain's election address it is clear that, like most of the other candidates, he stands for work for all, friendship with every nation, national reconstruction, national revival, higher wages, higher exports, higher imports, lower taxation, rearmament, peace, supremacy in the air, voluntary conscription, co-operation, co-ordination, and no closing hours.

BALLET (*Le Chauffeur Amoureux*)

When Tumbelova, moving like a bit of thistledown on an evening breeze, alights like the ghost of a fairy butterfly on the upturned face of Serge Trouserin one realizes that one is in for an intellectual banquet. What *soin*! What *soif*! What *coiffement*! Every *demi-volte-face* is a lyric. Every *pouffe* is an authentic avowal of unrecorded *grelache*. What *cru*! What *boulge*! What *viroflette*! Twirling anti-clockwise, *faisant le widdershins*, Tumbelova defies the *lois* of *gravité* at a single bound. When she leaps into the air one wonders if she will ever come down. It is the semi-sublimation of the Indian rope-trick, without Indian, rope or trick. *Ma foi*! Here is vintage equipoise with *bouquet*!

VOTE FOR FOULENOUGH – *And Voluntary Co-ordination*

Frenzied attempts are being made to rally all the Opposition candidates in the South Mince and Tiddlehampton by-election into one solid Opposition candidate. But, politics being a career like any other[1], none of the various shades of Liberals and what-not is willing to stand down. Captain Foulenough is reported to have said that a split vote is just as much fun as any other sort of vote. So things look promising for the Government candidate, Mr Thius.

Foulenough caused consternation yesterday while speaking in the Snabworth Aquarium by saying: 'If I were you people I should not hesitate to vote for the delectable Miss Flaring. After all, what is the difference between an Independent Progressive Liberal and an Independent Liberal – or whatever it is she is? Let us forget labels and stick to reality. This lovely creature would be an ornament to an Assembly not particularly renowned for the beauty of its lady members.' Here the Captain blew an imaginary kiss and sat down.

There have been many resignations from his committee following this incident.

A PLAIN STATEMENT

When the hunting people set out to pursue foxes, they will tell you that foxes are destructive vermin. But when farmers treat foxes as destructive vermin and shoot them as quickly as possible, the hunting people make a dreadful fuss about it.

Captain Screaming is the only M.F.H. I know at all well, and his explanation of this is that there are things one does and other things one does not do. I asked him by what signs one might know which was which, and he said, 'Either one does or one doesn't.' Whereupon I continued, 'Does or doesn't what?' To which he replied, 'Just does or doesn't.' Said I, 'Do you mean one does know, or there are things one does do?' Said he, 'Just does.' 'Or doesn't?' I added. 'Yes,' he said, 'or doesn't.'

I thanked him for his plain statement and went away musing.

---

[1] But more disgusting.

VOTE FOR FOULENOUGH—*And an International Register*

There was a disgraceful scene at the South Mince Steam Laundry Sports Ground yesterday. Before one of Foulenough's meetings began there was a hitch on the platform. Mrs Quaffle had said, 'Captain, you are neglecting the women in this constituency.' Foulenough at once linked his arm in that of Boubou Flaring, and replied, 'I hardly think so, dear lady.' A Mrs Worsted intervened. 'You should kiss some babies,' she said loudly. Whereat Foulenough seized the Independent Liberal candidate, Miss Flaring, in his arms and kissed her soundly. 'This is the baby I kiss,' he explained. But his chairman, the Hon. Borchart Vickett, flounced off the platform and the women began to chatter. The audience roared with laughter, and Boubou, blushing charmingly, said, 'I know we're supposed to be rival candidates, but I do so love my public.' This, the first speech she has made in her campaign, has disappointed her supporters.

'If this is democracy,' said a prominent councillor, 'then I'm the Queen of Iceland.'

It is democracy, but he is not the Queen of Iceland.

NARKOVER NEWS

Dr Smart-Allick, of Narkover, gave a powerful address in the Speech Hall last night.

He said that it was not always the timid fellow, with four conventional aces in his hand, who won the highest honours.

'It is often,' he said, 'the fifth ace that makes all the difference between success and failure.' He was loudly cheered from the fifth-form benches, and at the end of the address a young master swarmed up a pillar and threw playing cards down among the boys.

VOTE FOR FOULENOUGH – *And Democracy*

Captain Foulenough staggered his audience, disgusted what is left of his Committee, and roused his opponents to fury last night by reading out messages of support which he claimed to have received from nine Cabinet Ministers, Mr Clark Gable, Mr Noël Coward, Mr Anthony Eden, Mr Joe Louis, Bishop Mrs Riquette, Tubby Garstang, Mamie Dugold, Harry Armitage, Babs Thornycroft, Trixie, Vi,

Polly, Ethel, Madge, Bobo, Curly, Mabel, Dot, Irma, 'Coppernob' Halsey, Flo, Nan, Gert, Myra, and Olive.

ALCOHOL

'Father, what are these Dreadful Sounds of bottle-smashing that fill the house?'

'My boy, you must know that as Mr Beachcomber and I were taking the air yesterday we saw a large poster in a shop-window, telling us that No Man who touches Alcohol the Demon King, could be a Boy Scout.'

'What then, Father?'

'Why, boy, we decided that this Poison, one single drop of which can turn Man into a Raging Beast, should pollute our Homes no longer. I may add that tomorrow we go to buy our Uniforms.'

'And will you both Show your Knees, like grandma, and blow whistles like baby?'

'That is our Intention, boy.'

'An Intention, Father, which I cannot but Applaud.'

VOTE FOR FOULENOUGH – *And Duty-Free Lard*

There is no end to the Captain's enterprise. He now has girl-jugglers stationed at each corner of his platform. They throw up and catch coloured balls so skilfully that one hardly knows whether the applause is for them or for what the candidate is saying. His opponents, whom everybody has forgotten, are attacking him fiercely in the South Mince *Recorder*. They accuse him of undemocratic methods, but he merely points to the cheering crowds.

Miss Boubou Flaring appears to have ceased almost entirely from being a rival candidate. A telegram from the National Liberal Club asked, 'What are you doing?' Her reply – or perhaps it was the Captain's reply – raised a storm. It was: *'Nothing of which my mother would not approve a kiss here a kiss there a whispered word in the lanes were you guys never young.'*

ADVERTISEMENT CORNER

Will the gentleman who threw an onion at the Union Jack, and repeatedly and noisily tore cloth during the singing of 'Land of Hope and Glory', at the Orphans' Outing on Thursday, write to Colonel

Sir George Jarvis Delamain Spooner, late of Poona, telling him what right he has to the Old Carthusian braces which burst when he was arrested?

STOP PRESS

Foulenough in.

The astonishing victory of Captain de Courcy Foulenough in the South Mince and Tiddlehampton by-election is, if one may phrase it so, an unequivocal condemnation of the degrading policy of peace pursued by the Government since Democracy was thrown to the Fascist wolves at Munich.

('Liberal News')

The popular victory of a distinguished soldier in the South Mince and Tiddlehampton by-election is one more proof, if proof were needed, that the people of England are solidly behind the Government. It is a grievous blow for the critics of the Government.

('Towzer's Twopenny')

A triumph for Progressive Socialism.

('The Progressive Socialist')

The entry of this outstanding personality into the House of Commons cannot but impress those foreign critics who think that Democracy is tottering.

(Mrs Howler)

A blow in the face for Democracy.

('The Corker')

LITERARY NEWS

Mr G. J. Oyle is engaged upon an article for the *Mausoleum*. It is an examination of an article by E. P. Hoax dealing with an article by Henry Smelt on Wanda Brown's article on Esther Curry's article on Selena Hack's article on Brenda Gurle's review of Sidney Futtle's book on E. L. Bupp's book on the book by Robert Dreyfus on Marcel Proust.

CAPTAIN FOULENOUGH, M.P., D.T.

Captain Foulenough will take his seat in the House one day this week. His sponsors will be Mr Demetrius Bottle, the silent fool, and Mr Stichfield Gurnsey, the garrulous fool. The one never speaks at all, the other never stops speaking. The Captain will go through the whole tralala of kissing the knee of the Serjaunt-Herald in Puisne, bowing to Miss Wilkinson, holding up his left thumb backwards at the Speaker, grinning at the Chief Whipper-In, crawling backwards on all fours round the bar, and so on and so forth. He will then take an oath of fealty to our jolly unwritten (Ha! We are too wise to put the vile thing on paper, like those foreigners) Constitution.

HEROISM UNDER TORTURE

It is being said of a certain poet that though he tortures the English language, he has never yet succeeded in forcing it to reveal his meaning.

THE CAPTAIN DISAPPEARS

The theft of the Mace from the House of Commons, reported exclusively by every newspaper, has staggered Europe and dumbfounded Asia. 'Such a horrible occurrence!' was heard on every side. Speculation ran, or rather waddled, rife as to the motives of the theft. The name of Foulenough is being freely mentioned, and it is assumed that he walked off with the symbol of British umtarara in a fit of absent-mindedness.

Nobody can believe that he intended a deliberate insult to the majesty of the House, *et tout le bataclan du tralala.*

'One feels lost without the Mace,' said a woman Member remarkable for witlessness, tactlessness, public fuss, and private folly.

The police have so far found no trace of the Mace, and none of the intrepid Captain Foulenough, whose conduct in thus breaking one of the unwritten laws of the House before even making his maiden speech is condemned by all who have the welfare of our, etc., etc., etc., at heart and tumty iddly ido.

Chapter 9

A Foul Innuendo

THERE HAVE lately been complaints in the newspapers, from Civil Servants, that lodging-house keepers show favouritism to their regular clientèle. The accusation roused that well-known seaside landlady, Mrs McGurgle.

Dear Sir,
  I treat civil servants just like my other lodgers. No better and no worse. It is rapid eating and not social status that gets a second helping. If I see an empty plate, I fill it, be its owner a big panjandrum in Government circles or only a humble traveller in biscuits. Snobbery, I am thankful to say, has never cast its foul shadow across the threshold of Marine House. For though the late Mr McGurgle, by whom I had the honour to be led to the altar at St Philip's in this very resort, held an important position in a warehouse, he never to his dying day set up to be better than his fellows. An early decease, due to tainted cocoa partaken of at a French watering-place during a well-earned holiday, robbed me of my guide, philosopher and friend, but I flatter myself that Marine House is run today as it was in his lifetime, without fear or favour.
  All are welcome, from dukes to dustmen.
                                                  Yours faithfully,
                                                  Florence McGurgle.

THE BOARDING-HOUSE ROW

Dear Sir,
  As one who has had a long experience of lodging-houses by the sea, may I hasten to support Mrs McGurgle's contention that civil servants are human beings, and must be treated as such? But they are bad mixers. It takes the old habitué to come into the landlady's private sitting-room with a bit of a swagger, and maybe to pinch her ear in sheer camaraderie. Landladies don't like being treated as stand-off ogres, and are as

susceptible to a spot of flattery as the rest of us. What some of these establishments where there are civil servants need is a bit of a rough-and-tumble to break the ice – blind man's buff or something of that sort. That is the rule we have adopted at Beach View, and already it is no uncommon sight to see a gentleman from the Board of Works on all fours in the passage, begging a piece of kipper from one of the young ladies touring in 'Atta, Girl!'

Yours truly,
Herbert Cleft.

MRS MCGURGLE AGAIN

Dear Sir,

I can well imagine what the late Mr McGurgle – him that I have said fell a victim to tainted Continental cocoa and should have known better than to tempt fate by ordering it so far from home – would have had to say of a proprietress who graded her helpings according to the birth and education of the clientèle. Why, I remember once it was our privilege to receive as a paying guest at Marine House a very high official of the gas company. It is true we gave him a big room, him having so much luggage, but when it came to mealtimes, I can hear my late husband saying, as though it was yesterday, 'Flo, put the gentleman between the insurance clerk and the piano-tuner. He is only one of us while he enjoys the shelter of the McGurgle roof.' And I flatter myself that when I stood up to help the gravy, gas company or no gas company, his portion did not outweigh that of his neighbours, nor was the smile I directed to the least of our patrons, Miss Ansper, the orphan of a night-watchman whom diphtheria and complications carried to a premature burial in the north corner of St Oswith's cemetery, any less friendly than that reserved for the official who, be it added, for all his luggage and fine airs, knew no better than to stove his morning egg in at a blow with his thumb.

Yours truly,
Florence McGurgle.

MCGURGLE'S SENSITIVENESS

Dear Sir,

Barbed tongues, vicious as the serpent's tooth, are saying that my communications to you are only a vulgar attempt to advertise Marine House. Let me say at once that the late Mr McGurgle so detested even well-merited fame that on the occasion of his winning second prize in a South of England vegetable show, his entry being a gigantic turnip which he did my sister, Mrs Cage, the honour of presenting to her after-wards, when the local newspaper sent a young man to interview him *he refused to allow his photograph to be published, since he said he was not going to compete with film-stars for the public applause. Would such a man's widow be likely to go in for vulgar advertisement? On another occasion the late Mr McGurgle, a horticulturist if ever there was one, called a peony which he exhibited at Bognor the Mrs McGurgle, in compliment to me. But at the last moment he told me he could not bring himself to expose even so much as my married name to the sensation-mongers of to-day. So he changed the peony's name to Robinson, after a long-dead grand-uncle of his mother's. Perhaps I have said enough to defend myself from foul innuendo.*

Yours truly,
Florence McGurgle.

SUNDAY SUPPER AT MARINE HOUSE

Dear Sir,

It is difficult for a mere member of the public to fathom what is behind your extraordinary attempt to deify the late Mr McGurgle. I knew him quite well, when we were both with Clipper and Radlett. He was a very ordinary man, and had an annoying habit of cracking his fingers while he talked. Mrs McGurgle, for whose feelings as a bereaved widow I have every respect, is, I think, idealizing her late consort. I only once met her, being bidden to Sunday supper at Marine House. It was a gloomy meal, relieved only by the senseless giggling of a young lady, who appeared to be a filing clerk in the office of a hop factor. The food was terrible and scanty. I was allowed one glass of stout, and the whole time I was drinking it Mrs McGurgle kept on saying that, though she had never succumbed to the demon drink, she had no objection to others wrecking their insides and their morals by wallowing in alcohol. We broke up early, because the very silent sister of a commissionaire suddenly went into screaming hysterics.

Yours truly,
Oscar Suggridge.

SHE IS HURT

Dear Sir,

Mr Suggridge's letter is merely vulgar. When he complains that Sunday suppers were gloomy at Marine House, I will ask him to remember that this establishment is not a cabaray. Almost my mother's last words to me, as she lay a-dying in Hampshire, were, 'Flo, never let the French Sunday get a grip on your establishment.' As to the clicking of the late Mr McGurgle's fingers which so irritated this so-called Mr Suggridge, may I hasten to assert that my late consort only clicked them when he desired to emphasize a point? The giggling lady he refers to was my niece, who has been nervous ever since she was jilted by a man who sold scissors and knives at a booth at Hexham. I hope I have said more than enough to demonstrate that Mr Suggridge, whom I scarcely have the honour to recollect, is hardly what respectable people would call comeelfo. If one glass of stout on a Sunday night is not enough, his spiritual home is the bodeega.

Yours truly,
Florence McGurgle.

THE LATE MR MCGURGLE

Dear Sir,

If the Mrs McGurgle who writes to you is the Mrs McGurgle whose husband tried to get my brother Alfred to join the Lamplight League of Sunday Silence, she must have married a tartar. McGurgle used to come to our house gassing about the beauty of contemplation, and he always left leaflets urging us all to link our thoughts in a chain of pure gold to the Infinite. I never heard a man talk so much about silence, and I often wondered how the lodgers at Marine House took his jabbering. He gave my brother a snapshot of his wife when she was Miss Palmer. He said she was the ray of sunshine which filled the boarding-house with singing birds. I told him to save me a chaffinch, and he left off badgering us.

Yours truly,
E. N. Spillman.

A NOBLE DEFENCE

Dear Sir,

There appears to be a conspiracy to malign the late Mr McGurgle, even by those who, baser than the serpent's tooth, mark their ingratitude by attempting to bite the hand of the deceased man who fed and boarded them in the early days of Marine House. If stout did not flow like water at our table, is that not to the credit of the establishment? There are doubtless boarding-houses which cater for such as cannot pass a public-house without darting in to the detriment of their characters. Mr McGurgle used to say that his home was his public-house, and water his tipple, and that he required no bar in his front parlour. But I venture to reassert that he was no less gay and sporty than they whose veins run with distilled poison, whose eyes are bloodshot and restless, and whose limbs tremble at breakfast like the proverbial aspen. He is not likely to turn in his grave at the mud-slinging of mean natures.

Yours truly,
Florence McGurgle.

ANOTHER SUPPORTER

Dear Sir,

As sister to the late Mr McGurgle, I protest against this bandying of his name, as though he were a Casanova always diving into public-houses frequented by what my sainted mother used to designate harpies of the underworld. Mr McGurgle always abhorred strong drink, as exemplified on the 4.52 from Waterloo to Epsom one day, when a stranger changed hats with him unasked. My brother gave him a stare that would have turned a basilica to stone. The sot got out at Raynes Park, still reeking of the demon alcohol. My brother merely wiped his hat on his knee and began to hum nonchalantly. A fine example of manners and self-control.

Yours truly,
Freda Rumteigh.

MORE GHOSTS FROM THE PAST

Dear Sir,

Florrie Palmer that was has certainly sobered up a bit, no offence. My word! There were evenings at the Magpie which would have made her future lord's hair stand on end. Florrie used to sing, 'Tap, tap, tap! It's not the postman!' and then she and Fred Townham would do a Russian dance, splits and all, with two kitchen knives between their teeth. Ah, well! It's a far call from the Magpie to Marine House, which sounds to yours truly about as gay and giddy as a morgue. I wonder if Flo recalls the evening when Capper put a bloater down her back?

Yours truly,
Syd Telgrove.

THE EXCELLENT COG

Dear Sir,

Your correspondent who claims to have known me in my courting days seems to be surprised that I have not remained a giddy young girl whose god was pleasure. It is one thing to stand on the threshold of life's doorway and raise the bubbling cup of youth to inexperienced lips. It is another thing to be the chosen consort of a serious-minded warehouse overseer and to have an old-established boarding-house to manage. Of course, I take my work seriously, and proud of it. Success in the boarding-house world is the guerdon of hard work and nothing la-di-da about it. We landladies are but small cogs in the vast machine of the lodgers' world, but as one of the least of those cogs permit me to say that without cogs where would you get to?

Yours truly,
Florence McGurgle.

A TOUCHING TRIBUTE

Dear Sir,

I hasten to corroborate all that my old and esteemed friend and landlady says of her deceased consort, the late lamented Stephen McGurgle. I had many occasions, while on tour, to use Marine House as my peadertair, and I can say, with my hand on my heart, that the excellence of the grub and the downy softness of the beds were only exceeded to by the human warmth and benignity of the welcome voochsaved to all by that charming host and hostess. Only a very brave woman could have kept the flag flying after the untimely removal of such a skipper as Stephen McGurgle. May I add that by a happy dispensation of his will and testament, when his anniversary comes round there is not a dry mouth in the King's Arms!

Yours truly,
Edmund Pillinger.

SHE REMEMBERS MR PILLINGER

Dear Sir,

Mr Pillinger's tribute to the late Mr McGurgle is very handsome. I wonder whether he is the Mr Pillinger who boarded at Marine House while playing the miser in 'The Aftermath'. If so, I well remember him helping the late Mr McGurgle to add a few twirls to the 'Welcome' which was such a prominent feature of our door-mat. I fear we used to make a good deal of fun of him, as he was very much attracted to one of our patrons, a Miss Gowle, who afterwards married into a Steam Carpet Beating business, and only once returned to our humble Marine House, in a solid silver motor-car with the flags of all the nations tacked on to the bonnet. I understand that her stepson was a bit of a racer and covered even the furniture with plaques and medals. I wonder if Mr Pillinger ever married. He would have made a fine, steady mate for some decent girl who could appreciate art and culture, and though I was never a matchmaker, I tried to encourage a friendship between him and a girl who typed dramas. Nothing came of it as both became involved in a row about a loose board on the landing, and she left in a huff.

Yours truly,
Florence McGurgle.

*   *   *   *   *

AMONG THE NEW BOOKS

Passionate Eclipse, by Amy Trent.
Tells how Consuelo murdered the man she loved to save him from

betraying his ideals. Written with the command of detail and the detached humour which we have come to expect from Miss Trent.

Great Fish: A Survey, by Ernest and Ena Wrotte.
A comprehensive collection of monster fish, beginning with Jonah's whale. Of this book a well-known diplomat laughingly said, 'I wish I had chips to go with all these fish.'

Ninette, by Freda Gillip.
The story of a *grande amoureuse* who, nevertheless, had a very human heart. Miss Gillip is that rare thing, a writer who can combine breathless excitement with profundity of thought. A challenging book, vital, human and arresting.

Corpse in the Coffin, by Jory Heemers.
They looked everywhere for the corpse, but nobody suggested the coffin until the uninvited guest arrived and pointed out that that was the obvious place for a corpse. A thriller full of unexpected turns.

The Truth About the North Pole, by Gene Verneotten.
An authoritative and up-to-date account of what is really happening at the North Pole, written by an American journalist who met a man who had been there. It is written in a lively and exciting manner, and has been chosen as the Liberal Book of the Week.

Mockorpington, by Tristram Rutt.
A long and serious love story. It tells of the love of the last of the Mockorpingtons for the last of the Gippstones. He is an authority on Scandinavian mosses, while she is an Egyptologist. The clash of interests obscures the full moon of love for eight hundred and thirty pages. Then comes the dénouemong. They decide to go their own ways, and forget. Joe Louis wired the publisher, 'Great stuff. I look forward to reading it.'

STULTITIA'S COMEDY

Here is interesting theatrical news. Stultitia Cabstanleigh has had her little play produced at the Mayfair Theatre. It has no title – a fashion that may spread rapidly – and it is described as a *soufflé*. The first night audience laughed heartily at the witty lines, and the talented authoress herself, sitting on a dais in full view of the auditorium, rang a small bell before each joke or epigram, as a signal for the chattering to die down.

Several young men in the stalls were so enthusiastic that they demanded encores in the case of many of the epigrams. The action of the play was held up many times in this manner, and the authoress made a pretty speech, pointing out that the good lines would occur often during the last two acts – so that there would be no need to encore them.

I really cannot resist printing one or two of the more brilliant lines below:

> Life must be lived to be believed.
> A cynic is a man who eats the cherry and leaves the martini.
> All men love the thing they kill.
> Life is a trifle – but sherry makes it tolerable.
> Life should always be true to itself.
> Death is such a crude anti-climax.
> You can't be sure of a woman who sneezes.
> She has a Rolls body and a Balham mind.
> No woman of forty can afford to be happy.
> Life is so like an apple. Take off the peel, and it turns a drab
>   brown.
> Nothing is really worth doing.

MRS WHACKOFF'S RECORD

I am sorry to disappoint my readers, but the Princess of Sarawak has not broken the record by becoming a Mohammedan five thousand feet up in the air.

The record is still held by a Mrs Whackoff, who became a Shintoist while half-way up Mont Blanc, and then broke her own record by going Parsee at the amazing altitude of 9,734 feet.

IN WHICH I INTRODUCE MYSELF

What now, notable boobies! Ha! 'Twas not thus in the days when Guy de Beaumanoir held the Abbey lands of Montsoreau (by enfeoffment, enfiefment, socage, demiburgage, and half-seizin). Then would I as soon have spitted you like larks as scrawl drivel upon paper like any besotted notary. Not though you gave me a life-size model of the bridge of Cahors and all in red Numidian granite, would I have ceased my sword-play. Hum! Permafoy! I remember an eating-house on the Quai des Lunettes, and a raw lad from the Nivernais that trod upon my foot. Zounds! In those days I could ride ninety leagues and fight four men at the end of it – aye, and then sit me down to a meal of paving-stones, if need be. They called me Iron Heart (*Cœur-de-Fer*), and they were right, beshrew me!

CŒUR-DE-FER

'The Chevalier de Menfiche! Cœur-de-Fer!'

How often I have heard that awed whisper in the ante-chambers of the great. I will tell you presently how I wooed and won the Duchesse de Garaboust in a walled garden at Vaucluse. Ha! 'Twas nothing.

IN WHICH I PINK A CURMUDGEON

It was at Bourg-la-Reine that I first set eyes on Louise de Montfichu. She had drawn up at the posting-house of old Derclaze. Her husband, an ill-natured boor, pushed past me, as I stood in the doorway twirling my moustachios. 'Have a care, sirrah,' I said sternly. 'A fig for you!' he retorted. Whereupon I threw a cup of Beaugency wine in his face. In a trice we had drawn, I had parried his mad thrusts, and my blade had passed through his arm. 'Have mercy!' cried his wife. I bowed sardonically and called for wine, 'I grant you your worthless life,' said I to him. Then, raising my cup, I drank to Louise de Montfichu. She lowered her eyes, and a slow blush stole over her cheeks. She left the room in confusion, with a backward glance. I called for more wine, flung it in her husband's face, and, with arms akimbo, stood twirling my moustachios.

IN WHICH I ENCOUNTER FOUR KNAVES

One day as I lay drinking in my sleep, and singing as I drank, four bravos, four down-at-heel rogues, entered my inn, the Horse of Bronze in Remiremont under the Vosges. They came to steal my wallet, which contained letters to the Sieur de Coquille-les-Baraquins. With one bound I left my bed and, seizing my sword, slit the cheek of the first, gashed the forehead of the second, pierced the left shoulder of the third, and pricked the fourth over the heart. I then trussed them up like fowls and rolled them into the cellar. At Jarnac I fought until I had nothing left to fight with but a one-inch stump of sword. At Ivry I had eighteen horses killed under me. At Arques I broke in the great doors of the castle with a blow of my fist. Yet, let me not boast.

IN WHICH I FIGHT A MILKSOP

It was at Les Egletons, in the Corrèze, that I first met Lady Diane de la Souricière. A perfumed milksop of the Court pranced at her side. I sneered at him. He tapped my cheek with his glove. In a trice we had drawn. I drew him on with a feint I had learned from Cointreau, my old master. Flick! My blade slid under his, and his weapon clattered against the far wall. 'Spare him!' cried the Lady Diane. So, 'Pick up your skewer, little mouse,' quoth I – and I gave him a push which sent him reeling back twelve paces. Then, calling for wine, and looking my Lady full in the eyes, I toasted her. A slow blush mantled her damask cheeks, as she left the room with a backward glance. I twirled my moustachios and called for more wine.

IN WHICH I KILL DE BOBINOT

As I rode into Paris by the Gentilly Gate servitors in the livery of Bobinot and men-at-arms were crying, 'Way for the Sieur de Bobinot! On the King's business!' And they pressed back the populace against the walls of the houses. 'Way for the Sieur de Menfiche,' cried I, 'upon his own business!' The crowd laughed, but a Captain of the Musketeers advanced menacingly. As he drew alongside me I grappled him round the waist and threw him from his Percheron steed. 'You will answer to me for this!' shouted M. de Bobinot. 'At your service,' said I, bowing mockingly. 'Behind Blache's eating-house, an hour before sunset,' said he. Fifty-nine minutes before sunset I had driven my sword through his heart. 'Twas nothing.

METHODS

Talking of biography, which method do you prefer? The Lytton Strachey, the Maurois, the Ludwig, the Guedalla?

Each is unmistakable. Here, for instance, is the Guedalla:

'The leaves fell and the King returned. Birchendorff simpered, and the first faint violins of the reassembled Court mingled with the whispers of the women. Far away in Oberspilchen the master-plotter bent over his maps, his thin lips curved into the cruel line that Palm has immortalized upon the largest of his canvases; the one crook too many who spoilt the Queen's broth.

In the same week a rider came hotfoot into Warwick, and dismounted at the gates of the Castle. He carried under his doublet twenty years of chicane and the honour of a woman.

And in Querupt, that tumbledown Alsatian village, a boy dreamed.

The boy's name was Kaulenwurtz, and as he dreamed he gazed at a picture of Saladin, the Kurd, who, on the parched plain under Hattin, had his way.'

Here is the Emil Ludwig method:

'All night long the wind has howled in the tall pine-tops, and the black clouds have moved in serried masses over the small house at the foot of the hill. Towards dawn there is a stirring in the house. People come and go. And in a small room that faces the storm the infant Balzac opens weak eyes upon the world in which he is to live.

It is 4.26 by Mrs Balzac's old clock that stands beneath the framed portrait of her grandfather. The storm abates.

"*Taisez-vous*, little one," says the mother, drawing the counterpane over the diminutive body.

The child sleeps . . . perhaps dreams. . . .'

MORE WIT FROM STULTITIA

In response to a demand for a few more witty lines from Stultitia Cabstanleigh's play, I have pleasure in bringing forward the following:

Lady G: Who is it, Mary? Mary: I'm not sure, madam. It's dressed like a woman, but it has long hair.

My dear, marriage is a vulgar effort on the part of dull people to bring boredom to a fine art.

A woman is like a pencil. She must be led.

Eating *foie gras* with an unintelligent man is like dancing a tango in diving-boots.

It isn't meeting people that matters; it's making them meet you.
It's the price of things that keeps Life exclusive.
Every modern poet has his favourite Mews.
The fly in the matrimonial amber is generally a wasp.
She loves romance with a small 'ah!'
　　Love, my dear Sir John, is like a motor-bus – easy to get into, but the devil to get out of.

SONG

The Captain stood on his bridge alone,
　　With his telescope to his eye,
The ship she was sinking rapidly,
　　As the storm went howling by.
He saw the rush for the lifeboats,
　　And he noticed a peer old and grey,
Then a sailor approached and saluted,
　　And thus to the peer he did say:

Chorus:

Pray take my place in the lifeboat,
　　'Tis a gesture I willingly make,
Since I fagged for your nephew at Repton,
　　It's the least I might do for his sake.
And when next, sir, you're seeing your nephew,
　　Pray sing him this short refrain:
'Piddock minor went down like a Repton man,
　　And gladly he'd do it again.'

UPHOLDING THINGS FAR AWAY

Once Carstairs was crossing a river in the crocodile-infested Bwara country. He was half-way across, when he glanced at his watch and saw that it was 7.30 p.m. He at once began to change for dinner.

　　The porters had to lift him out of the water so that he could get his trousers on, but he arrived on the farther bank in tails and a white tie. He was very wet and muddy, of course, but not a man in his service could fail to recognize a gentleman when he saw one after that.

He got the O.B.E. later for wearing an opera hat during a night attack on a mutinous tribe.

KEEPING THEIR END UP

Not many of our old families can boast that a Savile Row tailor calls four times a year at their country estates to measure the scarecrows in the fields for new suits.

MADAME DUMAS

When the warm spring days arrive I say to myself, 'Does Mme Dumas still keep that lonely inn under the Col des Goules, in Auvergne?' If I shut my eyes I can see the uneven grey steps leading up to her massive oaken door, the cool, dark room, with stone flags worn by the boots of so many sturdy drinkers, and the orchard behind the house, where we sang:

> *. . . Ainsi font, font, font*
> *Blondinets et blondinettes,*
> *Font, font, font*
> *Trois p'tits tours et puis s'en vont. . . .*

And 'Il pleut, bergère', which poor Fabre d'Eglantine wrote.

O Mme Dumas, long may you remain with us, to pour that rough wine of yours into squat tumblers. Mme Dumas, that is indeed a wine for men whose bodies are weary; a distant cousin of that dark nectar which may only be drunk by those who have found their way across the frontier of fairyland, and been welcomed by the mother of the shepherd girl, among the secret meadows of Corrèze. O Mme Dumas, will you be there when I return?

PRODNOSE: This isn't very interesting.

MYSELF: No. But does it never occur to you that one cannot be for ever facetious, cracking silly little jokes to make fools giggle? And since one cannot discuss international affairs with you, unless one agrees with your own ignorant point of view, I must write of other things.

Chapter 10

The Adventures of Charles Suet

OUR HERO, Charlie Suet, was born in the tiny Cornish village of Polwaddle-in-Tretoothpic. His father, Henry Suet, was a humble fisherman who lived in a gem of Victorian architecture justly famed as the smallest house in England.

It was the house in which Henry had been born, and to it he brought his very large bride, Amanda Coopstake, of Balmoral, Chesney-St-Vitus, Bedfordshire. In attempting to carry her over the miniature threshold, Henry Suet cracked her head against the coping, and laughed heartily at the omen. She bore the mark to the day of her death.

When Charlie was born she pleaded with her husband to build on to their home, but he replied that there wasn't enough to build on from.

CHANCE ENCOUNTER

A chance encounter at Weymouth with an aged mariner who kept a model ship in a bottle turned Charlie Suet's thoughts to this humble occupation. He made a dainty ship, but every time he tried to push it into the bottle he smashed the yards and tore the sails.

Finally he overcame the difficulty by inserting into the bottle a very small canoe made of match-ends glued together. He gave the whole thing an original turn by leaving on the bottle the label, which said 'Rampound's Pale Foamy Ale'. He exhibited his work on the promenade, but nobody took much notice of it – chiefly because the canoe was too small to see, and they thought he was some eccentric, advertising beer.

Encouraged by this experience, C. Suet, Esq., obtained work with a clockmaker. At the end of three days the clockmaker, a Mr Towelbird, said, 'I have never met anyone like him for pulling clocks to bits. He is the best man I ever had for that branch of work. But he doesn't ever seem to put them together again. That side of the work apparently doesn't interest him. When I said to him, "Where is that grandfather clock you took to pieces for Sir Stephen Blood?" he said, "Ah, I know all about it now", and made no further reference to the matter. When I was forced to get rid of him he said ruefully, "I didn't just want to mer . ᵇs. I wanted to get behind the inner workings." So we parted rather c ᵈly.'

An eccentric peer, hearing of Charlie Suet's passion for knowledge, said, 'His energies must be curbed. He will never keep any job. He should devote himself to the study of abstract knowledge, and to do this he must withdraw from the world.'

So he sent for C. Suet, Esq., and informed him that he would place at his disposal a three-roomed cottage in a lonely part of the Cheviots, where he could pursue knowledge without financial worries or mundane contacts. Suet accepted, not knowing what the peer was talking about. On a bitter winter's night he arrived at the cottage with his carpet bag. He had no idea what he was supposed to study, and he nearly froze to death. On the second night he took the roof off to see what it was made of. Next day, with a bad chill, he decamped.

We next hear of the incomparable Suet in a public library on the outskirts of London. He said to the head librarian, 'I don't just want to know what people write. I want to see how the books are put together and bound.' With this purpose in view Charlie began to ignore those who asked for books, and spent all his time in pulling volumes to pieces and examining the fragments under his microscope (the gift of a foolish aunt). There were naturally complaints, and the whole affair came to a climax when an old gentleman who had asked for the Victoria *History of Surrey* found one hundred and seventy-nine pages torn out of Volume II.

C. Suet, Esq., was given his marching orders.

As an attendant at the Stockport Municipal Baths Charlie Suet was a resounding failure. To find out where the water came from he scraped a large hole in the side of the bath, carried it through the outer wall, and flooded the street outside. When dismissed he said, 'I didn't just want to see how municipal baths are run, and how people swim about. I wanted to know how the water got there.'

Influence secured for the man Suet a post in a well-known picture gallery. 'This,' said his friends, 'will give him a chance to study art — or, as he would put it, to find out what is behind art.' And indeed Suet's first words, on being presented with his uniform, were, 'I don't just want to look at pictures. I want to find out what—'

'I know, I know,' interrupted the proprietor petulantly.

On his first day Charlie stayed late. The proprietor admired his zeal and devotion to duty, and left him to lock up. Charlie at once got to work to discover what was behind art. Daylight found him amid a pile of canvases which had been taken out of their frames, scratched with a penknife, and thoroughly investigated. By ten o'clock he had handed in his uniform and keys.

Charlie Suet's passion for acquiring knowledge, writes Miss Dredger, led him along strange paths. He once took a job as a night-watchman at a large factory where water-tube steam-generating boilers were made.

On his second night he yielded to his old temptation and began to meddle. He had the whole place to himself, and it was not long before he had pressed a small button. Then things began to happen. A horizontal electric steam churn-belt slid rapidly along towards a super super-heater. This started a 250,000-horse-power pressure-boiler, and almost at once a hydraulic riveting machine burst its multi-drum geared rollers. There was a bright flash.

Next day Charlie Suet was sacked.

Charlie Suet was very fond of an evening at the theatre. He was not in the least interested in plays or in acting, but he had a theory that the seats could be made more comfortable. So, whenever he had the money, he would purchase a stall for an evening performance.

He always brought with him his bag of tools, and as soon as the lights were lowered, he would set to work on his stall, humming and whistling happily as he sawed and filed and planed and hammered. The management usually protested, in response to the complaints of his neighbours, during the first interval. And after Charlie had been asked to leave, a man had to come and clear up the bits of wood and nails and screws.

In the case of the noisier and more rowdy operas he was often able to work even through the intervals, thanks to the din in the stalls. His record was three stalls sawn in half and painted bright yellow on a Wagner night.

Suet's next job was as a toast-master. He had a resonant voice and a good appearance. But at his first banquet he got to work on the back of the chairman's tail-coat. When the chairman rose to propose a toast his coat came in two, the seam down the back having been picked open. His braces had been severed, and down fell his breeches with a surprising swish. Furthermore, Suet had done something to his collar, which came off the shirt. There were titters all over the room, but Charlie kept on shouting, 'Pray silence for your chairman', and finally the toast was proposed by the rubicund, indignant gentleman, who grasped his breeches in both hands in a manful effort to preserve his dignity.

Charlie Suet was once employed at a telephone exchange, but his interest in the mechanical side of the business exceeded his interest in the needs of the subscribers. At the end of his first spell of duty nine Kensington subscribers, all of whom had asked for London numbers, were amazed to find themselves talking to a dye works in Scotland. Flashes of blue light terrified his fellow-workers, as he pulled things to bits. 'No man,' he said, 'can do his job thoroughly until he has mastered what lies behind the machinery of it.' By tea-time he had melted down his earphones on a small stove. But it was only when he began to take the switchboards to pieces that the controller asked him to go. 'Any fool,' said Charlie, 'can get a telephone number, but it takes brains to find out the why and the wherefore.'

A report in the files of a certain railway company says: 'The idea of entrusting such an individual with the delicate operation of

112   *The Best of Beachcomber*

testing the wheels of train-coaches was little short of madness.' This
sentence refers to Charlie Suet's short-lived career as a wheel-tapper
in the west of England. On his first day he knocked seven wheels to
pieces, thus disorganizing traffic on the line and doing considerable
damage. It was only when he smashed the hammer that he reported
his misadventures to the station-master.

He wrote recently to the Ministry of Supply offering as waste
paper 43,726 perforation holes which he had cut out of tear-off
calendars. An official said, 'But if they are perforation holes, they
are just holes, and not paper at all.' Charlie replied that when cutting
the holes out he was compelled to leave little bits of the paper round
them, otherwise there would be nothing left. When he said that if
there was not enough paper he could paste small circular bits over
the holes, the official screamed twice and fell to the floor with a
sickening thud.

'There the matter rests at present,' commented an unimpeachable
neutral spokesman in touch with authoritative circles.

At a theatre the other night Charlie Suet decided to salvage a good
deal of metal. He stealthily cut off thousands of trouser buttons, thus
rendering the braces useless. At the final curtain, the hoosh of falling
trousers was mistaken by the leading lady for hissing. She left the
stage in hysterics, and the male members of the audience did their
best to hold up their breeches while making for the exit. Many a
man was forced to wear his shirt outside his waistcoat, while using
his braces as a belt.

*   *   *   *   *

BLOW THE MAN UP

The old sailors had special songs for special occasions, devised to keep
a strict rhythm in the business of hauling, and to make dreary toil
less unendurable. It occurs to me that writers ought to work like this.
And I for one intend to hum to myself as I write today:

> What shall we do with the young reporter,
> What shall we do with the young reporter,
> What shall we do with the young reporter,
>   Early in the morning?

Let him ask a bishop what he thinks of baldness,
Let him ask a bishop what he thinks of baldness,
Let him ask a bishop what he thinks of baldness,
　　Early in the morning.

Make him write a story on the Giant Pumpkin,
Make him write a story on the Giant Pumpkin,
Make him write a story on the Giant Pumpkin,
　　Early in the morning.

Make him quote the jokes from the newest Blue-book,
Make him quote the jokes from the newest Blue-book,
Make him quote the jokes from the newest Blue-book,
　　Early in the morning.

– with a suitable refrain in between each verse.

AGAIN

A golden-haired boy, tall for his age and with very good manners, knocked at the door of a house in the country and asked to see the owner – a handsome unmarried lady in the roaring thirties. The boy, whose courteous bearing made an excellent impression on the lady, described himself as an evacuated orphan who had lost his label. The lady at once made arrangements to house him, and he was shown to a comfortable bedroom. He asked if he might sit up to dinner for the first night, and the lady agreed. She was very touched to notice how he moved his seat close to her, as though for protection, and still more touched when, between courses, he squeezed her hand and asked if he might kiss her.

It was then that the golden wig came off and the outraged lady found herself in the presence of the wily adventurer – Foulenough!

BUSINESS AS WE GO

The railways of England are doing their best to make travelling pleasant for business men. I read that dictaphones and typists are installed on some of the expresses, so that the magnates may get through their correspondence during the journey from, say, Manchester or Glasgow to London. But that is not all.

On many trains an attendant sells wigs, false moustaches and beards, and thick blue glasses to any business man who does not want to be recognized. There is a special compartment for black-mailers, with soundproof walls, and there is also a little steel cage next to the guard's van, in which the company-promoters and share-shufflers are housed, to protect them from the fury of ordinary travellers on whom they have got to work during the journey.

There are tape-machines in every compartment, and, when the train stops in a station, loud-speakers bellow the state of the market.

Pictures of prominent usurers are given away during lunch, and anyone who needs a thug to pull off a dirty trick for him need only apply to the Business Manager of the train.

CAT'S FISH-HEAD WAISTCOAT DRAMA

Using nothing but a heap of fish-heads—

PRODNOSE: Not another of those News items!

MYSELF: This is a newspaper, and is concerned primarily with the dissemination of news. Were I to omit this some other paper would use it, and bring off a scoop. I should get a curt note, 'How did you miss this?' And if I said I thought it unimportant I should be drummed out of the Press Club.

PRODNOSE: Oh, all right. Well, what did he make out of the fish-heads?

MYSELF (*sulkily*): A waistcoat for a cat.

POOR FATHER

A dramatic critic, in a notice of a play about the Brownings, asks why the actor who played Edward Moulton-Barrett, Elizabeth's father, should have handicapped himself with a false nose.

The answer can be found in the third volume of Mr Rollo Harland's scholarly and exhaustive *Life and Times of Edward Moulton-Barrett,* pages 386–483.

Not even his own family knew that the dignified father's nose was a false one until the day when Elizabeth asked him to smell a rose which Robert Browning had given her.

The father went through the antics of smelling and appreciating the perfume of the flower, but a constrained look in his eyes revealed the truth.

'Oh, Father,' cried Elizabeth. 'Poor, poor Father. Was it a tavern brawl?'

'Your father was never in a tavern,' said Mrs Barrett, sternly.

When the sobbing had ended, the father said, in a cold, dry voice, 'I caught it in a door.' He then strode from the room.

DOMESTIC SCENE

Some years after the event described so poignantly in the foregoing paragraph, Elizabeth said to her famous husband: 'Mr Browning, I had not ventured to reveal to you a circumstance in connection with my respected father, being in fear that, should the said circumstance become general knowledge, your career might be in some sort jeopardized. Thinking thus—'

'Be brief, Mrs Browning,' said the poet.

'In a word,' replied the distraught wife, 'in a word, sir, the nose of my reverend parent is false, utterly false! Oh, how can I bear the humiliation?'

But Browning was laughing.

'If it comes to that, my love,' he said, 'so is mine.'

So saying he pinched his nose, and it emitted a faint squeak.

'I do not know where to look for very shame,' whispered the happy wife.

WHO IS IT?

Complaints are being made, by many people who own houses in the West End, of the activities of a certain gentleman of military bearing who claims to be an 'A.R.P. inspector from headquarters'. This gentleman's procedure is to enter a house after sunset, wearing an enormous brassard on his arm. He then talks of 'interior black-out', and orders all lights to be shaded, or even turned off. This is usually followed by a great deal of giggling in the servants' quarters, and sometimes by ridiculous words of love whispered in the very ear of the lady of the house.

Lady H— complains – or perhaps boasts is the word – that when she had switched off the lights in her drawing-room and lit a candle, she was aware of an arm about her waist, and of a low voice saying, 'Stolen kisses are sweetest.'

The police are looking for Captain Foulenough.

NARKOVER NEWS

The old school pawnshop, known to so many generations of Narkoverians, is to change hands at the end of this term. I interviewed the old pawnbroker yesterday. He said:

'You would be surprised if you knew how many famous names have been connected with the shop. But I think I can say that nobody ever got the better of me. I used to sell the articles left by the young gentlemen, and replace them by inferior imitations pinched from people I had a hold over. They couldn't blab, which just suited me. Great days! Great days!'

Into the dear old man's face came that look of sweetness and tenderness which bespeaks the clean conscience after a lifetime of service.

I asked him if provision had been made for his declining years.

He grinned.

'Dr Smart-Allick,' said he, 'is going to see to that, but he doesn't know it yet. I have some letters of his to a Certain Person.'

WHAT THE BOY SAID

'This is going to hurt me more than you,' said his father.

'Then don't be too rough on yourself,' answered the boy, 'I'm not worth it.'

LITTLE CYRIL: Oo-boo-boo, Daddy!

FATHER: What is it, boy?

LITTLE CYRIL: Beachcomber didn't make me laugh in that last bit, Daddy.

FATHER (*after my own heart*): You really can't expect him to make you laugh the whole time.

LITTLE CYRIL (*nasty little beast*): But I do, Father. That's what he's for.

'HEARTS AFIRE' by MARION SCALDER (First instalment).

SYNOPSIS

(Read this and get a concise and clear idea of the plot.)

Chapter XXVI

PRUDENCE LOVEJOY, a bashful and winsome young innocent, is madly in love with

SIR ALEXANDER MCWHINNIE, laird of Castle Cowlairs, whose valuable estates are heavily mortgaged to

ABRAHAM WEISSMANN, an unscrupulous moneylender, whose life ambition is to marry

ESTELLE DE PARMESAN, a notorious actress and society vampire, who is threatening breach of promise proceedings against

CAPTAIN HONORÉ TEMPERLEY, pronounced Timlee, a prominent rum-runner, who is in command of a schooner belonging to

PRUDENCE LOVEJOY, Queen of the Parisian underworld, to whom, in secret and at midnight, comes

SIR ALEXANDER MCWHINNIE, chief of the U.S. Police, who has designs on the fortune of

ESTELLE DE PARMESAN, a dairymaid, originally a chorus girl in the employ of

CAPTAIN HONORÉ TEMPERLEY, pronounced Timlee.

One day during breakfast at Castle Cowlairs Sir Alexander McWhinnie is about to crack the egg placed before him by his discreet butler.

(Read on from here.)

As Sir Alexander raised his spoon with the avowed intention of decapitating the unheeding beige-tinted egg, which had been placed before him by his discreet butler, he paused as though struck by a sudden thought.

(Another fine instalment tomorrow)

THE WORLD OF MUSIC

Badhat, the centenarian Turkish violinist, gave his first concert of the season yesterday. He is now so old and sleepy that sometimes, for ten minutes together, he sits in silence, snoring at his fiddle. The élite call this trick *rubato,* and praise him for his eccentric modifications of rhythm. Last night he sawed away at his arm instead of at the fiddle, until an attendant in knee-breeches pointed out his error. Once he fell forward heavily and knocked the conductor backwards into the lap of a lady who was feeding a monkey in the front row of the stalls. And since his shirt was outside his waistcoat, when they tried to haul him back to his seat his braces burst with a report like a sporting-gun in a covert, and several ladies screamed.

In circles where music is taken seriously, people are asking whether it is not time that Badhat gave his farewell performance.

OPEN LETTER

Dear Sir James Barrie,—

 I am known among my friends as the beetles' fairy godfather. I, alas! know only too well the look that comes into a beetle's eyes when a rude hand smacks the poor tiny creature. My purpose is to create an atmosphere of whimsicality and wistfulness, and to fill this dear, drab world with silver laughter. Have you ever explored the tiny dark corners of a beetle's heart, or glimpsed, as in a dream-mirror, the hidden world of beauty therein? Heigh-ho, Sir James! Behind every beetle you will find a good mother-beetle. Need I say more?

OVERHEARD IN TRAFALGAR SQUARE

'Mummy, who's that gentleman on the top of the column?'
'Hush, dear, that is Mr Victor Gollancz.'

Chapter 11

The Life and Times of Captain
de Courcy Foulenough

THE MEMOIRS OF FOULENOUGH, which have been held up
for a considerable time, owing to dirty work of various kinds, are
at last about to appear.

Captain Foulenough discovered that his agent, Balsam, was really
a man named Clodpepper, who had promised Smart-Allick of Narkover that he would appear in a favourable light in the Memoirs. So
Clodpepper cut out a long passage describing Smart-Allick cheating
at cards as a boy at Narkover, and substituted a passage about Foulenough stealing books. A man called Pudsey, also an agent, has sold
the rights of the Memoirs to five publishers, and a further agent
named Burgeon-Hawke is claiming half the money on the ground
that Foulenough owes him a large sum for coupons. As a leading
literary critic remarked yesterday, 'All this has little to do with
literature at its best.'

The news that the Memoirs were about to appear led me to crave
a glimpse of them. The first sentences are characteristic of the entire
work:

'I was born to the sound of breaking glass. Not because my father
was in the trade, but because it was his custom, learned from the
Austrian Grand Duchess who nursed him, to smash a glass when
he had drunk from it. And as there were few glasses in Europe from
which he did not drink as soon as he saw them, it may be readily
imagined that after the shock of his first big deal on the Stock
Exchange had worn off, and the bailiffs were quiescent for the
moment, he bought a glass-works. I remember well one of his pithy
sayings: "Animals drink whenever they get the chance, so why

shouldn't human beings?" My mother, a mild woman, said: "But they drink water, dear." "The more fools they," roared my father, hurling a brandy glass against the wall.'

Below I give some further extracts:

My father always said that I got my winning ways from him, and my mother's comment was that if he was referring to card-games it was true. For from earliest childhood I had luck with the cards. I had always noticed that if things were going against my father in a game he would get up from his chair, as though to fetch a pipe or a box of matches. The journey always took him to a far part of the room, and he would return to his chair from behind the chair of his opponent. Suspecting that he used to see more than he was intended to see, my mother took to leaving his pipe and matches within reach. This annoyed him very much, and seemed to put him off his game. But there were limits to what my father would stand, and the first beating I got was accompanied by a memorable epigram: 'No boy under twelve has any right to unlimited aces.' I treasured that saying – particularly when I had passed my twelfth birthday.

Once, after Newmarket, my father was missing for two days. My mother did not seem to be in the least worried. 'Newmarket,' she said, 'is always a special occasion for him. He was once away for eight days celebrating his losses.' It says something for my father's robust nature that he always 'indulged in festivities', as my aunt called it, whether he lost or won. This time he came back in a most boisterous mood. He had lost at the races, but had won at cards, and then lost again at billiards, and then won again at cards, and lost again at billiards, and won again at cards. He reckoned that he would have been 17s. up on the two days if he hadn't lost £2 at a final game of billiards. 'But it was a near thing,' he said. Then, patting my head, he said, 'We'll get the boy into Eton yet, if the luck holds.'

When I was quite small somebody said to my mother, 'Does de Courcy take after his father?' 'His father doesn't leave much for him to take,' replied my mother rather bitterly. My father always used to say, 'If you don't help yourself to what you want, nobody is going to bother about you in this world.' I said, blank outright, 'Does that mean stealing, Dad?' My father replied, 'Stealing is merely a word, my boy. It is used of petty affairs and hole-in-corner occurrences. If a man with modest ambitions takes a loaf of bread because he wants something to eat, it is stealing. But in the greater world of really ambitious men of business we do not use the word. Successful negotiations or deals, we say. Aim high, my lad, pull it off and nobody will use that small-minded word about you.'

As a lad, I went to stay with a rich uncle of mine on his farm, and I was amazed when he introduced me to his bailiff. That word had but one meaning in our family. I said, 'Uncle, you're very rich, why not pay that bailiff and get rid of him?' He got very red in the face and shouted at me, 'What the devil are you talking about, boy?' 'Well, let him have some of the furniture,' I said, 'you don't want him hanging round every day.' Then my uncle laughed. 'Your father,' he said, 'doubtless forgot to tell you that there are bailiffs and bailiffs. I think it's time you went to some decent school.' 'I understand,' I said, 'that my name is down for Rugby.' 'I dare say it is,' said my uncle, 'I expect you've heard the story your father tells, beginning, "My people wanted me to go to Eton and Oxford."' 'And where did he go?' I asked. 'Cranston and Fulmer, steam carpet beaters,' said my uncle acidly.

My father's prosperity began when he opened a night club called the 'Silver Mulberry'. I was sent to a preparatory school, and my name was put down for Narkover. My father regarded Narkover as more go-ahead than the older schools, and he had met and become very friendly with old Dr Smart-Allick, father of the present headmaster. I remember the old Doctor saying to my father, 'Card tricks are more than a merely academic accomplishment. They have a practical application, and belong to life rather than to art. In the modern world you have only to set down a Latin or Greek scholar at a fair, or in some reputable gaming-house, to perceive at what a disadvantage he is among more progressive minds.' During my last term at my preparatory school my father gave the Doctor a free pass for the 'Silver Mulberry', and the next week I was awarded a scholarship at Narkover. One of my schoolmates was the Doctor's son, young Smart-Allick, so famous today.

I well remember the day my father won money at the Lewes races. He returned home in a new brown bowler, and he was singing loudly. He said to my mother, 'We'll enter the lad for Eton and Oxford and the Guards. Nothing's too good for a son of mine. Connie, my love, how would you like a big house-boat at Maidenhead? Eh? And a day trip to Boulogne from Brighton? Eh? I must get a secretary. I'll buy you a new umbrella in the morning, with a silk cover. A large one. And we'll get the boy a pair of skates. What about building on a bit? A sun-room? I might buy you some horses, if we had a stable. I must get a stable-boy. Remind me to buy you some antlers to go over the mantelpiece. Sport's the word, my dear.' And with that he fell asleep. My mother, after twenty years, knew how to take all this, and next day she discovered that he had won £4 10s., but had spent it all on the way home.

A frequent visitor at our house was a man named Grubb, whom my father called the Marquis. It was understood that he had come down in the world. My mother always said that he couldn't have come down much farther. She hated his visits, which always resulted in my father backing a loser. The Marquis wore enormous cuff-links with his crest on them. My father said they were an heirloom, but my mother said you could pick them up at eightpence a pair outside the Red Lion. 'What do you know of the Red Lion?' my father would ask. And my mother would then remind him of the night she was summoned to help him home, when, as his story went, he fractured his elbow on a tankard, and the pain made it difficult for him to walk. Remarking that he surely didn't walk on his elbows, my mother put the Red Lion out of bounds. But Dad bought a dog, and had to take it for walks. . . .

When I was still a youngster I came across, in a drawer at the top of the house, a large number of slips of paper, with the letters I.O.U. on them, followed by large sums of money. I questioned my mother, and she said, 'Your dad uses these when the tradesmen get nasty. They are all signed with imaginary names. We had a milkman once who spent his holidays trying to trace one of these imaginary people, to collect some money on Dad's behalf, in order to get his bill paid.' 'Is that what's called financial transactions?' I asked. 'Yes, dear,' said my mother, and added, 'In this house, anyhow.' 'Mother,' I continued, 'are we very poor?' 'No, dear,' she answered, 'but we ought to be.' 'Then why can't we pay our bills?' I asked. 'You'll understand one day,' said she. 'It all comes under the heading of financial transactions.'

My father was a very sociable man, and was always getting into conversation in trains. The conversations often ended in a friendly game of cards, to while away the time. He was also so interested in horses that he said the mere atmosphere of a race-train delighted him, and he would often travel to and fro on these trains without bothering to go to the meetings. I remember once when I was with him the police boarded the train, but when they reached our carriage three of the players were discussing welfare work, and my father was reading *Little Lord Fauntleroy*. I shall never forget my mother's horror and my father's cry of joy on the day when, for the first time in my life, I said angrily to my father, 'That's not the hand I dealt you, Dad.'

Some indication of the light way we took our education at Narkover may be gathered from the fact that one boy, answering in an examination paper the question: 'What do you know of the Asiatic races?' wrote: 'Indian races take place on elephants, so the weight of the jockey does not matter so much as with us.' He then went on to describe a race-meeting he had attended at Doncaster during the holidays, and ended up with a tip for the Oaks. As the horse won, Dr Smart-Allick marked this boy's paper very high, and had a long conversation with him in his study. That boy was made Head of the School and Captain of Cricket, two positions which carried with them a right to a percentage of the takings at the school roulette-rooms.

I print here one of my Narkover reports, to show how unconventional my schooling was.

LATIN: He has made some progress at Nap, but pays little attention to Cicero or anybody else.

MATHEMATICS: If his ability to add up his card winnings were applied to the more academic side of this subject he would be quite promising.

ENGLISH: Atrocious. He must have brought most of his bad language from his home.

FRENCH: Ruff's Guide to the Turf seems to be his French Grammar judging by the contents of his desk, and his answers to M. Destouches.

HISTORY: If history consisted entirely of the race-meetings of the last five years he would soon be Regius Professor at Oxford.

GEOGRAPHY: Anyhow, he seems to know where Newmarket and Epsom are.

In my form there was a bishop's son, and I remember the day when his father came to see him. The bishop said: 'If I play my cards properly, I ought to be able to get that boy of mine into the Colonial Office.' Smart-Allick paid attention only to the first part of the sentence. 'I had no idea, my lord,' he said, 'that you were a card-player. How about a game of bridge before you go back to town?' 'I was speaking metaphorically,' said the bishop. To which the headmaster replied rather rudely, 'Whoever heard of metaphors getting anyone anywhere?' 'I trust there is no card-playing in your school,' said the bishop. Smart-Allick choked, 'You might as well ask if we back horses,' he said. 'Ah, of course not,' said the bishop. 'I was not seriously suggesting any such thing.' 'Cards, drink and horses have ruined many a home,' said the Doctor, 'but not mine, I am glad to say. I have done quite well for myself – er – without them, of course.'

My father seemed to be very anxious that young Smart-Allick and I should be chums, but we were continually quarrelling. I noticed that when we were friendly I did very well in all subjects. Old Smart-Allick was very kind to me, and always added a message when I wrote home. 'Fawcus for the 3.15,' or 'Soldanella for the 2.30', or something of the sort. Sometimes the messages were very mysterious: 'Get Clapiron to sell the stuff to Ned', or, 'If Wivenhoe squeals, put Manderby and the gang on to him.' It was only later that I realized what all this was about. And I shall never forget the day when my father sent a message in his letter to me: 'Tell your thug of a head-master to lay off Wright or I'll spill the beans.' The next week I was bottom of my class, got caned five times, was dropped from the football team and refused credit in the tuck-shop. Apparently the row blew over, for at the end of the term I was awarded a history prize for which I hadn't even entered.

I find among my papers this letter from my headmaster, old Smart-Allick, to my father:

> 'You say that Joe can't plant the stuff on the Grangers because he owes Ned for the last lot. Well, why can't you get Tom to tell them it was paid to the others? They were working together at the time. As for Bertie's threat, I should get Bullock on to him – you know, the old police threat. I happen to know that Bullock's got a hold over him, through the Chadler affair. Mabel squealed to me. All this is very tiresome, especially as the Governors are kicking up a row about the necklace I gave the matron. She's a real corker, and makes me sick of Greek verbs, I can tell you. Your lad is doing fine. He and my youngster ought to go far together. The farther the better. They know too much about me. I suppose you still keep up the respectability pose with your youngster. He probably thinks you make your money out of Sunday school teaching or clothing Nigerians or something. . . .'

When I was seventeen our great family tragedy occurred. My father, through no fault of his own, was discovered monkeying with the cards on a race-train. As the head of the gang, or, as old Smart-Allick put it, the Chairman of the Company, he had no chance to establish what he called his innocence. And down he went for a long stretch. Smart-Allick preached in chapel on the following Sunday a very moving sermon on the importance of not getting caught. 'Life,' he said, 'is always very hard on the man who gets caught, and all our existence is an attempt to outwit fate. That is what Darwin meant by the survival of the fittest.' After chapel the headmaster sent for me and told me that I owed £174 for school fees, and introduced me to a new boy, the son of a wealthy band-leader. 'Soak him for your dad's sake – and mine,' whispered Smart-Allick in my ear, putting a pack of his own cards in my pocket.

In the Christmas term a conjurer used to give a performance in the school Concert Hall. I remember once how he was disconcerted, during a card-trick, by young Smart-Allick. The conjurer, stepping down amongst the audience, produced a card from Smart-Allick's pocket. My chum retaliated by producing a card from behind the conjurer's collar. The conjurer then took half a crown from my chum's ear, and my chum took a ten-bob note from the conjurer's wallet, three shillings from his trousers pocket, and a fountain-pen from his waistcoat. The headmaster interfered, and took a pound note from his son's coat pocket. The son at once got his father's watch. In a touching speech, the conjurer complained that he was four pounds down, and had lost his overcoat, a dozen stamps, his hat and his set of trick-cards.

My father's imprisonment was a great blow to my mother and me. We both thought he was too clever to get caught. And it meant that I must leave Narkover and become the family breadwinner. Through an uncle of my mother's I got my first job – with a dealer in second-hand carpets. My job was to label the carpets 'Genuine Bokhara', 'Old Kermanshah', 'Antique Thurralibad', and so on. The owner of the shop, a Mr Custard, got me to dress up as a young Turk, and told the customers that I had brought the carpets from my father's firm in Constantinople. With the aid of Mrs Dubbick's *Turkish Days and Turkish Ways,* I was able to answer awkward questions about my adopted country, and we did a good trade. It was only when the police found the mark: Birmingham, 3s. 6d. under our priceless 200-guinea Bokhara prayer-mat that my job came to an end.

When I left Narkover, at the age of eighteen, I had not done badly, thanks largely to my friendship with the headmaster's son. Young Smart-Allick was kept short of pocket-money, his father's theory being that it is up to a boy to make his way on his own, as soon as he can play cards. Consequently young Smarty, whenever he was having a run of bad luck, was always willing to get a look at examination papers and copy them for his chums, for a small consideration. And I soon found that if you can look up the answers to questions before an exam, the exam loses it terror. The only danger was that if the headmaster suspected that someone had been at the papers he would change them at the last moment – a dirty, underhand trick, if ever there was one. This battle of wits between father and son went on all through my stay at Narkover.

It has often been asked how I became a Captain, a rank and title which, I am glad to say, I have never abandoned. Well, after leaving Narkover, I did some odd jobs for my father, and one day he said he wanted me to take charge of a little motor-boat which plied on one of our lovely English rivers. I used to do two runs a day between two fair-sized towns, in the summer months. Its passengers, of which we could accommodate about nine, were usually holiday-makers or local couples. My father owned the boat, and had an agent to run it, a local ironmonger. The ironmonger was a busy man, so I took charge of the actual voyages. I had a fine uniform of naval design, with a smart peaked hat, and I was addressed as Cap'n Foulenough. Our occasional cargo never varied. It was a heavy sack which I took over from the ironmonger and delivered to a man in a remote alley in the other town. My father said, when I questioned him, 'It's a certain sort of goods – contraband, one might say – and nobody in these parts has ever thought of getting stuff by water to a fence.' Later, I discovered we had quite an organization at work.

I was very proud of myself in my uniform. The ironmonger's two boys would hand me the sack, which I'd stow away behind my over-coat. Then I'd say, 'All aboard! Cast her off, Mr Kemble!' and the man who owned the punts would untie the bit of rope, and I'd start her up. Old Kemble would shout, 'Aye, aye, Cap'n!' as we moved out into the stream, and every day the widow at the tea-shop window would yell, 'Take soundings, Admiral!' and the old gentleman on the lawn of the bowling-club would shout, 'Bring us back a Burmese idol.' It was all good-natured fun, and though my job wasn't particu-larly nautical, I was young enough to try to behave like the com-mander of a big ship. Often I'd frighten girl passengers by wetting my finger, holding it up, and then saying gravely: 'It's blowing up a bit, ladies.' I remember one girl who asked me if I'd ever been round the Horn. Thinking she meant the public-house at Bulminster, I said, 'Round and round it.' She thought I was making fun of her. I afterwards discovered that this girl, whose name was Ethel, was a detective's daughter.

Ethel's mother was an extraordinary woman. She was determined to get her daughter married. If I said to Ethel, 'It looks like rain', her mother would wink, giggle and remark to Ethel, 'Doesn't he say awful things?' If I said, 'Hello, Ethel, how are you today?' her mother would cry, 'Go on, now, you two!' But I had been too well brought up by my dad to go and marry a detective's daughter. So I cooled off a bit, but not before her father had made a trip on my boat. He sat down on the sack (which was full of silver jugs and things like that). 'It feels very nobbly,' he said. 'It's junk,' I said. He seemed satisfied, but I could see that he was a bit puzzled. His mind worked very slowly, and it was ten minutes before he said, 'Why junk?' I tried to laugh it off by saying, 'Why not?' 'Yes, that's true,' he said. 'Why not, indeed?'

Ethel's father's mind worked so slowly that I thought he had forgotten all about my sack. But three days after his trip on my boat, he said suddenly, 'I think I'd like to take a look at the contents of that sack.' I said with a laugh, 'I hope you don't suspect me of anything illegal.' 'Who said anything about illegal?' he replied, staring hard at me. 'Take a look whenever you like,' I said. 'Thanks,' he said, 'I will.' Next day he came aboard and you can bet the sack contained a suit of my clothes and a few odds and ends of braces, ties and boots. 'Why do you carry your clothes in a sack?' he asked. 'Because I haven't got a suitcase,' said I. He then went ashore, but I could see that he wasn't satisfied.

Chapter 12

The Saga of the Saucy Mrs Flobster

THOSE WHO HOPED that the *Saucy Mrs Flobster,* Headquarters and Flag Ship of Admiral Sir Ewart Hodgson, Governor of Lots Road Power House, would be towed to her resting-place, to be broken up, are likely to be disappointed. She is to be sold to Afghanistan for £341 12s. 8d.

There was a scene in the House when a Liberal member protested that this was no moment to sell our ships. A Ministerial reply revealed that the famous craft could hardly be called a ship any longer, being neither seaworthy nor river-worthy. Not even stagnant pool-worthy. Boys on the embankment have removed her stern bit by bit. There is no port-side to the after deck. The Captain's bridge is a yawning cavity. The anchor has no chain, and lies in the mud, independent of the ship. When the Afghans see her it is doubtful whether we shall get the 114 tins of onions promised in exchange, much less the £341 12s. 8d.

In answer to a suggestion that the *Saucy Mrs Flobster* should be broken up, the Minister of Bubbleblowing said: 'I understand that this ship is already as much broken up as possible.' Asked why we did not sell her to some foreign government, the Minister said: 'We were offered sevenpence for her by the principality of Lichtenstein, but on seeing a photograph of her, the intending purchasers called off the deal.' Asked why she was not used for fuel, the Minister replied: 'I understand she's too wet.'

Mrs Withersedge, caretaker on board the *Saucy Mrs Flobster,* has received orders to make all shipshape and Bristol fashion in readiness for the visit of inspection of Captain Gharikhar Girishkand of the Afghan Navy. She will begin by driving the hens off the poop, and nailing bits of felt over the holes in the deck. A new chain has been bought for the anchor, but it does not fit. Four steps are missing from the main companion-way, and the stump of the only remaining funnel is stuffed with rotten wood. Admiral Sir Ewart Hodgson, attempting to adjust the ceiling of his cabin, fell over a dead cat into a bucket full of mouse-traps, tins, sacking, and fish-scales. But today the Lots Road burgee flutters from an old piece of stove-pipe tied to the smashed roof of the chart-house.

A knock on the side of the *Saucy Mrs Flobster* brought Mrs Withersedge on deck. It was Professor Hugetrouser, who had arrived to examine the old hulk for signs of erosion. The Professor said grumblingly, 'This is more like a heap of rubbish than a ship.' He then attempted to take soundings, and found that 'while the front part of the ship is stuck fast in mud, what remains of the back part peters out into slime. She can hardly be said to be afloat, unless there is some water under her middle portion. The railing at the blunt end is missing, but this is not due to erosion.' Mrs Withersedge obligingly pointed out the nest of a bearded tit, but the Professor snapped, 'Even that doesn't make the thing seaworthy.'

Before leaving the *Saucy Mrs Flobster* Professor Hugetrouser asked to see the log. 'We don't burn wood,' said Mrs Withersedge. 'Of course not,' said the Professor. 'But I want to see the reel and line with which you record the ship's speed.' Mrs Withersedge laughed. 'We 'aven't 'ad any speed, as you might say,' she replied, 'since we was blown a mile down the river in a storm and fetched up crack against the embankment near Chelsea Bridge. Since then we're an 'ome-lovin' craft, as you can see.' 'I wonder she has not sunk long ago,' said the Professor. 'She couldn't sink much more,' said Mrs Withersedge, 'an' the rats seem to think she's safe enough.' The Professor blew his nose in embarrassment.

An unexpected message from Admiral Sir Ewart Hodgson to his ship, the *Saucy Mrs Flobster,* anchored off the Embankment, near

Lots Road Power Station, threw the caretaker into a state of frenzy yesterday.

The boy who brought the message said, 'You're to put to sea, Mrs Withersedge.' 'Put to *what*?' shouted the lady. The boy surveyed the miserable hulk. 'There's an 'ole in the deck, Ma,' he observed maliciously.

'There's 'oles everywherest,' replied the caretaker. 'Why, you couldn't float this muck-heap in a public bathin'-'ouse. Not at the shaller end, neither. What does 'e think we are, 'im and 'is puttin' to sea? Hadmiral my foot!'

Mrs Withersedge, caretaker of the *Saucy Mrs Flobster,* was confronted by what looked like the remains of a sailor – a scraggy, whiskered scarecrow in a jersey marked 'Blackburn Rovers'. 'I bin sent,' said the seedy mariner, 'to get 'er ready to sail.' 'Sail?' thundered Mrs Withersedge. 'And what d'yer think she's goin' ter sail with? The last sail we 'ad aboard was used to plug 'oles in 'er stem when she rammed 'erself against the embankment. Why, I'll bet even 'er keel's bin et by fishes.'

'Any rope?' asked the gloomy salt, with the air of having a hanging in mind. 'Only a bit what's used to tie a lot o' loose planks to 'er sides where she rammed 'erself against an old dray the boys pushed into the water on Guy Fawkes' night, when they burnt 'er mast.' The sailor scratched his head meditatively.

'D'you reckon,' asked Mrs Withersedge, 'as 'e *reely* means to put to sea in this old skow?' 'No knowin',' replied the disconsolate sailor. 'Maybe 'e'll get 'er towed down-river.' 'Towed my foot!' said Mrs Withersedge. 'Why, the 'ole thing'd come apart. This mornin' one o' them 'ens pecked a hole in a smoke-stack. Soft as blottin'-paper everythin' is 'ere.' ' 'Ow's the engyne-room, Ma?' 'Like a scrap-'eap. You could run 'er with a couple o' typewritin' machines as easy as with all that worm-eaten junk.' 'Steerin' gear O.K.?' asked the sailor. 'There's a bit of a wheel with no spokes, but it don't connect with nothin'.' 'Leaky?' 'Leaky! Why, down below there's a reg'lar swimmin'-pool for all 'Ollywood.' The sailor sat down gloomily on a stanchion, which broke, and the pieces rolled noisily across the so-called deck.

Admiral Sir Ewart Hodgson had rung up from Lots Road Power Station to say that he would come aboard at 11 a.m. Mrs Withersedge and the disconsolate sailor received him, and helped him to clamber over a heap of broken crockery and torn rigging to an almost roof-less chart-house, where two hens were kept. 'Where's the wind?' inquired the Admiral, wetting his finger and holding it up. 'You'll need a 'urricane to dislodge this lot,' said Mrs Withersedge.

The Admiral then studied an inventory of ships' fittings, which included a cat's basket, three old cycle tyres, a roller-skate confiscated from a boy who fell through a hole in the deck, a stuffed raven given to Mrs Withersedge by her son-in-law, a painter's ladder with eight rungs missing, a Brazilian oil-stove without any inside, and a fire-man's helmet won in a raffle by the late Mr Withersedge. The Admiral then went back to Lots Road.

Captain Garikhar Girishkand of the Afghan Navy was surprised when, expecting to be taken out in a launch to look over the *Saucy Mrs Flobster,* he was shown into Admiral Sir Ewart Hodgson's office, near Lots Road Power House.

'Here she is, as she was in her prime,' said the Admiral, pointing to a photograph on the wall. 'You'll find her changed.' An hour later the Captain, having put his foot through the deck twice, considered this a gross understatement. 'Does she float at all at high tide?' he asked. 'As much as she ever floats,' replied the Admiral. 'And where,' inquired the visitor, sarcastically, 'might her stern be?' 'It *might* be in its usual place,' said the Admiral, 'but it isn't.' The Afghan cursed softly under his breath.

'Do you go with the ship?' asked the courteous Afghan mariner.

'Go?' repeated Mrs Withersedge, mystified.

'Yes,' continued the dusky seafarer. 'I mean, when one acquires the ship and she sails for her new berth, do you sail with her?'

'Don't make me laugh!' retorted the caretaker. 'This 'ere ship stopped goin' years ago. As for sailin', St Paul's is just as likely ter sail.'

'Put it this way,' said the sunburned foreigner. 'Are you a member of her crew?'

'I'm all the ruddy crew I ever seed,' replied Mrs Withersedge vigorously. 'But now she's crumblin', I'm gettin' ready to go back to 'Oxton.'

The Afghan surveyed the preposterous craft in gloomy silence.

The following significant passage from a leading article in the *Jamrad Jokhta* (the journal of the Afghan Navy) speaks for itself, but not for me: *Ghazi bustan shutargi vemul 'Zaucy Misses Vlobster' wana han Kandahar, kala bist landi diaram.* As I haven't the faintest idea what this means, as Seymour Hicks used to say when he recited a 'Czech poem', we will turn to matters more easily dealt with, smiling through our tears as we do so, for we are jolly good fellows, and so say all of us.

'Come in,' cried Mrs Withersedge, forgetting that she was on board the *Saucy Mrs Flobster*. The knocking was repeated. The caretaker went on deck and craned over the side. There she saw the errant anchor knocking against the ship. Moreover, mud had given place to water under the so-called bow, and the good ship was as nearly afloat as possible. Mrs Withersedge had a sudden vision of being washed out to sea and round the Cape before she could say sausage. She ran forward, nay, forrard, and pulled on the rope which hoisted the flag, so that the Admiral, from his room in Lots Road, might see the signal. But it was not a flag, but a blue flannel night-dress which fluttered from half-way up what was left of the mainmast. The Afghan Captain, arriving for a second tour of inspection, clicked his heels and saluted the ensign. 'These English are mad,' he muttered.

'Mrs Withersedge speakin', Hadmiral . . . yes . . . I thought you'd like ter know about the hanchor . . . we was pullin' at it, me and that sailor, like you said, to see if it would come up by itself, like, and there wasn't no hanchor at the end, so we think, as you might say that the hanchor's got lost in the mud, and there ain't nothin' to 'old the old tub firm but that bit o' rope the policeman tied to the seat on the embankment, an' the sailor says that if there's a storm an' a bit of a off-shore wind the 'ole caboodle's goin' ter get dragged out from 'er moorin's, so I and 'e got a bargeman ter twist some wire off of the 'en-coop amidships round a lump of stone, and there she rides as easy as you never saw. . . . Hi! You've cut me orf! . . .'

As the *Saucy Mrs Flobster* lay, or rather mouldered, at her so-called moorings, there came alongside a little boat rowed by a fat old man in a peaked hat. From the stern floated the flag of Lots Road Power Station. The fat man heard the voice of Mrs Withersedge and approached an open port-hole. *'It hadder be you,'* sang Mrs Withersedge as she emptied a pail of fish-scales and dirty water over the fat man, who was standing up in his boat. 'Yus, it had to be me,' retorted the visitor, wiping the muck from his head and clothes. He then delivered a letter from the Admiral. 'Sealed orders, I suppose,' said Mrs Withersedge, 'to be hopened at sea.'

'The front part of the *Saucy Mrs Flobster* is now afloat,' said an official spokesman in touch with tomfoolery yesterday. The back part has got wedged under the embankment wall, and is loaded with garbage and rubble and refuse well above the Plimsoll line. Ignorant workmen have glued the rudder on to the front part, but as there are only two temporary spokes (made from saucepan handles) of the steering-wheel left, this will not affect life on board, particularly as the wheel itself has come off.

Last night's theft of the anchor chain from the *Saucy Mrs Flobster* is regarded in naval circles as a comparatively trivial event, owing to the droll fact that there was no anchor attached to it. Mrs Withersedge, the caretaker who sleeps aboard, heard noises which she attributed to roving vermin, or to the usual disintegration of the bounding barque. The proximity of what is left of the stern to the embankment makes it easy for marauders to scramble aboard. 'She's still anchored securely,' said Mrs Withersedge in an interview. 'Least-aways, what I mean is the anchor's stuck in the mud orf of what the Admiral calls 'er starboard beam. For all the good it does us it might as well be 'angin' from the roof o' the National Gallery. Them Afghans won't 'ave to 'aul it up when they sail away for the Spice Islands, an' yo ho ho an' a bottle o' rum served ice-cold in the crow's nest.'

Rumours that the *Saucy Mrs Flobster*, crack and only craft of the Lots Road squadron, was about to waddle to sea, reached the public houses both north and south of the river.

The local wits taunted the gloomy sailor with requests that he would bring them back a bag of groundnuts or a giant baboon. Mrs Withersedge coming ashore for a breath of fresh air, was heard to admit that another bit of the stern had dropped off at high tide. 'Dessay as 'ow that won't matter much,' she added. When asked if it was true that seafaring folk got to love their ship like a home, she said, 'Not me! I'd rather go to sea in a disused railway kerridge.' 'Steam or sail this trip, Ma?' asked a jaunty young landlubber. 'It'll 'ave to be oars,' replied Mrs Withersedge, 'an' the only one left 'asn't got any blade.'

Yet, at that very moment, welders and blowers and plate-rifters and cordwainers and caulkers and baulkers and keel-haulers were swarming over the ship, and getting her ready for the great moment, when her snout would once more sniff the tempestuous brine. Mrs Withersedge came out on deck and stared incredulously at all this activity. Approaching Admiral Sir Ewart Hodgson, who was leaning nonchalantly against a forward bunnion, she said: 'Then we hare reely outerd bound, Hadmiral?' The Admiral slapped his thigh breezily with his telescope, and replied, with nautical bonhomie, 'Shipshape and Bristol fashion, my dear.'

At 11.23 ship's time a wisp of dirty smoke stole gingerly from the worm-eaten funnel of the *Saucy Mrs Flobster*. A moment later a thudding and a shuddering and a rattling announced that the engines had started. The siren emitted a hoarse note, like an old crow with laryngitis. The Admiral, on the bridge, was thrown to the ground. The gloomy sailor, standing by the wheel, put his elbow through the spokes and got it stuck there. Mrs Withersedge, who should have shouted to a pavement artist on the Embankment to cast her off, remarked instead, 'She's blowin' up! All 'ands to the boats, if there was any 'ands, if there was any boats.' Before the pavement artist could do anything, the ship had swung round, the cable had parted, and there was that queen of the inland seas more or less headed for distant landfalls, notably the Surrey shore.

Orders and counter-orders poured like water on to a duck's back from the lips of Admiral Hodgson. And like the same water off the same duck's back, they poured unheeded by that gloomy sailor at the wheel.

Having banged into the Surrey shore, the *Saucy Mrs Flobster* suddenly lurched sideways, swung round and lumbered back to the muddy spot she had left. Still trailing the parted rope, the damnable craft sank to rest with an almost audible sigh of contentment. The engines spluttered and died. The sailor spun the wheel derisively and mopped his forehead. 'The old place 'asn't changed,' said Mrs Withersedge with a broad smile.

'She is no longer seaworthy,' said the Admiral breezily to the Press, 'or even riverworthy.' 'Mudworthy's the word,' added Mrs Withersedge. As the sunset gun boomed from Lots Road Power Station, Admiral Hodgson saluted. Mrs Withersedge approached with an egg. 'One o' them 'ens laid during the voyage,' she said. The Admiral shook his head reflectively. Nothing was heard but bits off the ship slithering into the dirty water, and the sailor whistling 'Rolling down to Rio' as he clambered on to the Embankment for shore leave.

An unfavourable report on the *Saucy Mrs Flobster* having been made to the Afghan Government, the deal has fallen through. The part of her which was afloat at high tide came to bits at low tide, and Captain Girishkar Garishkand said sardonically: 'If my country is ever to have a navy, we must make a better start than this.' The whole question as to whether Lots Road Power House really needs a ship at all is to be thrashed out in Parliament soon.

* * * * *

INTERLUDE

O cuckoo calling through the rain,
  I knew by heart, in other times,
  The old grey wall, the grove of limes
  That soon will store the sun again—

PRODNOSE: Hi! What hoggery is this?

MYSELF: Supposing I told you it was by Tennyson.

PRODNOSE: Then, naturally, I should apologize and say it was good.

MYSELF: Well, it's not by Tennyson. It's an unimportant thing by an obscure fellow.

PRODNOSE: There you are! That just shows. It is chronically bad. None of these obscure people can write for nuts. Give me the big names. They pull it off every time.

MYSELF: Very well.

When the sun goes down in the blazing Orient—

PRODNOSE: Ha! Excellent verse. What did I tell you? A sip is enough. That's the real thing, hall-marked.

MYSELF: Yes? Do you think so? I've just this moment made it up. Do you like your suns to set in the east, Prodnose? You should join the Penny Bizarre School, my little dolt.

(*The fool shuffles away in shamed silence.*)

ANSWERS TO CORRESPONDENTS

EDNA: No, Edna; it is only when the poor gamble that gambling is wrong.

MABEL: No, Mabel; it is only when the poor drink that drinking is wrong.

DAISY: No, Daisy; it is only when the poor avoid going to school that avoiding going to school is wrong.

CLARA: No, Clara; it is only when the poor have large families that having large families is wrong.

BIRDIE: No, Birdie; it is only when the poor make a disturbance in public that making a disturbance in public is wrong.

FLO: Yes, Flo; the poor are always wrong.

PRODNOSE BITES

Laryngitis. *A slight attack, which unfortunately forces me to write, as it were, in a hoarse whisper. In fact, it is a great strain to write at all, as all who have suffered from this ailment will readily underst——*

PRODNOSE: One moment! Surely laryngitis doesn't affect the size of one's writing. It's the voice, the capacity of speech which is affected.

MYSELF: ANYHOW, I WAS ONLY SHAMMING.

CENTURY OF THE COMMON MAN

Dame Gertrude Glapiron, O.B.E., opened today an Exhibition of

Prefabricated Homes. Each house consists of a television set, a room for keeping forms, a garage, a dog's bedroom, and a mat of artificial grass on the plastic roof, for sun-bathing. The houses fold up into a small space, and are bright yellow. They have courageously modern names, such as Owaryer, Wattaboutit, Avanutha, Ereweya, Dunwanderin, Pilgrim's Nest, O.K., Sezu, etc. Dame Glapiron made a hearty tea, and when called on to speak, said, 'My mouth is too full for words.'

THE BATTLE OF WITS

A semi-official account of a game of cards played at Narkover between Captain Foulenough and Dr Smart-Allick says: 'For every ace which Foulenough had up his sleeve, the headmaster had two inside his waistcoat. For every counterfeit half-crown the headmaster produced, the captain produced a forged ten-shilling note. The battle of wits went on far into the night. Cards of every denomination lay ankle-deep round the table. The floor was littered with IOUs and cheques, sham postal orders, forged money-orders, bottles and bent coins. Towards dawn the two experts were so red-eyed and exhausted that Dr Smart-Allick trumped a cigarette-card of one of our biggest battleships with the visiting-card of a Miss Ruby Delamotte, and claimed the stakes, which included three trouser buttons, a cream caramel, a metal label from a dog's collar ('Frowstie'), a sardine's head, an enamel sign marked 'No Exit', a bone collar-stud, a tooth, a steward's badge, a door-knob and a cistern-stamper.'

SPECIAL SCOOP

David Burghley carried the hooked nose of the Cecils triumphantly through Eton.

(News item)

Eton High Street was thronged. From the early hours of the morning crowds had been assembling, and fragments of sandwich lying beneath camp-stools told of many a Spartan snack. Shortly after nine, as though to grace the scene, the sun flashed from behind a bank of cloud. A second later, distant cheering announced that the old ceremony of the Carrying of the Nose had begun. Presently, craning forward behind the lines of soldiers, we could see the Hooked Nose, borne on its red velvet cushion by David Burghley, surrounded by twelve mounted Cecils. The massed bands of the Brigade of Guards crashed into the opening bars of the old song, 'Go, Lovely Nose'.

Ten minutes later a thirsty but proud people crashed into the opening bars of Eton and Windsor.

Once more the Nose of the Cecils had been carried in triumph through storied Eton. 'This,' said a laughing mother, as she wiped a tear from her eye, 'this could only happen in England.' Then she added, in a low voice, quivering with emotion, 'Dear isle, set in a silver sea.'

THE DANCING CABMAN

Alone on the lawn
  The cabman dances:
In the dew of dawn
  He kicks and prances.
His bowler is set
  On his bullet-head.
For his boots are wet,
  And his aunt is dead.
There on the lawn,
  As the light advances,
On the tide of the dawn,
  The cabman dances.
Swift and strong
  As a garden roller,
He dances along
  In his little bowler,
Skimming the lawn
  With royal grace,
The dew of the dawn
  On his great red face.
To fairy flutes,
  As the light advances,
In square black boots
  The cabman dances.

Chapter 13

Mr Justice Cocklecarrot: Home Life

COCKLECARROT always refers to his retiring and very silent wife as Mrs Justice Cocklecarrot. For the first eight years this raised a wan smile on her face, but the joke has now worn thin, and he gets no encouragement when he trots out the phrase. Since, however, it is his only jest, some of his friends still greet it with a short and insincere burst of laughter. One or two mutter, 'Jolly good!' Others sigh heavily and turn away. And she, the source of the phrase, sits as impassible as a lump of earth, listening, always listening, but taking no part in any conversation. Which explains why the servants were recently staggered to hear her say suddenly, in a loud, clear voice, to her lord and master: 'Wivens fell down a manhole on Christmas Eve.' Cocklecarrot was in the hall, about to set out for his club. He turned in astonishment, gazed at his wife, said 'Thank you, my love', and went out dreamily into the street.

Ten minutes later he returned, with a puzzled frown on his face, and sought his wife in her boudoir. 'What Wivens was it that you were speaking of?' he asked. 'E. D. Wivens,' said his wife. 'I see,' said Cocklecarrot, who had never heard of the man. Silence fell. After a quarter of an hour, Cocklecarrot, happy in this new talkativeness of his wife, said pleasantly: 'Did you know him, my dear?' 'No,' said his wife. So Cocklecarrot again set out for his club.

Many times in the next few days Cocklecarrot endeavoured to recapture the first fine careless rapture of that conversation. He would say, 'Now, this Wivens you mentioned, my dear . . .' But the fish always refused the bait. Sometimes he would try a different opening gambit. 'Wivens was the name, was it not, my love?' But all he got was a solemn nod of assent. Whatever volcanic eruption, deep in that massive frame, had thrown up the glittering lava of small-talk was now quiescent. Somewhere in her secretive brain the Wivens incident died of inanition. Quiet reigned in the house once more.

Mr Justice Cocklecarrot was convinced, after the incident described above, that Wivens was the magic word which might one day again open the floodgates of Mrs Justice Cocklecarrot's eloquence.

There was something a little pathetic in the way he would watch her large, empty face as he uttered the word Wivens, now coaxingly, now indifferently, now with vigour and decision. But it was of no avail.

Who, he asked himself, was this Wivens, whose fall through a manhole had made so profound an impression on his wife? The name began to haunt him. He awoke in the night, from dreams of vast landscapes pitted with manholes, and heard himself cry 'Wivens!'

Sometimes he would try a new tactic, and say, 'Talking of manholes, my love . . .' But stony silence met him. It seemed that nothing would ever again make so strong an impression on Mrs Justice Cocklecarrot as the misadventure of this unknown man. One day he entered the breakfast-room breezily, and began at once, 'My love, I do wish you would tell me about this man Wivens,' hoping to surprise her into speech. But her only reply was to point to his chair and hand him a cup of tea. 'Damnation!' he roared, as his nerves snapped. Mrs Justice Cocklecarrot laid her finger to her lips. Half an hour later, as he was going out, she said, 'Every swear word goes through me like a spear,' turned, and went upstairs.

As time passed, Cocklecarrot began to forget his suspicions, and the customary silence settled over the house. Then one day, as he was going out, and his wife had come into the hall to speed him on his way, he heard words which froze him in his tracks. The voice of Mrs Justice Cocklecarrot said languidly, 'Wivens fell down that manhole again yesterday.' Cocklecarrot, after recovering from his first shock, turned to his wife and said, 'Pray repeat that, my love.' She did so. Then, speaking very gently but firmly, Cocklecarrot said, 'Is this Wivens – E. D. Wivens, I think you told me before – a great friend of yours?' Mrs Justice Cocklecarrot smiled happily. 'He's adorable,' she said. Cocklecarrot winced. 'You should see him lap up his milk,' she said. Cocklecarrot started as though stung by a hornet. 'Who – what is this Wivens?' he said. 'A cat, dear. The Marshams' cat.' 'But cats don't have initials.' 'This one does,' The relief was so great that Cocklecarrot thought he was going to faint.

The *dénouement* of the Wivens affair led Cocklecarrot to try again to draw out his silent wife. Very briskly he said to her at breakfast, 'Well, has E. D. Wivens fallen down that manhole again?' 'Yes,' said his wife. 'They ought to keep it covered,' said Cocklecarrot. Exactly twenty-three minutes later Mrs Justice Cocklecarrot replied, 'They do.' 'Then how does the accident happen?' he asked. But this time there was no reply. A heavy silence pressed on the room, and the judge had to leave home with the slender hope of the question being answered that night.

This 'delayed-action' form of conversation often results in Cocklecarrot receiving answers to questions long forgotten. His wife will say, out of the blue, 'Not necessarily,' or 'They didn't, though,' or 'If you really think so.' To all of which he usually answers, 'Of course, my dear.' And then silence falls again.

One day a cat made its way into the Cocklecarrot mansion. Believing it might be E. D. Wivens, and therefore an agent for the restoration of speech to Mrs Justice Cocklecarrot, the judge began to call softly, 'E. D. Wivensy-Pivensy, then! Diddums! Come up, now, there, Wivy-Pivy, did he, then!' The cat ignored these puerile advances, and the judge shouted louder endearments, hoping to bring his wife downstairs. When she arrived, he said, 'My love, we have a visitor! Look! Wivens, I take it, eh?' His wife, drawing her skirt aside with disapproval, went on into the dining-room. Cocklecarrot remained to play with the cat, though he was much disheartened. Two hours later his wife said, 'That was not Wivens. It was Scrounger.' And once more silence reigned supreme.

Thirsting for conversation the other day, Cocklecarrot sought to kindle his wife's imagination and awaken her enthusiasm by saying at breakfast, 'My love, hasn't E. D. Wivens fallen down that manhole again yet?' He awaited the answer anxiously, uncertain whether he hoped for a yes or a no, and tempted, as the silence remained un-broken, to admit that it really didn't matter much, either way. Presently his wife looked up and spoke. 'He has tried to,' she said, 'but the manhole was shut.' 'Did he always do it on purpose, then?' pursued the judge, intoxicated with this unaccustomed babbling. But there was no reply, and he returned with a sigh to his unexciting porridge-powder. Twenty minutes later she startled him by saying, 'Why else would a cat fall down a manhole?' Having no reply ready, he grinned happily.

*   *   *   *   *

MY OWN DEAR PAGE
(*For My Own Dear Public*)

Do, please, write to me, all of you. Then I shall feel I know you, and we can get together and contribute our little effort towards the better-ment of this weary world.

A dear old great-grandmother, by the fireside, in the winter mists. Her face is furrowed by time and care, but in her heart is wistful tranquillity.

Those words, spoken by the girl next to me on the bus, made me realize what a power for good a conscientious journalist can be. I at once rang up a dear little old lady who lives in such a lovely little cottage near Chertsey. She was out, so I went out into my garden and looked up at the stars.

That girl on the bus haunts me. One day she may be somebody's great-grandmother. Will she remember the bus, and the journalist who just longed to be decent to somebody's great-grandmother?

Let us, you and I, try to be what we might be. 'Nothing,' said Emerson, 'is difficult to do when once it is done.' Everywhere I go I see people who are longing and yearning, as I am at this moment, to *understand*. For if we can but understand, then our problems and difficulties fade like snow before the sun.

I wish you could see my charwoman's mother. Such trust, such confidence, such bravery. Oh, why must the world be full of crime and cruelty, when there is this love and understanding waiting for us, if we only get together?

Soon spring will come like an army with banners. What are we going to do about it? Please, please try to realize that I want to help.

Tomorrow I will tell you how a girl called Ann cried despairingly yet happily as we stood side by side by a cab shelter and watched, through the park railings, a small bird murdering a worm. Through her tears shone faith and hope, and for her the dark winter of discontent was over. She was on her way to marry a stoker from Christchurch. And I said to her: *'Be happy, and then everyone else will be happy. Tears are the jewels on time's fingers, and all our troubles are but chaff before the wind.'* I think, I hope, I pray that my words helped her a little.

She told me, as we stood on the terrace, gazing at the moonlit sea, the most harrowing story I have ever heard. It was a love story, but the love was thwarted, and all her world was Dead Sea fruit in her mouth. I longed to bring comfort. I said: *'Never laugh at people who tell you that every cloud has a silver lining. It is literally true. Try to concentrate on the lining instead of on the cloud. There is a sweetness in sorrow which softens shattered souls, and in suffering we learn to understand.'* I spoke eagerly, for I knew what she was feeling. And when she turned her face to thank me, I knew that somehow, stumbling, blindly, I had been of use to a fellow-creature. And suddenly my world was irradiated with beauty. So true is it that a good deed, however small, is God's golden boomerang. It bounces back and blesses the doer.

Of all those millions who wrote to me in reply to my appeal, I think I understand Mrs Hoofe best. Mrs Hoofe, of Leytonstone, says: *'Nothing in my life has helped me more than what you said about your charwoman's mother. I think many of us forget that charwomen have mothers. The hurly-burly of daily existence takes toll of our tender thoughts. It was not thus with my mother's sister, Mrs Towty. She always had a kind word for charwomen's mothers. So I just want to thank you.'*

Thank *you*, Mrs Hoofe. This morning the grass in my tiny garden seems greener than ever before, and all because of our deep understanding.

All day long I have been thinking of Mrs Hoofe. One day, when the silvery mist is clothing our mellow London in a garb of sombre gossamer, I shall take a bus along the lonely way to Leytonstone. For

I do ask you to believe me, and I am not ashamed to ask it on my bended knees, that Leytonstone is only every other place under a different name. And its folk are our folk, just like you and I. They laugh and suffer and die like us. And love, too, touches Leytonstone with its daffadown wing.

She was playing Beethoven – just a silver-haired lady at an oh so little piano. My thoughts took wing. I seemed to see you all, my readers, and somehow we were all smiling through our tears because we were together, and understood what the music was struggling to say. And I said deep down in my heart, *'Joy and agony are but two sides of the same medal.'* And echo wove a soft answer on the loom of peace.

Stop Press: Financier Caught by Nose in Rat-trap says, 'Cheese Makes Him Sick.'

CONTRETEMPS IN THE BILLIARD-ROOM

A pathetic story lies behind the latest experiments of Dr Strabismus (Whom God Preserve) of Utrecht, in the matter of growing hair on billiard balls.

Some years ago the Doctor was staying at the country house of a certain Colonel Sopper. The Colonel and his most intimate friend, General Tumult, liked to play billiards together after dinner. Both were bald and short-sighted.

The Colonel was a small man, and had often been tapped on the head by the spoons of short-sighted guests at the breakfast-table. One night he laid his head on the edge of the billiard-table to judge an angle, and the General potted him rather hard.

The mistake was taken with great good nature by the Colonel, but when it happened every night, he grew tired of it. It was then that the Doctor designed wigs for the balls, in order to distinguish them from the heads of the military gentlemen. But it was observed that the wigs fell off when the balls were struck.

So the Doctor tried to grow real hair on them, but without success.

THE TALKING FERRET

Professor Stowte (since we are in scientific mood today) spent twelve years trying to teach a ferret to talk. He used to hold up a large alphabet before it, and record the noises it made. At the end of the twelve years a committee of scientists was summoned to hear the ferret (Palmer was its name) do its stuff. All present agreed that, when bidden good-day, Palmer replied 'Swuth', or words to that effect. Professor Stowte interpreted this as an attempt to say 'Very well indeed, thank you, Professor.' One of the committee, Dr Boldox, wrote a book about Palmer. It was called *Ferrets and the Future*, and he looked forward to the day when other words besides 'Swuth' would pour in a silvern cascade of melody from the lips of Palmer's descendants.

SIXTY HORSES WEDGED IN CHIMNEY

The story to fit this sensational headline has not turned up yet.

LONDON DAY BY DAY

A deputation of dwarfs waited on Lady Cabstanleigh yesterday and presented her with a copy of the Access to Mountains Bill. 'What has this to do with me?' she asked. 'You are a mountain,' they chanted in chorus, 'if ever there was one, and we would like to scale your northern shoulder and boil our little kettles on your crest.'

A SONG ABOUT WORDSWORTH

Now ole man Wordsworth, so they say,
'E loved to roam the 'ills,
Wiv 'is butterfly net an' 'is botany book,
An' a sixpenny packet o' Wills.
An' when 'e come 'ome in the twilight,
You'd 'ear 'is missus cry:
'Now, Willie, me lad, where the 'ell 'a you bin?'
And Willie, 'e'd reply:

> *'I've been looking for daisies:*
>   *A daisy drives me wild,*
> *An' whenever I see a primrose*
>   *I giggle just like a child.'*
> *Then 'is wife says, 'Chuck yer kiddin',*
>   *I can't swaller that stuff—*
> *The only daisy that tickles you*
>   *Is a bit o' mountain fluff.'*

One night 'e come 'ome extra late
Wiv 'is eyes all glowin' bright
An' 'is wife says, 'Where you bin to, mate,
T' come 'ome this time o' night?'
An' Will 'e answers 'er promptly,
'I'm nearly orf me 'ead,
For I've found another new kind o' bird'—
But 'is missus ups and said:

> 'You an' yer bloomin' daisies,
>   An' yer different kind o' bird,
> Is about the fishiest story
>   Wot ever I 'ave 'eard,
> 'Op off, then, back to yer 'ill-tops
>   An' yer innocent nature-stuff—
> An' I'll warrant the bird that sings to you
>   Is a bit o' mountain fluff.'

BOOK NEWS

Messrs Huxter and Huxter are issuing shortly a tasteful little anthology of cricket prayers. It has been edited by Bishop Jardine, and includes not only some of his own work, but much of Archdeacon P. F. Warner's heart-rending prose.

The Rev. H. W. Austin is represented only by one very beautiful little prayer, urging us all to carry the spirit of tennis on to the cricket field.

INTERLUDE

'Don't tickle my leg, Viscount, the Marchioness is watching.'

The words, spoken hurriedly in the luxurious salon of Rose Rambler, the star of 'Seething Moments', arrested the nobleman thus addressed in the midst of his puerile dalliance.

'O.K., little chief,' he retorted, indolently stroking his iron-grey moustache.

PRODNOSE: What on earth is this nonsense?
MYSELF: A pastiche of life above stairs.

Chapter 14

Big White Carstairs and the M'Babwa
of M'Gonkawiwi

BIG WHITE CARSTAIRS has been busy preparing a list of the
names of African chieftains who might be invited to attend the
Coronation celebrations in England. The most picturesque personality on the list is the Yubwa of Yubwabu, who stamps all his
letters with the skull of a warrior dipped in boiling dirtibeeste's-milk
cheese, and has thick hair on the soles of his feet.

His grandfather travelled 4,000 miles through dense jungle to meet
Livingstone near the Victoria Falls. After a journey of eight months
he arrived at the meeting-place, only to find that he had missed
Livingstone by fourteen minutes. He ran after him, but was too tired
to go far, and so he and Livingstone never met.

Livingstone was told the story years later at a reception given by
Lady Berrington. He laughed a good deal.

If the Coronation festivities include a processional march of the
representatives of the Empire, will the M'Babwa of M'Gonkawiwi
be included? And will he insist on being accompanied by Ugli, the
witch-doctor and perhaps by Jum-Jum, the sacred crocodile? A special
committee of M.P.s is meeting at the House of Commons to consider
these questions.

There is a feeling in some quarters that if one curious potentate
and his entourage are to be honoured, then the claims of others must
be considered. And that brings us to the fascinating question of what
is to be done with the Wug of Noonooistan and his Holy Apes,
Buruwo and Buruwa; with the Baffomi of Gopahungi; with the

Padalu of Pokmo; with the Hereditary Snevelinka of Ridolulu and his Dancing Bear; with the Bhopi of Sliwiziland; with Mrs Elspeth Nurgett, M.B.E., and her corps of Swuruhi Girl Guides; with the yellow harbour-master at Grustiwowo Bay; with Hijiwana, the Queen of the Waspidili pigmies; and with Plakka, the roving ambassador of the Nopi of Buttabuttagatawni.

A message from Big White Carstairs has reached the Colonial Office. It says that the M'Babwa of M'Gonkawiwi insists on marching through London, so that people may see him. His party, which will accompany him on the march, is to include Jum-Jum the sacred crocodile, Ugli the witch-doctor, eighteen wives, thirty-eight devil dancers, forty-one pigmies, a sorcerer, an astrologer, four idol-carriers, six head-hunters, a dwarf wrestler, the Zimbabwe Wanderers Cricket team, the Umpopo United football team, Mrs Roustabout, the missionary, the old tribal hedgehog, a mad spearman, a baboon, a herd of dirtibeeste, and a native actress.

The M'Babwa of M'Gonkawiwi, who has hitherto taken no part in the controversy which is raging over his visit to England, broke his silence yesterday with a strong expletive much used by his tribe. When Carstairs told him that the Great White Mother Over the Sea might not be too pleased to welcome Ugli the witch-doctor and Jum-Jum the sacred crocodile, the M'Babwa said, 'Ufganoola.' A rough translation of this would be, 'I hope you and your Great White Mother may be roasted over a slow fire of dirtibeeste's wool.' He later insisted on bringing his team of devil dancers, his eighteen wives, his magicians, and his pigmy poisoners. Carstairs at once cabled to the Colonial Office as follows:

M'Babwa threatening bring devildancers wives magicians poisoners stop what action advised stop.

The Colonial Office cabled back:

Impossible include poisoners magicians wives devildancers in official welcome stop must come as private tourists stop.

There has been a spirited correspondence between Big White Carstairs and various Government departments on the subject of the visit for the Coronation of his Serene Highness the M'Babwa of M'Gonkawiwi, M'Gibbonuki, M'Bobowambi, Zimbabwe, and the

Wishiwashi hinterland, comprising Wowo, Nikiwawa, Wibbli-wambi, M'Hoho, M'Haha, M'Tralala Zogomumbozo, Moponambi, Nambipambi, and Sockemondejaw.

In answer to the application for an invitation, the Colonial Office wrote to Carstairs:

. . . We have been unable to find some of the places mentioned as being under the jurisdiction of his Serene Highness on any map. Nor have we been able to trace a ruler with such a title as the M'Babwa claims. Is the M'Hoho mentioned in your report the M'Hoho near Zumzum or the M'Hoho near Wodgi? Should he travel as the ruler of the places mentioned he will be allotted a seven-and-sixpenny seat in Shepherd's Bush. If, on the other hand, he travels as Mr Posworth, we can promise him nothing nearer than Slough High Street. The suggestion that he should bring with him a tribal witch-doctor and a sacred alligator is not favourably viewed. There is no accommodation for witch-doctors or animals, though doubtless the latter could be temporarily accommodated at Whip-snade, and the former in Bond Street, in the parlour of Mme La Zophitella, star-gazer. . . .

Carstairs replied:
. . . *Of the utmost importance not to offend the M'Babwa. Discontent among the tribes in his territory might mean a rising of the Slobga pygmies and the Ushawiri head-hunters. Could not the sacred crocodile be held up at the Customs until a doctor's examination had certified some infectious disease? As to the witch-doctor, why not get him into some Mayfair set? Plant him on the rich women as a new craze. They've never met anyone who can foretell the weather from the entrails of a goat . . . Most of the M'Babwa's possessions are not on any map yet, but the M'Hoho mentioned is the one near Wodgi . . . You can't put him as far off as Slough. There'd be a rising here. . . .*

The Colonial Office has just been thrown into as fine a state of panic as ever seized a flock of Limousin sheep by another despatch from Big White Carstairs.

It appears that the M'Babwa of M'Gonkawiwi has assimilated huggermugger and helterskelter and hotchery-potchery a certain amount of Western usage – just enough to make things awkward for everybody. He has, for instance, determined to travel to England as plain 'Mr Hurst', while his wives have been saddled with the names of English football teams, such as Oldham Athletic, Sheffield Wednesday, and so forth. Ugli, the witch-doctor, is to travel as Herr Goethe, and Jum-Jum, the sacred crocodile, as Fido. Carstairs has pointed out that this is not the right procedure for the occasion. But the M'Babwa is as stubborn as a Numidian goat. Furthermore he insists on wearing his cricket cap (Zimbabwe Wanderers) while in England.

Yesterday Miss Whelkstone (Soc., Wriggleminster) asked the Minister of Transport whether the system of lights applied to sacred crocodiles. The Minister replied that he did not anticipate that the crocodile would be allowed to go out unaccompanied. Major Thruster (Con., Thostlehampton-with-Buckett) said he thought foreign visitors would get a very queer idea of the Empire if they found the hotels and restaurants filled with the magicians and devil dancers of dubious potentates. The Home Secretary, or someone made up to look like him, said that His Majesty's Government had never at any time contemplated filling hotels and restaurants with magicians or devil dancers. There would, at most, be a round dozen, and arrangements were being made to shove them on to the Boy Scout organizations.

MISS WILKINSON: Shame!

MISS RATHBONE: Yes, shame!

THE SPEAKER: Will you two ladies kindly stop talking rubbish?

MR HATT (*Lib., Pomphbury*): In the event of the M'Babwa of M'Gonkawiwi seeing fit to include cannibals in his suite, will the Board of Trade give an undertaking that no foreign visitors will be eaten?

MISS RATHBONE: Are they to eat the English, then?

MISS WILKINSON: Yes, are they to eat the English, then?

No answer was given.

AT THE BOARD OF AGRICULTURE AND FISHERIES

MEMO: What is all this about an African chief and his crocodile? What are we supposed to do?

MEMO: It's a sacred crocodile. I don't see where we come in.
MEMO: What do you mean – 'sacred'?
MEMO: I don't know. I suppose they worship it.
MEMO: If so, it comes under the Established Church. Better pass all
this correspondence on to the Home Office.

Mrs Wretch, supported by the P.E.N. Club, Auntie Edna's International Pacifists, Mr Aldous Huxley, Mrs Wurfie, and the Neo-Liberal League, is making a last frantic appeal to the Home Office to keep the M'Babwa of M'Gonkawiwi out of England. From a photograph in her possession she has established the fact that he wears a black shirt. But Big White Carstairs has cabled: 'That is not a shirt stop it is his chest stop'. Mrs Wretch, however, is still convinced that he is a Fascist, and that his mission is to annoy Professor Laski, and to carry on secret propaganda against the National Liberal Club.

Unless the Home Office can be persuaded to act, the M'Babwa will arrive in England shortly.

The following statement was made in the House yesterday with reference to the M'Babwa of M'Gonkawiwi:

Unless our dusky cousin from overseas intends to appear in London naked to the waist, the blackness of his chest should not give offence to that progressive and enlightened part of our population which, very naturally, sees in this colour an organized international menace to progressive Liberalism and enlightened Marxism.

Dear Sir,
  Much as I love our great British Empire – I had a cousin once who was rescued from drowning by an Australian – I do not see why the M'Babwa of M'Gonkawiwi should be given facilities for seeing the Coronation when so many white people will not be able to see it. Furthermore, by extending hospitality to an animal and a witch-doctor, we are carrying democracy to absurd lengths.

I learn that an official of the R.S.P.C.A. has objected to the sacred crocodile Jum-Jum being lodged in an aquarium, where it would have to mix with ordinary animals. It is further pointed out that much cruelty is needed to train a crocodile to be sacred, and the suggestion is that if the beast comes to London it should be looked after by a Mrs Gespill, whose lodging-house in the Camberwell Road is a haven for creatures of the deep, including the toothless shark from Dumeira, captured by Rear-Admiral Sir Ewart Hodgson during manœuvres in the Red Sea.

Asked yesterday whether the M'Babwa of M'Gonkawiwi, etc., had a seat reserved for him at the Coronation, Mr Ramsay MacDonald said: 'What we have to do is, at present, according to what we can do, is to see that in the allocation of seats, that is, of seats for various people at the Coronation, is to see that the seats are sufficient. The question of the M'Babwa being allowed to have his crocodile Jum-Jum next to him is a question which must be decided by those who are competent to make such a decision, that is, by those who have the competent authority to make a decision on this matter. Such decisions can only be made by the people who can make decisions of this sort in such matters, not otherwise. What we have to do is to see that this is done, or to see that somebody does it, who can do it, in such a matter, I think.'

Mrs Borgholtz asked today in the House whether it is a fact that the chest of the M'Babwa of M'Gonkawiwi is really black, and if this is not Fascist propaganda designed to prevent the British public from knowing that he wears a black shirt. It is suggested in progressive quarters that Miss Wilkinson and Miss Rathbone and Canon Ball should make a journey of investigation to find out to what extent Fascism is prevalent among the M'Gonkawiwi tribes.

A sad voice interposed: 'But who will pay for the trip?'

Another voice replied: 'The Moujiks, Ltd, Travel Agency.'

The affair of Carstairs, the M'Babwa, and the Colonial Office has reached such gross proportions that the Colonial Office has ceased attempting to push the whole thing on to the Board of Agriculture and Fisheries, on the plea that Jum-Jum, the sacred crocodile, is a beast to be dealt with by that department.

Meanwhile Carstairs has received the following letter from Lady Cabstanleigh:

Dear Major Carstairs,

I trust you will forgive the liberty I am taking, but a mutual friend of ours, young Hoofe of the Colonial Office crowd, tells me there is some hitch about one of your local big pots bringing his witch-doctor to England. I understand the fellow's name is Ugli. Is he more of a witch than a doctor or vice versa? Well, I thought I might help you all by putting the fellow up while he's here. What does he eat and drink? Will he have dress clothes? I suppose he's not utterly savage – not that one really cares, but there'll be a sort of bishop in the house, and I don't want any exorcism stuff. And I hope he can behave decently. I mean, I've never forgotten that Rumanian gipsy singer who bit the neck off a magnum of Yquem 1904. By the way, I suppose he's plumb black. If he's yellow I shall unload him on to Sybil, who loves 'em yellow ever since she was rescued from a snake by a Chinese chef. But it turned out to be jaundice. Forgive me for bothering you. . . .

Carstairs has replied to Lady Cabstanleigh's offer to accommodate the witch-doctor:

Dear Lady Cabstanleigh,

I'm afraid the witch-doctor Ugli would be rather a handful for you. He chants incantations all night, picks his teeth with his spear, and lights bonfires whenever he can. One does one's best, but all one's efforts to make him change for dinner have so far failed. He simply doesn't seem to understand, and, under his influence, even the M'Babwa himself won't go beyond a dinner jacket and a black tie. He seems to think a white tie is some sort of symbol of the domination of the white races – as indeed it is. For these reasons I hesitate to put him on to you. And he might start sacrificing one of the ladies to Bok, the headless god of the Boopi jungle. And then the bishop you spoke of would have to intervene, I suppose. And you couldn't have the papers getting hold of a story of human sacrifice at Cabstanleigh Towers. I'm rather inclined to get him into some quiet hotel in Kensington, where the retired Army and Naval officers might be able to manage him. . . . I understand that the Galashiels Aquarium has offered to house Jum-Jum, the sacred crocodile, temporarily.

Professor Roosch, Tollemache Professor Comparative Folk-Lore at Oxford, has written to the Colonial Office to point out that the housing of the sacred crocodile Jum-Jum in the Galashiels Aquarium would most certainly be resented all along the lower Poopoo, and might start a Garumpi, or holy crocodile war, since Jum-Jum is supposed to be a kind of deity. To which the Galashiels Aquarium replied that they already have a sacred codfish from Bali and that it is treated just like any other cod, except that on the occasion of the first full moon after August Bank Holiday it is exchanged for a dwarf jelly-fish in the Bodmin Aquarium, according to a proviso in the will of the donor, Captain Marabout.

Carstairs landed at Southampton from the *Megatherium* yesterday morning. He was met by his mother, and motored straight to his home near Brocklehurst. His mother said, in an exclusive interview, 'I am so glad to have my son home again.

'It is so good to have him back. Naturally I am delighted to have him back home again, and to see him again. It is so good to see him back that I am overjoyed to have him with me once more, and to have him back again, so that I can have him home again.

'I am so glad to see him back again, and so glad that he is home once more. It is so good to have him back, and to see him home again once more. I am delighted to have my son back home, and to see him again. It is so good to see him back home, and I am delighted to have him back.

'Naturally I am very glad to have him with me once more, and to see him back. And I am overjoyed to be able to have him home with me again, and to see him once more, now that he is back home again with me. It is so good to have him back home again and to see him back.'

Carstairs said, 'Every one has been most frightfully decent, and I must say I think everybody's been awfully good.

'Naturally I am fearfully glad to be back home again with my mother, and to see her again, now that I am back home again once more. It is so good to see her again, now that I am back home, and I'm naturally pretty pleased to be back again, so that I can see her now that I am home again with her once more.

'It is frightfully good to be home again with my mother, so that I can see her, and I am awfully glad to see her now that I can be back home again with her again.'

A trick which reflects no credit on our far-flung (the farther the better) cousins was recently played upon Big White Carstairs.

He had arranged to review the Gogo Light Infantry, and at the bugle's note the dusky warriors began to march past the saluting-base (a large sugar-box). But a dusky sergeant-major with a sense of humour arranged that when each company had passed the base it should double round behind the bungalow (Mon Repos) and march by again.

After half an hour Carstairs, whose saluting arm was growing weary, said to his assistant political officer, 'This is a very big battalion indeed.' After an hour he was still saluting, and it became doubtful whether he would have time to dress for dinner.

Night fell, and still he stood at the salute, while the tired warriors staggered by. Finally the sergeant-major gave in and the review came to an end.

'That,' said Carstairs, 'is the biggest battalion I have ever seen.'

Write to your M.B.E. about it.

Chapter 15

Dead Man's Alibi

(Introducing Inspector Jack Malpractice)

NOT IN THE LIBRARY!!!

HERE BEGINS what I think I may call the most 'vital and human' detective story ever written. It is about a rich man, living in the country, who was not murdered in his library. *He was not murdered in his library.* That is the key to this astounding mystery. No wonder it baffled not only the local police, but also the picked brains of Scotland Yard. The absence of a body in the library, slumped over the desk, was so far beyond their ideas of anything that could possibly happen, so crazily fantastic, that they called in veteran detectives who tore down the whole library, floor, walls and ceiling, to discover what everyone believed must be there – the body of the murdered man. But to no avail.

Begin this story today or some other day. It is called *Dead Man's Alibi,* and is by a new writer called Nollington Faggott.

DEAD MAN'S ALIBI

I

Old George Booby, the village policeman, was not at all surprised to see a bright light shining through the tall french windows of Sir Henry Fuzzock's library. The little hamlet of Swigney-St Vitus was asleep, for it was 4 a.m. But George Booby knew why that light was burning. He was a well-read policeman. He did not hesitate, but walked straight across the beautifully cut lawn of Swigney Hall to the lighted windows. All the rest of the house was in darkness. The members of the house-party were asleep. But Booby knew what lay, slumped over the desk, in that lighted room. He knew he would find the body of Sir Henry – murdered. Bracing himself, note-book in hand, he stepped through the window, which was half-open. Then he stopped dead, his eyes staring at the desk, staggered at what he saw. The room was empty! There was no body in the ornate chair. There were no signs of a struggle. There was not even a blunt instrument lying beside the telephone. Rushing into the hall, Booby belaboured the great Burmese gong, intent on rousing the household.

II

So vehemently did Booby beat the Burmese gong that everybody in Swigney Hall was awake within twenty seconds. They crowded out of their rooms and came tumbling down the stairs, rubbing their bleary eyes. Booby summoned them all to the main hall and lined them up. Little Mrs Cuffling kept on screaming, 'I know it's a murder. Someone's been murdered.'

'Are we under arrest?' drawled Lord Slaver.

'Not exactly,' retorted Booby. 'But I must hold you all. Nobody must leave the premises.'

'What has happened?' asked Joan Toyle.

'There is no corpse in the library,' rejoined Booby.

'Why should there be?' inquired Mabel Leathart.

'Light full on at 4 a.m.,' read Booby from his note-book. 'No signs of disorder. No blunt instrument.'

'But whose body isn't there?' asked Prunella Trivett.

'Sir Henry Fuzzock's,' replied Booby. 'The question is, if he has not been murdered, where is the body?'

The two under-parlourmaids, Sayers and Christie, went into hysterics at this point, while Booby rang up Scotland Yard, at the express wish of the local Chief Constable, who had said over the telephone that he could not understand the case.

III

'See here, my boy,' said one of Scotland Yard's Big Twelve, Sir Benjamin Corke ('Big Ben' to the force). 'See here, you'd better get out your long, low sports car and go down to this god-forsaken hole.'

Handsome Jack Malpractice, the youngest thingamebob in the force, grimaced, as though he smelt a rancid hen pheasant.

'What is it this time, sir?' he asked.

'They can't find Sir Henry Fuzzock's body in the library. No trace of it at all.'

'Anything to suggest foul play?'

'Nothing. That's the whole point. If there was, and he wasn't there, we'd know where we were.'

'Wasn't he even slumped over his desk, sir?'

'No.'

'Any motive, sir?'

'For what, my boy?'

'For his body not being there.'

'That's what you've got to find out.'

An hour later Jack Malpractice was doing ninety-four along the Great West Road in his long, low Sports Thanatos Six.

IV

Jack Malpractice paced the library at Swigney Hall. He had measured everything twice, shaken finger-print powder over every article, and examined things under the microscope.

'There is nothing,' he said to Booby, 'to suggest that anybody has ever been in here – except you, Booby,' he added with a keen glance. 'There is the footprint of a raven in the avenue, but that is hardly an explanation of the absence of a corpse from the library. I think I will question Mrs Kekewich.'

Mrs Kekewich, a handsome brunette, appeared in the doorway in answer to Booby's summons. She seemed to be flustered.

'Now, my dear lady,' said Malpractice, 'where were you when the gong awoke you?'

'In bed,' said Mrs Kekewich haughtily.

Cunning Jack Malpractice tried another approach.

'Fond of jewellery?' he asked, gazing at the ceiling.

'Naturally.'

He suddenly lowered his gaze and faced her, speaking like a whiplash.

'Where did Sir Henry keep his jewels?'

Each word was like a scorpion gone crazy.

'He had given them all to me last year,' said the brunette triumphantly. 'May I go?'

Jack Malpractice bowed irritably.

v

Jack Malpractice was still in the library at Swigney Hall. He had measured everything four times by now, but was still puzzled.

'If we reconstruct the absence of the body,' he said to himself, 'we shall get no farther. Since there is nothing to show that Sir Henry was in here when he was murdered, how do we know he was murdered? Simply because the body isn't here now. Is that sufficient proof? Or again, suppose he was in here when he was murdered, is the absence of his body sufficient proof that he was really murdered? It is extremely unlikely that the owner of Swigney Hall would be murdered anywhere but in his library, and if he wasn't here when it happened, why were the lights on? The absence of a blunt instrument is a mere blind, to make me think that he was murdered in some other room. Therefore, if he had been murdered in some other room, the murderer would have left the blunt instrument in here, to mislead me. Again, why do I assume that it was a blunt instrument? Because I have found no other kind.'

After this piece of logical reasoning the young detective felt better. He was about to measure everything again when a cold voice spoke from the doorway.

'Does it occur to you,' asked the voice, 'that the absence of a dead body from a room does not necessarily prove that someone is dead? Your dead body is not in the kitchen, but you are not dead.'

Malpractice swung round to face the door. Lord Slaver sauntered in.

VI

'Lord Slaver,' said Malpractice firmly, 'I understood you to say that the absence of Sir Henry's body from this library does not prove that he has been murdered.'

'That is so,' replied the peer suavely.

'Whom are you trying to shield?' flashed back the detective, every nerve and sinew alert.

'Why not ask Miss Grosser what she was doing in this room at midnight?' replied Lord Slaver with a mischievous smile.

'I will,' said the detective. 'Booby, fetch Miss Grosser.'

The village policeman was about to leave the room when the telephone bell rang.

'Answer that call,' said Malpractice, 'unless the wires are cut.'

Booby picked up the receiver, listened, and then replaced it.

'It's something about two shirts,' he said.

'Trace that call,' thundered Malpractice.

After some inquiries Booby said, 'It was the Snow White and Seven Dwarfs Steam Laundry.'

'Check it,' said Malpractice, 'and now get Miss Grosser. Lord Slaver, you may go.'

And the lynx-eyed detective once more measured the distance from the telephone to the coal-scuttle.

VII

Malpractice decided to try shock-tactics with Hyrcania Grosser, a timid spinster of some forty-five summers – aye, and winters. The moment she had crossed the threshold, he shouted at her, 'What were you doing in here at midnight last night?'

Miss Grosser looked mildly surprised.

'Borrowing a book,' she said nervously. 'I am a guest in this house. And there's no need to shout.'

'What book?' barked Malpractice.

'Meredith's *The Egoist*.'

The detective sprang to the bookshelf. His eyes narrowed to points of steel.

'Then,' he cried triumphantly, 'perhaps you can explain how that book happens to be still here, on the shelf.'

'I put it back five minutes later,' said Miss Grosser.

'Why?'

'I didn't care for it. I came back and replaced it, and took Jane Austen's *Northanger Abbey*.'

Malpractice again dashed to the shelves.

'It's not here,' he said triumphantly. 'How do you account for that?'

'I haven't put it back.'

'Was there a body in here on either occasion tonight?' asked the abashed detective.

'Of course not,' said Miss Grosser, testily.

Malpractice dismissed her with an angry word.

VIII

Inspector Malpractice sat in the library and stared gloomily at his notes. They bore witness to the lack of progress made with the case. He seemed to have got nowhere, as the following scribbled entries show: *Motive? Motive for what? No marks of struggle. No blunt instrument. Telephone wires intact. Raven's footprint in drive. Why lights on? Why not? No fingerprints. No blood. Is this book-borrowing by Miss Grosser genuine? Why not? Everybody seems to have been in the library that night. Everybody except murdered man, which doesn't make sense.* At that point Malpractice looked up and saw a half-smoked Virginian cigarette in an ashtray on the desk. He wrapped it in his handkerchief and dropped it into an envelope. Then he went on reading: *Door to north wall 16 ft. Telephone to hearth 12 ft 6 ins.*

With sudden determination he threw aside his note-book and summoned Booby, who was on guard outside the door. 'I want them all here at once,' he cried. When the twenty-three guests were assembled in a row he said bitingly: 'Hands up all those who smoke Virginian cigarettes!' Twenty-three hands shot up. Hiding his chagrin, Malpractice waved them out of the room. Mr Carver, a thin hardware magnate, remained behind.

'I think I ought to mention that I was in here last night,' said Mr Carver apologetically.

'Why?' thundered Malpractice.

'I followed Miss Ganting,' said Mr Carver.

'And what was she doing in here?'

'I think she had a rendezvous with Mr Cliff.'

'Well?'

'Well, on my way in I passed Mrs Transom coming out.' Malpractice groaned. 'Was anyone with her?' he asked. 'Yes,' replied Mr Carver, 'two girls and three men.' Malpractice groaned again.

IX

The sky was growing grey above the beeches in Swigney Park. The guests were sitting on the stairs yawning and grumbling at their ordeal. But in the library Jack Malpractice was working like a demon.

He had established the fact that every one of the twenty-three guests had been in the library that night, shortly before Booby had discovered the absence of a dead body. Every one of the twenty-three had admitted hatred of their host, whose food and drink they appreciated, but whose company they detested. 'Twenty-three motives,' mumbled honest Jack Malpractice, counting them on his fingers. Perhaps they had all set on Sir Henry. But where was the body?

And then, slowly and sleepily, down the stairs came the twenty-fourth guest – the lovely Petronilla Belmonte. Malpractice caught his breath uneasily. 'Who are you?' he asked. At the obviously foreign name the inspector frowned. He knew what foreigners were. She explained that she had only just awakened. Skilful and rapid questioning elicited from her the admission that she, too, had been in the library, that she loathed her host, and that she was only there because her friends had brought her. 'As a matter of fact,' she said, 'we had words last night, Sir Henry and I. He was insulting. I could have killed him!'

This passionate utterance sent the maids, Christie and Sayers, into hysterics again. Malpractice darted a fiery glance at her as she breathed hatred through set teeth.

'And did you kill him?' he asked.

'Don't be silly,' said Petronilla.

'Come into the library a moment, please,' said Malpractice suavely. She preceded him. The door closed. He swung round and faced her, his chin set in a hard line.

x

Malpractice, taut as a bowstring, faced the beautiful Petronilla Belmonte in the library.

'I shall have to hold you on a charge of murder,' he said curtly, 'and anything you say will be used in evidence against you.'

'Then use this for a start,' replied the astonished girl. 'I don't know who you are, and I don't much care. But you must be a lunatic.'

'I am Inspector Malpractice of Scotland Yard, and this is a serious business.'

'And whom did I murder?' asked Petronilla.

'Sir Henry Fuzzock.'

'And the evidence?'

'You told me you loathed him, and often wanted to kill him, and that you had a row last night.'

Fear and horror stole over her beautiful face, as she realized that this was a deadly serious matter. This man's hard eyes, cold as steel, were watching her as a mouse watches a bit of cheese. Fear became panic.

'Where did you find his body?' she blurted in a hoarse whisper.

'We haven't found it yet,' replied the detective menacingly.

'Oh. Then I think I can explain,' said Petronilla, with a sigh of relief.

Jack Malpractice, too, was relieved to hear her say that. For, in spite of himself, he was human, and this lovely young creature had made his pulses hammer like a series of piledrivers.

'Won't you sit down?' he asked courteously. 'Now, tell me all you know.'

XI

Jack Malpractice was only human, I repeat (and barely that). When he found himself confronting the beautiful Petronilla Belmonte in the library at Swigney Hall, or whatever the place was called in earlier instalments, he found it difficult to maintain an official attitude; still more so when he remembered that he was holding her for the murder of Sir Henry Fuzzock. He was about to start questioning her, when she said, 'Now, let us straighten this out. Who is it I'm supposed to have murdered? Tell me again.'

'Sir Henry Fuzzock,' said Malpractice.

'Where is the body?'

'I don't know – yet.'

'Then how do you know he was murdered?'

Malpractice faced this awkward question for the first time.

'George Booby reported it,' he said, 'and Scotland Yard sent me here.'

'George Booby reported what?' she asked.

'The murder.'

'Didn't he merely say there was nobody in here and that therefore Fuzzock was murdered?'

'Well – yes,' said the detective uncomfortably. Then, with an attempt to save his dignity, he said, 'But, look here, *you* seem to be questioning *me*.'

Petronilla turned her lovely face to him, and smiled frankly. 'Do you mind?' she asked, in a low voice.

Honest, human Jack Malpractice smiled back.

'Not much,' he said.

XII

'Now that we're friends,' said Petronilla in her gentle, musical voice, 'I hope you won't go on regarding me as a murderess.'

The detective in Jack Malpractice gave one last kick and then died, leaving a young man bewitched by a beautiful girl.

He grinned foolishly.

'Now listen,' she went on.

'I am all ears,' said Malpractice.

'Enough to be recognized in a field,' riposted Petronilla maliciously.

'Oh, I say,' answered Malpractice deprecatingly.

'We all hate Sir Henry,' the girl continued. 'We only stay here because one must stay somewhere. And he hates us. When we move in, he moves out. That is to say, he tries to avoid us. He sleeps in the cellar when the house is full. If we come into a room where he is sitting he goes out. He was in the library last night, but he went out when we came in. That explains the mystery of the absent body, I think.'

'I begin to understand,' said the detective, quailing before the battery of her eyes.

'Splendid!' said Petronilla.

'But,' resumed the dolt, 'where is Sir Henry now?'

'Probably asleep in the cellar,' said Petronilla.

At that moment there was a knock on the door.

'Come in,' said Malpractice.

George Booby entered. 'Here's the murdered man, sir,' he said, standing to one side.

XIII

The gentleman who entered had clearly used the cellar for other purposes than sleep. His waistcoat was outside his coat, and he had only one shoe on. His hair looked as though he had been sweeping the floor with it, and he carried in his right hand a lump of butter.

'Sh!' he said, with finger to lip. 'Don't wake them, they're not asleep yet. How are they all? The house is full of them. Look here, can't you clear out? It's daylight now, you know. Damn it, you can't expect me to stay in that cellar all day. Isn't the week-end over?'

Malpractice had risen and was about to explain his presence, when Petronilla forestalled him.

'This is Sir Henry Fuzzock,' she said.

'Of course I am,' said Fuzzock.

'And this is Inspector Malpractice.'

'Too many inspectors,' said Fuzzock. 'No gas meters here. At least, I hope not. Who brought you?'

'Scotland Yard,' said Malpractice. 'We thought you were dead.'

'Who's dead?' shouted Fuzzock.

'Nobody,' said Malpractice.

'Of course not,' said Fuzzock. 'Who said he was? Who said who was? You all talk too much.'

Sir Henry then solemnly handed the lump of butter to the girl, saluted and went unsteadily from the room.

'A pretty good alibi for a dead man,' said honest Jack Malpractice.

When the detective drove away in his long, low sports car, Petronilla was by his side.

Chapter 16

The New Boy at Narkover

NARKOVER REASSEMBLES on Monday for the new term. Not for a long time has a new boy caused so much speculation as Mountfalcon Foulenough. A history master said yesterday, 'If his uncle has taught him all he knows, there won't be much left for us to teach him.' A reporter asked whether the master was referring to scholastic attainments, and received the reply, 'No. I was thinking of a general knowledge of life and its conduct.'

All over England loving hands are packing trunks and tuck-boxes for the young gentlemen of Narkover, who reassemble today. Eager voices are heard shouting, 'Mater! Don't forget to put in that pack of cards with the nicked aces,' or 'Auntie Frances, where have you put my dud half-crowns?' From many a home the father is, alas, temporarily absent, behind bars, but the lonely mother has the consolation of seeing her boy develop in the way his father would have wished. Meanwhile, Narkover awaits Mountfalcon Foulenough with bated breath.

Considerable surprise has been caused by the announcement that young Mountfalcon Foulenough has won a scholarship at Narkover. One of the Governing Body said yesterday: 'Since the boy has not tried for a scholarship, the word "won" must be a euphemism.' When questioned, Dr Smart-Allick, who is on holiday in the Fulham Road, denied that there had been any arrangement between himself and the proud relative. 'Even if we were to arrange anything,' said the headmaster, 'we should only double-cross each other as usual at the first opportunity.'

Mountfalcon Foulenough is described by those who know him as a very quiet boy, whose mild look probably conceals a character infamous enough to satisfy his famous uncle. He lives in a remote Devonshire village with his widowed mother, née Lavinia Foulenough.

The rumour that a relative of Captain Foulenough is entering Narkover next term has created great excitement in the scholastic world. It is known that the Captain and Dr Smart-Allick met a few days ago, and their conversation is said to have turned on the financial aspect of the affair. The Captain, not unnaturally, wants some guarantee that if he gives the boy a large allowance, the money will be used to cover such expenses as a place in the football team and a few prizes and cups, and not to feather the nauseating nests of the more venal masters, some of whom charge as much as ten pounds for a good half-term report.

The opening of term at Narkover has been awaited with considerable excitement. The name of Mountfalcon Foulenough is on every lip. It was assumed that the famous Captain would coach the boy for a few weeks, but this has not happened. Mountfalcon has remained quietly at home with his mother. Any information that can be gathered shows him as the most dangerous type of boy – the devilish little terror who wears a mask of innocence. In the absence of definite knowledge, there are already wild stories of his prowess at cards and of his intolerable pranks in the villages of the locality. He is said to be utterly uncontrollable. Foulenough, when questioned, says, 'I have not seen the lad since he was a baby. No doubt he is a true Foulenough.'

Lavinia Foulenough, mother of Mountfalcon, is a cousin of the famous Captain Foulenough. She married a certain Plumhurst Foulenough, belonging to what de Courcy calls a minor but reasonably notorious branch of the family. That is why the boy has always called Captain Foulenough Uncle de Courcy. Plumhurst made a fortune out of bad boots at the age of thirty, went bankrupt at thirty-two, founded a steam carpet-beating business at thirty-three, absconded with the capital and the carpets at thirty-five, went to America, and died there at the age of forty-two, having left his wife and young son in England. So, as the Captain says, Mountfalcon is simply crammed with Foulenough blood.

Dr Smart-Allick has received from Lavinia Foulenough a letter which he regards as a masterpiece of satire. The mother says she is most anxious that her dear boy shall not be tempted into gambling, 'which is the family failing'. She draws a picture of a simple, trusting nature, and says that she has been much perturbed by reports of wild behaviour and dishonesty at Narkover, and that she would not like to think of her little Mountfalcon being bullied, or cheated out of his pocket-money. Smart-Allick replied gravely, assuring the widow that an unarmed baby could carry the Crown Jewels openly down the High Street without being molested by anyone except the boys and the masters.

Eight new Narkover boys arrived at the Headmaster's House for the new term yesterday, but nobody had eyes for any but the quietest and most unassuming of them all.

Owing to the reputation which had preceded him, the senior boys treated him with unwonted respect. As for the younger boys, they locked away their wallets, and gave him a wide berth. Even Dr Smart-Allick, when he shook hands with him, and 'hoped he would settle down happily among us', kept his free hand on his watch-chain, and seemed to be surprised when he emerged from this first encounter without any article missing. Mountfalcon's silence and his obviously feigned modesty and timidity terrified even the Soames gang, accustomed to impudent new boys, who produced packs of cards on the first evening, in order to curry favour. 'He's a deep customer,' said Smart-Allick to himself.

'Please, sir,' said Mountfalcon to Mr Snudder, his form-master, 'some boy has stolen my fountain-pen.' 'And what did you steal of his?' inquired Snudder pleasantly. 'Nothing, sir,' said Mountfalcon. 'I'm surprised at you, with such a name,' said the master. When he later mentioned the incident to Smart-Allick, the headmaster said, 'I see what his game is. He is determined to play the innocent. He needs careful handling.' A little later another master reported that one of his spies among the boys had suggested a game of poker to the new boy, and that Mountfalcon had refused, pretending that he did not know how to play the game. Meanwhile the boy who had stolen Mountfalcon's fountain-pen got no praise. 'He's leading you on,' they said. But the Soames gang was getting impatient.

Dear de Courcy,

I can't see my way to putting the lad into the football team the moment he arrives here for his first term. It would savour too much of favouritism. As Edward III said at Crecy, 'Let the boy win his spurs.' In other words, let him pay up like anyone else. If he is a genuine Foulenough he's sure to win enough at cards to get his place in the team by the middle of the term. I'm sure you will understand that we foster the competitive spirit at Narkover, and the big prizes, both in games and work, fall to those who can show the enterprise of the old Elizabethan adventurers. No favouritism. Money talks, and we are always listening.

> *Yours ever,*
> *Smarty.*

Dear Smarty,

I hope I have too much pride ever to ask for any special privileges for the lad which he cannot buy or contrive to get by his own cunning. I know nothing of the boy Mountfalcon, except that his mother has brought him up so piously that he's probably a roaring terror by now. However, I recall how you said, when the two sons of my old friend 'Flash' Mullins broke open the desk in your study, 'Narkover can take it', and I have no doubt that whatever the lad gets up to, he will meet his match, either among the older boys, or among the masters. Tacknoe (who now runs an airport smuggling concern) was asking after you the other day.

> *Yrs always*
> *de Courcy.*

The attitude of the more daring spirits at Narkover towards Mountfalcon Foulenough is not unlike that of a boxer who is longing to attack, but it is not quite sure that his opponent's unaggressive manner may not conceal a murderous left. A puzzled classics master said yesterday: 'The boy *looks* like a milksop, but his name alone teaches respect.' When one of the Soames gang engaged the new boy in conversation, Mountfalcon was so friendly that a trap was suspected, and everyone is now on guard, the burning question being, 'When is this cool customer going to begin to operate?' When Redvers major produced a pack of cards and shuffled them expertly, Mountfalcon walked away, as though to say, 'Pah! Anyone can do that.'

The prefects yesterday decided that it was time for a showdown with the new boy. Using his own pack of cards, one of them managed to win £17 11s. 6d. from Mountfalcon. The general impression at first was that Mountfalcon was allowing his opponent to win, and so to become over-confident and careless. The new boy played like a novice, and made the most ludicrous mistakes. When asked for the money, he said he would have to write home for it. Forty-three offers of a loan at the usual interest were refused. Mountfalcon said he thought it wrong to borrow money. By this time everyone was thoroughly annoyed with this continued pretence of priggishness.

A ring of flushed and angry faces surrounded Mountfalcon. 'Why should you refuse to subscribe to a fund to get Moodie into the team?' shouted Peplo major. 'Listen,' replied Mountfalcon patiently, 'Bonnington told me that last term you made this collection, and Moodie was passed over. Why? Because a science master stole the money and used it to get his own candidate into the team. He then swore you had tried to bribe him, and if you hadn't paid someone to go through his desk you couldn't have threatened him with the letter he had stolen from Mr Horsepath. Now isn't all this a lot of trouble for nothing? And isn't it disgraceful?' The group broke up into smaller groups. Quarrels began. Whether it was disgraceful or not nobody cared, but certainly many agreed that the present system seemed to be a lot of trouble and expense for very little return.

Dr Smart-Allick regarded the Soames gang as the rich cream of his shock-troops. Soames, the leader, was a horrible overgrown lout of nineteen, who had only twice seen his father – fleeting glimpses between his parent's long prison sentences. The Doctor thought the moment had come to counteract 'this namby-pamby nonsense', as he called it. The gang set to work with a will, and for a week even the most hardened thugs among the masters were aghast at the utter lawlessness of school life. Boys who had been inclined to listen to Mountfalcon were knocked down, informed against, framed, robbed, terrorized. Two brothers paid, in protection money alone, £74 which they had won at the races. It was 'a victory for the progressive forces', to quote a classics master, when six forged half-crowns, a pack of marked cards, and a stolen ring were found by Soames himself in young Foulenough's overcoat pockets.

With a smile of triumph which he could not conceal Dr Smart-Allick said, 'Well, young Foulenough, they tell me you're in trouble again. What's this I hear about rings and marked cards and forged money being found in your pockets?' 'They were put there by some-one, sir,' replied Foulenough. 'You're telling me!' said the head-master under his breath. Aloud he said, 'You don't say so! How odd! How droll! How truly bizarre!' Then he went on, 'Why not put all the stuff in someone else's pockets? Eh?' 'It would be wrong, sir,' replied Foulenough. The headmaster made a gesture of despair. 'It was done to you,' he said. 'Two wrongs,' said the impossible boy, 'do not make a right.' 'Who told you that?' snapped the pedagogue. 'Not your uncle, I'll warrant. Run off, now. You repel me, my lad.'

My dearest boy,

What on earth are you doing with your money? I want you to enjoy yourself at school, but I cannot afford to keep on sending you more pocket money. I do hope you are not over-eating at the tuck-shop. And how do you manage to lose so much clothing? Is the school laundry at fault? Every garment was properly marked, I'm sure. Try to be more careful. You tell me that Fuddock, your room-mate, is a receiver or fence. Is that a football term? And really, dear, you must not refer to any group of boys as a 'gang'. It gives a wrong impression. It is very nice to think that the Headmaster himself is taking an interest in you, but I don't quite understand his talk of cards. Is he one of those 'patience' addicts? Perhaps it rests his mind. I hope you are doing well at your work.

Your loving Mother.

SMART-ALLICK TO FOULENOUGH

. . . What the devil is your game? This nephew of yours is the most horrible little milksop we've ever had in the school. At first we thought he was playing a part, but it seems he doesn't know the first thing about cards or horses or greyhounds. I don't care to think what kind of a home he comes from. One or two weak-minded boys think it clever to copy him, and yesterday I had a deputation of the smaller boys, calling on me with a protest—a *protest*, if you please!—against the Soames gang. It wasn't friendly of you to assure us that Mountbreadandmilk was a holy terror. Meanwhile, I lent him some money which he had lost, thinking he'd win it back. But he lost again, so you owe me £39 14s. od., exclusive of the interest. . . .

FOULENOUGH TO SMART-ALLICK

. . . You are always too impetuous. You should have kept the Soames Gang in reserve, while you gave the boy time to find out that milksoppery would get him nowhere. If you want to get a man to put money into a dud company, you don't knock him down and sit on him until he signs his cheque. The Soames Gang are the hard-hitting, direct type. You should have put someone subtle and sly on to my young relative, and instead of planting all that jewellery and stuff on him, you should have been content at first with giving him a taste for cards, by letting him win for a while, using an unmarked pack. As it is, you've given him a strong distaste for the Narkover way of life and made him distrustful. I'd have made a better headmaster than you. . . .

MOUNTFALCON WRITES HOME

My dear Ma,

I hope you are well. I am. I hate this school. The shoes you sent me were soled by Fuddock to pay his card detts, and he says he has his eye on two of my new shurts to sell, and I found a saphier ring in my cote pockett yesterday, and two boys fought about it, and a master took it, and he tried to get me to buy it back from him. The ink pots in our form are full of red wine, and Cadson minor, who's always been last in everything is first now because he says he has a letter written by Mr Hubberwick our form master to a grayhound trayner. There was an awfull row this week because someone stole the Head's watch, we were all searched, and a pile of post orders was found in my pejarmers pockett. I hate this place.

Your affectunatte son.

Dr Smart-Allick sat in his study, with a disconcerting report from his secret agents before him. It appeared that there had been several cases of boys refusing to pay for places in teams or for good weekly reports. The takings of the School Roulette Club had fallen off, and letters to parents, complaining of the financial aspect of school life, had been intercepted. 'There is no doubt,' said the report, 'that this new trend can be attributed, in part, to shortage of money, and, in part, to the influence of a new boy, who by sheer, incredible innocence and a rather dangerous priggishness, has caused unrest in certain quarters.' Smart-Allick digested this grim news. Was even Narkover, he asked himself, to be hit by a slump? 'Meanwhile,' he murmured, 'the pernicious activities of Mountbreadandmilk must be curtailed.

In the Sixth Form Hall the headmaster delivered an address, calling attention to the tendency of a few deluded boys to call in question the sporting traditions of Narkover. He said: Nothing is more demoralizing and stultifying to youth than the idea that honesty must be lowered to the level of a doctrinaire system of universal frustration. Honesty should be the basis of an adaptable code of behaviour, allowing for imagination, enterprise, ambition. . . . You will note that the objections to gambling come from the losers. Do the winners ever complain? Does the boy who acquires a place in a school team, by a wise outlay, ever snivel? No. It is the boy who has not the wits to get on who talks of bribery and corruption. Boys, if killjoy priggishness raises its hideous head here where our fathers drank of the Pierian spring, we must cut it off! . . .

It was with some consternation that Dr Smart-Allick picked up a disquieting rumour yesterday. According to Mr Transom (alias Bathurst), a mathematics master, it is being said loudly that Mountfalcon Foulenough is *not* playing a part; that he is as innocent as he looks; and that when the boys find this out there will be the devil to pay. 'The thing is impossible,' snorted the headmaster, 'with such a name as his.' 'How do we know it's his real name?' replied Mr Transom (alias Bathurst) who was rather sensitive in these matters. 'We have Captain Foulenough's word for it,' said Smart-Allick; and then both men laughed at the absurdity of having the Captain's word for anything. 'Anyhow,' added the headmaster, 'the prospect of the whole school being demoralized by a pious prig is not one we need take seriously.'

Dr Smart-Allick's secret agents have reported to him that Foulenough's odious relative appears to have discovered a way of protecting himself from exploitation by the boys or ill-treatment by the masters.

'He spends all his spare time,' says the report, 'in eavesdropping. Whatever he hears, he passes on, with, very often, the most deplorable results. Members of the same gang find their attempts to double-cross their friends forestalled and made public. Masters can never be sure that the boys in their forms will not get to know of their private affairs. This boy does not even try to sell his information. He gives it away free, which makes it impossible to get any hold over him. Mr Kellaway injudiciously offered to make him Captain of Football if he would promise not to repeat something told him by Mr Grant. The boy refused. Next day Mr Kellaway was knocked down by a friend of Mr Grant.'

> *Dear Ma,*
>
> *I am getting on better now. I find that if I can tell the bigger boys and the masters things they want to know they stop bullying me and giving me no marks, it isn't telling lies Ma because I only pass on what I overhear, and I don't invent anything, and some of them are so pleezed that they try to reword me, but I tell them its a plessure. Whenever I get threttened now I get let off for giving bits of news, and I got full marks at Latin last week, and I don't reely think it was because Mr Clatchett was favuoring me, but he was pleezed with me for telling him what Mr Boyle was going to do about some letters. For telling Bates that Fuddock was going to break open his tuck-box I got a bar of chockerlet, but he took it back later to sell to Crawford. . . .*

SMART-ALLICK TO FOULENOUGH

. . . Look here! Have you been writing to this nephew of yours? He's invented the lowest form of sneaking I've ever come across in fact, he's an unpaid informer. The Soames gang is split in two over it. Soames lost his head, and we had the police in – a new lot we hadn't squared. Your nephew even came to me and told me that P— was working against me with L—, and when I offered him a quid, he said, bold as brass, that S— had told him I always used forged notes to bribe boys with. I caught him by the ear, and asked him if he imagined I was trying to buy his silence. And he said, 'Yes. That's what Parker warned me against.' The little beast is impossible. Before he left me, I said as graciously as I could, 'Here's a *real* quid for you.' He replied, 'Real or forged, it's bribery, sir.' I was so angry I couldn't speak. . . .

FOULENOUGH TO SMART-ALLICK

. . . So, you see, it ends by my odious nephew getting the better of you all. I must say I never suspected him of such ingenuity. A free information service – what a sublime idea (provided he makes a bit on the side). Sheer philanthropy doesn't pay. I really cannot pretend to be sorry for you. You all set out to get what you could out of him, and he's turned the tables on you, and I laugh loudly when I think of your toughest lads being beaten by this sanctimonious little horror. The least you can do is to put him into the first eleven this term, and I bet you won't get a penny out of him even if you make him Captain. By the time he realizes that the smart thing for him is to cash in on all his knowledge, some of you are going to have to fork out to a fine tune, believe me. . . .

> *Dear Ma,*
>   *Will you ask our vicker if it is wrong for me to take money from boys who want to buy my silence about bribery and stealing and then to tell on them all the same, I don't do it to get the money but there is no other way of getting them to tell me what the others want to know about them, for instuns yesterday I got ten shillings for telling one boy I wouldn't say where he had hidden a wotch he stowl, and a master gave me a quid to tell him where it was hidden, and I was thuss able to do my duty, and the master told on the boy and sold the wotch to someone else. I tried at first to do my duty without taking money but the head told me it was very wrong and upset the school truddition, so now I take the money. I have just over three hundred quid.*
> *Your loving son,*
> *Mountfalcon Foulenough.*

Dr Smart-Allick sat in his study and contemplated with disgust and contempt the snivelling new boy. Mountfalcon nauseated him. 'This pose of yours has gone on too long,' snarled the headmaster. 'It was funny for a day or two, but we're all tired of this pretence of being a nasty little prig.' 'But, sir,' said young Foulenough, 'I tell you I've been cheated out of more than my pocket-money for the whole term.' 'Then go and win it back like a man, instead of whining to me,' said the headmaster. 'This isn't a lame cat's home. What use will you be in life's hurly-burly if you can't lose a few quid without blubbering? Why, when I was your age – but never mind that. Now, stop pretending to be a little martyr. I'll let you have what you lost, at five per cent, and you can go and skin the swi – er, boys who swind – er, beat you.'

Mountfalcon was surprised to find his Latin translation marked 'Disgracefully bad', especially as the master, Mr Whaup, said: 'It's not so much your mistakes, of which there are only a few, as that you make no attempt to co-operate.' 'Co-operate?' repeated the astonished boy. 'Don't pretend you don't understand,' said Mr Whaup, pocketing a ten-shilling note handed to him by the head boy of the form. 'You seem to think education here is free,' sneered Mr Whaup. 'Masters have to live, you know.'

FOULENOUGH TO SMART-ALLICK

My dear Doctor (of Divinity, I presume),
I'm amazed to hear this about Mountfalcon. I told you I hadn't seen him or his mother for years. As to your hopes of getting back from me the money you were crazy enough to lend the young ass, they are as leaves before the wind. And if you feel like getting nasty – if you could ever get any nastier than you are – pray remember that I still have the juiciest bits of your correspondence with H. about the coupons. Verb. sap. Accent on the sap – meaning you, my revered twister. The letters cost me a tenner, and it looks like money well laid out, eh, my old scorpion of the schools? What's come over Narkover? Are you losing your nerve? Surely you're not going to let this little cherub get away with it . . .

The Soames gang seem to have stamped out the rebellious attitude of the poorer boys, and there is no longer any danger that the priggishness of Mountfalcon may undermine the traditions of Narkover. The new boy's uncompromising honesty has brought him to the bottom of his form, and the study which he shares with a go-ahead son of 'Flash' Fuddock is beginning to look like a pawn-shop in a back street in Middlesbrough. As one of the prefects said: 'You can pick up anything there from a dud fiver to a fountain pen, and as Foulenough isn't in the business, Fuddock is doing well enough to have a shot at buying a place in the Soames outfit.' Yesterday Mountfalcon had the doubtful honour of seeing his braces sold for five and ninepence in aid of a fund to pay Fuddock's card debts.

Narkover appears to be settling down after the recent alarm. The progressive elements have the upper hand once more, and the disturbing influence of an uncommon type of boy has been swiftly counteracted. His effect on Narkover has been unimportant. What effect will Narkover have on him? Will he, in self-defence, abandon his deplorable rectitude? Or will he face expulsion for 'obstruction and refusal to co-operate'? As a master said yesterday, 'There's something about the little blighter that makes virtue seem even more horrifying than usual.'

Chapter 17

If So Be That

If So Be That—A Romance of the Spanish–American War
by HELPA KITCHEN

Synopsis

*The Silver Monster is pounding along the metals to Quebec at
seventy miles an hour. Unknown to the passengers dining luxuriously
in the restaurant car, a murder has been committed in a packet-boat
plying between Abbeville and Leeds, with a cargo of lawn-mowers.
Stark and cold on the deck lies Okuno Pigiyama, the Japanese Pleni-
potentiary Extraordinary, with or without portfolio at the court of
Athens. Beside him are the corpses of 'Red' McGuire and Toby Slews,
gunmen and gangleaders from Cambridge. Farther on, reading from
left to right, are the bodies of sixteen other men. The mate's lifeless
body is prone beneath a sack of wheat.*

*But on the footplate of the Silver Monster, all unheeding, Ingeborg
Maelstrom, the first Norwegian woman renegade politician to cross
the Rockies, is braising carrots.*

CHAPTER ONE

Burgeonings

Julia crouched back against the locked wall of her bedroom. She
was terrified . . . terrified . . . *terrified* . . . terrified . . . trembling
in every pore. Her breath came and went. Then . . . in the depth
of the great and vast silent mansion she heard a footfall echoing
through the raftered halls. Steps were mounting the vaulted staircase
to the loft. There was a smell of lamp-iron . . . coming ever nearer
in the gloom. Now they were at her door, and the handle began to
turn. She—

PRODNOSE: Stop! I have been in consultation. Nobody, not even your editor, has the vaguest notion whither all this tomfoolery is leading.

MYSELF: I understand from Miss Kitchen that the mystery has not yet begun. Your puzzlement proves how good a story it is.

PRODNOSE: Well, I must ask you to discontinue the serial. Miss Kitchen shall be compensated. No offence is intended to her; in fact, I suspect that you have been playing the fool with her work, and I am not alone in my suspicions.

MYSELF: But I—

PRODNOSE: That is enough! Pray consider the whole episode closed, and let your readers know that the serial will not be continued. Thank you.

KITCHEN V. BEACHCOMBER

As I expected, Miss Helpa Kitchen, whose serial story was so unceremoniously interrupted and brought to a premature conclusion by the ubiquitous Prodnose, has, after taking legal advice, decided to bring an action against me for breach of contract and recovery of damages. She points out in a dignified letter to me that such treatment as she has received is bound to be prejudicial to her career, particularly as the story has not progressed far enough for anybody to have an inkling of how it was going to develop. The fact that I received so many letters complaining that the whole thing was unintelligible certainly bears out her contention.

The case will, I believe, come up for hearing early in the next week, before Mr Justice Nagge. Miss Kitchen's case will be conducted by Mr Henry Boodle, K.C., while mine is entrusted to Mr Ernest Dross, K.C. Several well-known witnesses are to be called, notably Dr Strabismus (Whom God Preserve) of Utrecht, Mrs Wretch, and Prodnose.

The first hearing of the case Kitchen *v.* Beachcomber, in which Miss Helpa Kitchen, author of the serial recently occurring in these columns, seeks to recover damages for breach of contract, was marked by several regrettable irregularities. From very early hours the court was crowded from roof to floor, one enterprising young man clinging to the former until ordered to leave the court. Miss Kitchen arrived early, in a neat suède costume looped up with ruchings of old apricot, and wearing one of the new gas-meter shaped hats of crisped Viennoise. She carried in her hand a copy of her last novel, *Flaming Phyllida*. I myself arrived later, in one of our plain vans.

When Mr Justice Nagge entered the court there were cries of 'Good Old Splutterface!' and a bag of peanuts was thrown into the well of the court, narrowly missing the junior clerk of the rolls, and gliding into the top ink-pot off the elbow of the senior serjeant-at-arraigns, at which there were cries of 'Good shot! Pass me the jigger!'

Order being restored, there was the usual almost inaudible swearing.

Opening for the prosecution, counsel, Mr Boodle, said, without any preliminaries:

'M'lud, I hope to prove not only habendum, free warren, botany and citation, but also gross bailiment by desuetude.'

There was a slight pause, while the judge glanced at a piece of paper passed up to him from one of the inky men under his dais. On the paper was written, 'Put your shirt on Asterisk for the 2.30.' Mr Justice Nagge coughed and ordered a reporter to stand down. Then Mr Boodle said:

'When two or more parties to a contract, under Sub-section 17, *volenti non fit injuria—*'

'What?' said the judge.

'*Presumptio componendi,*' continued Mr Boodle, 'their separate estate being bound, agree by malfeasance to the rights of the mortgagor – as in Northcote *v.* Linnet, H.3.96 – then the puisne devolves automatically on the heirs in chancery and co-legatees of the marshalling assets. The messuage being thus enfeoffed—'

'What?' said the judge.

'I must explain, m'lud,' continued counsel, 'that an *interesse termini terminator non sub rosa equidem quia noli emptoribus de heretico comburendo vel de medietate linguae necnon solvens dum jurat in partibus si quisquis valuit nemo in loco ferae naturae ex officio durante bene placito dona amicus curiae* has already been applied for.'

'Who by?' said the judge.

'My client, Miss Helpa Amabilia Kitchen,' retorted counsel.

'M'lord, is this in order?' cried Mr Dross, counsel for the defence, springing to his feet.

The judge then rang his bell, and amid cries of 'Muffins! Seconds out of the ring!' and so on, the court adjourned for lunch.

The hearing will be continued.

The hearing of this case was continued yesterday. The court, as before, was crowded with celebrities from every walk and crawl of life. Immediately the court had assembled the judge rose and addressed the jury as follows:

'Gentlemen, the onerous duty laid upon you of determining what designs may or may not be registered, under the law of patents, designs and trade marks, will, I am sure, be discharged with your customary honesty. A design, in the meaning of the Act, is any design applicable to any article for pattern, configuration, shape, form, ornament by printing, painting, casting, embossing, engraving, staining, scratching, scrawling, scraping, or—'

The junior provost of Assizes here informed his lordship that he was reading from the notes of another case. At this point the judge sat down, and a piece of paper was handed up to him. On the paper was written, 'Shove a fiver each way on Morning Bath.'

Counsel for the prosecution intervened to say that he understood his client was a novelist of international status. (Mrs Wretch: 'Hear! Hear! Dear Helpa!' Shouts of 'God bless you, Miss Kitchen!' and 'Ugh! the old toad!') A woman who threw an orange at counsel was removed kicking and screaming. When order was restored counsel for the defence said: 'I propose, m'lud, to read one or two letters which will show how the interruptions of Prodnose have prejudiced my client, Beachcomber, in the eyes of his public.'

'They have surely prejudiced *my* client, too,' interrupted counsel for the prosecution.

'That is as it may be,' rejoined Mr Dross. 'Now here I have a letter from a resident of North-West Ealing. She says, "We did so like the serial. What a pity Prodnose interfered." A Miss Voulder, of Balham, says, "Prodnose must be a nasty, interfering man." Mrs Scowl, of Penge, says, "What a pity Prodnose is allowed to interfere with

Beachcomber." There are many more like that,' added Mr Dross, 'for instance—'

'Lunch!' roared the judge, madly ringing his bell.

After the luncheon interval a sensation was caused by a suggestion made by the counsel for the defence that the whole case was a Post Obit Reversion, following on False Custody. 'In that case,' shouted Mr Boodle, 'I shall call Dr Strabismus (Whom God Preserve), of Utrecht.' While this important witness was being sought, the judge read a brief résumé of the case Nuik *v.* Stargett, which was similar to the present one of Kitchen *v.* Beachcomber.

The following passage of arms then took place between the doctor and the counsel for the prosecution, Mr Boodle, K.C.:

MR BOODLE: Dr Strabismus, you are, I believe, an eminent scientist?

DR STRABISMUS: I am, sir.

MR BOODLE: Resident in Utrecht?

DR STRABISMUS: Certainly.

MR BOODLE (*harshly*): Please answer Yes or No.

DR STRABISMUS: No.

MR BOODLE: You are not resident in Utrecht?

DR STRABISMUS: Yes.

MR BOODLE: (*eyeing the jury and the judge alternately*): Will you tell the court where you were on the evening of October 24, 1927, at 6.14 p.m.?

DR STRABISMUS: I was in an airplane, on my way from Hamburg to Rotterdam.

MR BOODLE (*triumphantly*): You hear that, m'lud?

THE JUDGE: I do. But what on earth has this to do with the case?

MR BOODLE: I hope to show a chain of evidence, m'lud. Doctor, was there any reason for your making this journey?

DR STRABISMUS: I was to lecture in Rotterdam on the Deflected Angle in Bridge Construction under the Roman Empire.

MR BOODLE: Ah! Exactly! The Roman Empire! Doctor, are you acquainted with the plaintiff or the defendant?

DR STRABISMUS: The defendant has often taken articles on scientific subjects from me.

MR BOODLE: And paid for them?

DR STRABISMUS: Always.

MR BOODLE: And were those articles ever interrupted by a certain Prodnose?

DR STRABISMUS: Never, to my knowledge.

Here Miss Kitchen fainted, and the court adjourned.

*   *   *   *   *

THE CHEYNE THALIANS

What a deplorable state the theatre is in! On Sunday night the Cheyne Thalians produced, for one performance, at the tiny Lilliput Theatre, Ulric Hausenfurth's enormous drama, 'Fatuousness', which lasts for seven hours. Is it credible that we who call ourselves a civilized country should prefer the buffooneries of the music-hall to this immortal play – the very cream of genius, which Badger has called 'A pinnacle of European art'?

Miss Boubou Flaring's reading of Agatha, the wronged rocking-horse-maker's daughter, left nothing to be desired except death. The scenery, by Spox, was phenomenal, and the costumes, by Flugel-spitter, might have stepped straight out of the canvases of Wimp – in his later period.

A select audience, following the play in their little books, applauded vociferously, and I, for my part, would like to see this almost incredible work put on for a run at a West End theatre.

It may seem churlish to criticize such a perfect performance, but I cannot but wish that the supers had removed the dead more quickly in Act 14.

FLEET STREET FASHIONS

It is the fashion today to write about everybody's clothes, but nobody ever considers the men of Fleet Street. Their clothes, though not as expensive, are quite as remarkable as those seen in Mayfair or Hoxton.

The notes that follow were written by a well-known *flaneur* and man about Shoe Lane.

Undoubtedly Mr— is one of the most amusingly dressed men in Fleet Street. He has chosen for spring wear an old sports coat with slit pockets, and large spots on it. With this he wears a daringly torn collar of cotton, one of the new stringy ties, and short trousers with frayed edges.

The new drinking hats are very popular. The wide brim gives privacy, and the sweeping turn-up in front allows the face to sink easily into the tankard.

Very effective and striking was a pair of boots I saw worn by a noted journalist yesterday. They showed an intriguing amount of sock, and the uppers were held together by marine glue, string, and drawing-pins.

STRABISMUS ON THE HALLS

The astounding success of the recent Strabismus expedition to darkest Africa has resulted in many attempts by theatrical agencies to persuade the Doctor to appear in public as a 'turn'.

It was first rumoured that the learned man had consented to appear with an African dirtibeeste. The rumour turned out to be true, the Doctor having, with great patience, taught the dirtibeeste to sit up and beg for a piece of meat.

Unfortunately, the first appearance was a fiasco. The Doctor rather absent-mindedly forgot the meat. At the carefully rehearsed words 'Up, Paul!' the expectant dirtibeeste sat up on its hind legs. When the meat was not forthcoming, the animal made a scene, and the curtain had to be rung down.

The dirtibeeste bit a scene-shifter's leg, smashed a castle, and went through a trap-door. It has since been sent to the Zoo.

The Doctor's next appearance was made in a provincial music-hall, where he was announced as a conjurer.

His first trick was to cover a bowl of goldfish on the left of the stage with a red silk handkerchief, and a block of ice on the right of the stage with a blue silk handkerchief. Each article was on a small table, and the Doctor stood between them.

'At the words, "Hey! Presto! Pass!"' said the Doctor, 'the ice will be found in the bowl, and the goldfish where the ice was.'

'Hey!' said the Doctor, and paused with a smile, 'Presto!' he continued, grinning. 'Pass!' he concluded, beaming.

Then he walked softly towards the red silk handkerchief, caught his foot in the table, and brought the bowl tumbling to the floor, where it broke into a thousand smithereens.

With an oath the learned man approached the other table, lifted the blue silk handkerchief, and disclosed – the lump of ice.

The Doctor scratched his head with his wand, and the curtain was rung down.

The Doctor next consented to appear as Caligula in a series of living tableaux. Being even more absent-minded than usual on the first night, the learned man, in the garb of a Roman Emperor, was one tableau too soon, and took his place among the 'Swedish Fisherfolk At Home'.

Discovering his error, he scratched his head with the metal fastening of his laurel crown, and the curtain was rung down.

MUSIC IN THE HOME

There was a plea yesterday in a newspaper for a 'revival of real music' in the home. Whenever I think of real music in the home, my memories play round old tea parties, with this kind of programme straggling all over them.

My Barque of Dreams … … … (Encore!) Laddie o' mine … … …	The Colourless Young Lady.
Tom's at the Mill … … … … (Encore!) Men o' Wiltshire … …	The Baritone in the Tail Coat.
The Rachmaninoff Prelude … … (Encore!) No. 16 'Lieder Ohne Worte' … … …	The Usual Girl.
Recitation: 'Birdies in the Wood' … … … … … (No Encore! No fear!) … … …	Little Daughter of the House
Roses, only Roses, Love … … … (Encore!) Thy Rose, my Rose … … (Encore!) His Rose, her Rose … … (Encore!) Our Rose of Love … …	An Appalling Widow.
Mattinata … … … … … (Encore!) Poi che sole … … …	The Smooth-Haired Tenor in Spats
Open-air Jack … … … … … (Encore!) Sloggin' Home … … …	The Pimply Pallid Youth.

DR STRABISMUS AT SALZBURG

The Doctor was dissecting a fish in the laboratories of the Baumgartner Museum at Salzburg yesterday, when some friends called to carry him off to the opera. He absent-mindedly stuffed the fish into his pocket.

The anaesthetic wore off during the second act of *Faust*.

The fish, a large whiting, leaped from the Doctor's pocket and out of the private box on to the stage.

Marguerite dived, and brought off an exceedingly difficult catch, throwing Mephistopheles off his balance as she did so, and pushing Martha against the scenery.

Amid cries of 'Safety Faust!' the diva flung the fish back, but it struck the ledge of the box and rebounded into the orchestra, where the conductor stunned it with one blow of his baton.

Next day it was eaten, *en colère,* by the Mayor.

COCKLECARROT CALLED IN

The case of the man who put handlebars on a cow after dark and wheeled it without a rear light is more serious than I thought. It is having our old friend repercussions, and Mr Justice Cocklecarrot has been called in by the Government.

Last night Cocklecarrot explained, with his customary lucidity, that if a cow with handlebars is a bicycle, within the meaning of the Act, then a bicycle with four legs instead of two wheels is a cow, within the meaning of the Act. Again, quoth he, if a torch flashed in front of a cow is claimed to be a rear light on a bicycle, then a torch flashed behind a bicycle is a front light on a cow. And still further, averred he, if a cow with one handlebar is half a bicycle, then a bicycle with two legs is half a cow. All, all within the meaning of the Act. What Act? Almost any Act you like to mention, as in the case of the Princess Rhama-Bul-Bhag *versus* Orkney Rolling Stocks and Mr Cosmo Fewtrass, in which Mr Justice Spaddlewidge held that a rhinoceros driven along a railway line is not rolling stock merely because a cloud of red, sulphurous smoke issues from its ears. But the same rhinoceros – let us call it Travers[1] – may be held to be

---

[1] Or Bestwick.

rolling stock if it be used to draw a train, however small and dirty. All, all within the meaning of that thrice accursed Act.

HOME CORNER

There are two ways of telling the age of a rhinoceros. The first is to examine its teeth. The second is to collect the evidence of those who remember the beast when it was young, and may even have kept some newspaper cutting recording its birth. The disadvantage of the first method is that it requires an expert, a man who is used to rhinoceroses, and knows exactly how to examine their teeth without danger to himself or inconvenience to the animals. The disadvantage of the second method is that very often those in a position to give information are unwilling to come forward, and to embroil themselves in what they consider to be a rather highbrow discussion, and one that has little relation to the average man's life or activities. They argue that the exact age of a rhinoceros cannot matter very much to most people. And though this represents an egotistical point of view, it is understandable. The real question is – do those who have known a rhinoceros all their lives always make a point of ascertaining its age? Or are they content to leave the matter undecided?

ACCORDING TO EGGILBIRD

Glancing through Eggilbird's *Perpetratio Imbecillitatis, Vol. IX*, I find the case of a man who became web-footed through the drinking of strong ale during the summer solstice (with Agrippa already entering the Sign of the Hairy He Goat and Compasses) and failed to assert broffage during a nine-week hearing at the Market Harborough Assizes (Mr Justice Otter up). This forms an interesting sidelight on the much-debated ruling of Cocklecarrot in the matter of non-ferrous stair-rods, *et alia mobilia secundum artem*. For then, as now, there rose a great clamour of the people, demanding the explanation of *quod sensu percipi non potest*, and battering of court doors with cries of *'Ut dummodo!'* and *'Tanquam imperfectis!'* and other snacks and driblets from Porridge's Common or Garden Law for the Common or Garden City Masses', with a thumping great index and a foreword by a bottle-nosed Hindu from the Inner Temple.

But stay! An injunction *ab loco*, and pending

fraxin	porgole	mivvick
vellum	gripe	techy
dortmany	initial outlay	abulbol
cludder	toggo	frank albacy
aspen-traverse	gurney	adequitio
greengroan	teleolo	firmatio
orchimandry	supprasition	relt
grossness	aerial rights	double relt
evellience	yardson	gaming-light

must, of its own *exquisitio*, be supposed to pre-suppose *abhinc* and *abhunc*.

Chapter 18

Hôtel McGurgle et de l'Univers

MRS McGURGLE, boarding-house landlady *par excellence*, is already planning. 'Just like everybody else,' as she says. Having read that the Government is going to make an effort to start a prosperous tourist industry in England, she is trying to introduce one or two Continental touches into her establishment. It will no longer be called Marine House, but 'Casa McGurgle', or 'Hôtel McGurgle et de l'Univers'. She has already written to a Miss Kelvick, who used to sing 'Where My Caravan Has Rested', to her own accompaniment. It is thought that this lady might introduce a kind of cabaret or café chantant atmosphere into McGurgle's. The cabbage, she tells me, will be cooked in a new way, 'with a lot of sauce', and the breakfast kipper will appear on the menu as *Kipper maître d'hôtel*.

The McGurgle's preparations for tourist traffic are the talk of the town. She has engaged an artist of local renown to do some rather daring mural paintings in the coffee-room – including one of the Mayor's wife in a backless bathing-dress. To make the atmosphere more bohemian than of old, the window-boxes, which used to contain dusty geraniums – gerania to Mrs McGurgle – will henceforth be filled with cardboard orchids and passion-flowers, and the mat which bore the word 'Welcome' in the entrance hall will now say, with Gallic naughtiness, 'Entrez.' Moreover, the McGurgle has unearthed from an attic a gay little round table with a yellow and red umbrella to fix above it. This will stand outside the entrance, to encourage the clientèle to take their stout in its shade.

As chef the good landlady has engaged a buxom woman who has twice made a day-trip to Boulogne, and is being encouraged to read

One Hundred Real Continental Dishes, by Mrs Cranston Bopchalk
('Germaine' of the *Seaville Argus*). The question of wine has arisen,
and Mrs McGurgle has laid down some dozens of the new Anglo–
Saxon Sparkling Near-Burgundy-Type called Château Frotho. She
herself has begun to wear long red ear-rings (a souvenir from sunny
Llandudno), and an enormous five-pointed beauty-spot in the middle
of her left cheek. As her married sister remarked, 'And what, pray,
is that blasted starfish for?'

A second interview with her new cook has left Mrs McGurgle
without much hope of 'making her cuisine less insular', as a highbrow boarder puts it. Good, honest Mrs Trudge says plain fare is
the best, and by plain she means very plain. 'I can get all the sauces
I want out of bottles,' she said yesterday, 'and as for Yorkshire
pudding, well, I'd back mine against the whole Rooderlarpay with
the Ark do Triumph thrown in.' Mrs McGurgle pointed out that all
she asked for was a touch of imagination in the cooking. 'Imagination,' cried Ma Trudge. 'Well, reality's what people like in their
grub. They can imagine they're eating frogs fried in sparkling champagne if they like, but the hotpot's more homely, to my way of
thinking.'

'As to soups—' began Mrs McGurgle. 'Same as sauces,' said Ma
Trudge, 'out of the bottle or the packet. And none of your ladida
liquids with all the letters of the alphabet floating in 'em.' 'I was
thinking of Consomays—' 'Oh, you can call 'em what you like,
Mum. You give me the packet and I'll make the soup. What you call
it is no affair of mine.' 'But don't you remember any soups you had
in Boulogne, Mrs Trudge?' 'Soups? D'you think I went there to
drink soups? Not me. We took a flask o' tea, some bull's-eyes, a
packet of chips, a few sardines, and two bars of chocolate cream.
Soups!'

Mrs McGurgle has had another talk with the new cook. Having
recalled that Mrs Trudge had twice made a day-trip to Boulogne,
Mrs McGurgle was surprised to find her so stolid and dowdy. The
landlady said with a sweet smile, 'What we want here is a kind of
light touch with the food, something almost naughty about the
dishes.' To which Mrs Trudge replied, 'I can't say there's anything

very naughty about my cabbage. I cook it like my ma used to.' 'There are other dishes besides cabbage,' said Mrs McGurgle. At which cook raised her eyebrows, and seemed to be saying, 'Are there? I have yet to hear of them.' 'What can you do in the way of sweets?' asked the McGurgle. Mrs Trudge frowned and thought for a moment. 'Well,' she said, 'there's always blommonge, isn't there?' 'Yes,' said Mrs McGurgle, with a sigh, 'always.'

Tremendous excitement was caused the other day by the arrival at Hôtel McGurgle (et de l'Univers) of a dreamy gentleman, who announced that he had a week's holiday, and was going to paint. Mrs McGurgle at once had visions of letting her attic to a nest of starving poets, who would sing as they worked. It was only when the artistic boarder explained that he painted coloured pictures of dogs for a firm of postcard-makers that the excitement died down. He wore a dirty cloth cap instead of a floppy béret, and a made-up bow tie instead of a flowing cravat. And his name, to crown all, was Miggett. Any hopes that the ladies of the establishment had entertained of being taken to a 'fast' tea-house faded at once. The only romantic thing about Miggett was his habit of rolling his eyes. But that audacity was reserved for his food.

Still bent on helping the tourist agency, the exquisite Florence McGurgle is beginning to leave about the house books in foreign languages, or translations, which she picks up in a second-hand bookshop. Imagine the surprise of old Miss Felspar on finding a guidebook to the Velay and the Vivarais; conceive the horror of Mrs Twapsey on being confronted with a Spanish novel by Pedro Galdos; consider the shock to Mr Pursecraft on seeing in his bedroom *One Hundred Thoughts from d'Annunzio*. And, finally, pray sympathize with Mrs Chelmsworth, who, while looking among the music in the parlour for 'Bird-Song – And you,' came across 'Allez-y, Toinette!'

The appearance and even the personality of Mrs McGurgle seem to be undergoing a change. The vision of her establishment playing its humble part in building up a prosperous tourist industry is leading this English rose (McGurgle was an Aberdeen auctioneer, but Florence was a Gurricle, from Crabhampton) into extravagances of manner and behaviour. In her glossy dark hair she wears a vast

Spanish comb, and is already calling the baker's boy *amigo*. To emphasize a point she lays her finger along her nose, and recommends her rooms to inquirers by blowing kisses skywards on the tips of her fingers, and saying, 'What would you?' all of which seems comically out of place in a solid, good-natured English landlady. No doubt it will make the tourists feel at home, especially as she is already hinting at a youth spent abroad.

Something tells me that all the McGurgle's attempts to contribute to the building up of a tourist industry in this country are doomed to failure. She has grown too like her lodgers for the adoption of a Latin levity to sit lightly on her. Her feet are planted too firmly in toad-in-the-hole and nondescript stew. She is too deeply rooted in frightful vegetable matter. No daring frescoes of girls shrimping on a foreign shore can change the honest dullness of her furniture and her decorations. Her gigantic ruby ring is more evocative of the pedlar's tray outside the 'Magpie' than of 'A runaway match in old Madrid'. Her Spanish comb has an air rather of the bargain basement than of 'A token of esteem from a Castilian nobleman'. As for the anklet which made Mrs Purvis ask, 'Have you, pray, been sold in the market-place at Bognor or elsewhere?' – this anklet, could it speak, would say, not 'Cap Ferrat', but 'Curtain-ring from Hammond and Pyecraft'.

The irrepressible Flo McGurgle has begun to practise, on the sly, simple Italian songs. From her private sitting-room comes:

> *Lar don-nar ee mobilee*
> *Cwal pum al ve-hen-to* . . .

Or,

> *O-o-o-o solly me-ho* . . .

Which brings young Mr Solomon Farragut to the door with a tell-tale blush.

The baker's boy has complained to his father of being called 'amigo', and the baker has asked for an explanation, and has been told it is French for 'my little man'.

A boarder at the Hôtel McGurgle has complained that a bottle of stout which he ordered for lunch was brought aslant in a basket with a napkin round it.

Dear Beachcomber,

Exaggerated reports of my attempts to help the tourist industry would almost suggest that I am arranging for bullfights on the Promenade, and that the floors of my establishment are awash with champagne. Let me hasten to assure the public that the one or two cosmopolitan touches introduced by me will not banish the sane English decorum of this tested house of entertainment. There is no truth in the report that my chef, Mrs Trudge, was a dancer at the Moulin Rouge. On the contrary, she was a washerwoman at Nuneaton. And Mr Trudge, as his name might have indicated, was not so much a rich Parisian Boulevardier as a rather needy Birmingham pawnbroker's assistant. Surely that will set at rest the fears of mothers of impressionable sons or daughters.

A colleague of Mrs McGurgle's, Mrs Faddick, who runs Rest Haven at Bucktooth-by-Sea, has protested against what she calls 'the tendency to make the tourist industry an excuse for Continental practices'. She maintains that we ought to show foreigners the 'innate respectability of English boarding-house life rather than attempt to emulate the indiscipline of flightier races'. She continues: 'Let Mrs McGurgle plaster her walls with frescoes of underclad adventuresses. "Love Me, Love my Dog" is good enough for Rest Haven.'

The mayor's wife depicted on Mrs McGurgle's wall has objected strongly to being called an underclad adventuress.

And from Mrs Clabham, mine hostess of Rock Bower, Nudging-on-Sea, comes this sturdy lump of common sense:

. . . Rock Bower will remain what it has always been, the home of simple English fare for English connysirs. Those who come from abroad to see the ruins of our castle can stay at Larch End, where my colleague, Miss Upchurch, new to the business, does not scruple to include among her clients a cosmopolitan gentleman who plays the violin, and has been seen with his arm round the waist of two of the barmaids at the 'Rifleman'. Rock Bower has healthier ideas of fun – witness the straw hats with 'Sez You' printed on the bands which we distribute gratis during the season. . . .

Dear Mrs McGurgle,

All we old-timers want is for your place to stay as it was. We long to return to your sermons about gravy-stains, and to hear you say, in a voice that reduced us all to dumb terror: 'No lady or gentleman, I presume, wishes a SECOND portion of Yorkshire?' And do you remember when a novice held up his hand and said, 'I could do with another go'? The way in which you affected to be unaware that anybody had spoken was magnificent. And how about when Eames, the steam carpet-beating clerk, threw a potato at the cat Mibbins? And the old gent who said, 'If this is curry, I'm the Emperor of Iceland'? And Wedger, who pinched the cheese from the mousetraps? What days! May they soon return!

Yrs gratefully,
Monty Clowdes.

Dear Mrs McGurgle,

It is with regret that I tell you that we shall not be coming to your boarding-house any more. I have to think of my daughter, who must not be exposed to all this continental frivolity. You may imagine my feelings, and my wife's, when I heard that in place of the picture of cattle drinking which we admired so much, you now have a half-nude figure of the mayoress on your wall. This will no doubt attract the Latin races, but you will lose your old British clients. I have often praised and recommended your Yorkshire pudding, but I suppose from now on it will be snails and garlic. What a pity!

Yours faithfully
M. D. Numpley.

* * * * *

FOUNDLING

As a very pretty woman stepped out of her London house yesterday she nearly fell over a basket. Sounds of crying came from beneath a pile of clothes. Stooping to investigate, and to comfort the derelict baby, she was surprised to receive an adult kiss, resounding and carefree. As she stepped back, Captain Foulenough rose from the basket, demanding asylum. 'I'm an orphan,' he said. 'And you, I know, are on the committee that runs a large orphanage. Practise what you preach, my lovely one. Take me in.' The woman was too dumb-founded to reply. A second adult kiss restored her speech, and Foul-enough and his basket retired to the house of another beauty.

ADVTS.

Society lady would sell enormous red wig, part worn, suitable for bald giantess or judge of High Court. Could be used as child's bath-mat.

Would the gentleman who left a fried egg as a bookmark in Byron's Poems (page 84) at the Westbrook Public Library last week com-municate with finder?

Mr James Sossidge draws the attention of his clients to the correct spelling of his name, as above. 'Sausage' is *not* a permissible alter-native.

Christmas. – Give umbrella ferrules and be the most popular man at the party.

BALLET

Le Spectre du Fromage

Here is modern balletography at its most evocative; a tenuous lyric replete with the *fromagerie* which we have come to expect from the productions of Commissarmutzky. From the opening *pas de cheval*, during which Tumbelova rises dreamily from the Cheese like a sleepy night-watchman on the frontiers of Fairyland, to the closing *ricochet* of the Marquis, who has been thrown against the dungeon wall, the spectacle is a feast for eye, ear, heart, brain, and that aesthetic sixth sense of the *aficionado*. Serge Trouserin, who has little to do but shoot his imaginary arrows at the huge Cheese, contrives to suggest, particularly in his *demi-pas*, his *retroussements*, and his irresistible *chinoiseries*, a spirit out of tune with mundane *affaires*.

(Tomorrow: Chuckusafiva in *L'oiseau sur le Chapeau de Nelly*.)

STRAIGHT BAT WEEK

Many have suggested that crowds should be encouraged to sing the Narkover School Song on every possible occasion during Straight Bat Week.

For those who may have forgotten the song I reprint it below:

THE SCHOOL SONG

When we who played for Narkover
  In happy days gone by
Are parted by the piteous foam,
  And, 'neath an alien sky,
Recall the glad, the joyous time
  When youth was at the spring,
God grant that in our hearts may chime
  The song we used to sing:

Refrain:

    Straight is my bat,
    Aye, straighter year by year,
    Life's googlies spin,
    Break out, break in
    But I can have no fear.
    Loud comes the call
    Across the world to me,
    I laugh at Fate,
    My bat is straight
    As e'er it used to be.

When we who played for Narkover
  Are laid beneath the loam,
May breezes bear to us once more
  Some echo from our home,
May we recall the hour of pride
  When life was on the wing.
And boys who played to save the side
  Were not ashamed to sing:

Refrain:

    Straight be my bat, etc.

STRANGE GOINGS-ON

'Only a poor waif.' Thus read the label on the basket which Mrs

Tangsten, a former belle of West Mimms, pulled from the doorstep into the hall. The Captain lay still.

'Who,' said the lady, 'could be hard-hearted enough to leave 'oo outside, then?' 'Who, indeed?' echoed Foulenough, rising like Venus from the basket, and folding the lovely creature in his arms as though to the manner born. Struggling free, the Mimmsian Mona Lisa cried, 'But you are no infant! What foolery is this? Spangrove! Show this baby out!' Hastily taking final toll of a pair of lips painted as thickly as the statue of Cobden in Rashleigh Gardens, the Captain sold the basket to the cook for 12s., and repaired to the 'General Abercrombie'.

'Bring the little darling in, Ada.' The basket, from which the whimpering came, was carried from the doorstep, and deposited in front of a large fire. Ugly Mrs Townslow then began to sing a lullaby. Foulenough sat up and threw aside the sacking in his basket. He had expected to see the beautiful Mrs Vuttle. Mrs Townslow uttered a yell. 'Wrong house,' said Foulenough. 'Sorry. My mistake.' And he picked up his basket and strolled out of the house, leaving the hideous young châtelaine in a swoon.

An auction of brandy was proceeding without incident, when a man at the front of the hall suddenly took out his handkerchief and began to wipe his forehead. Then he sighed, clapped his hand to his chest, and sat down. There was a sympathetic murmur. 'Taken ill . . . poor chap . . . looks pretty dicky . . .' Feebly the sick man cried, 'Brandy! brandy!' A gentleman in the front row who had just seen twelve dozen knocked down to him could hardly refuse aid. With grudging chivalry he uncorked a bottle, and handed it to the patient. 'I think . . . a little air,' said the patient, and getting to his feet, he walked to the back of the hall. 'Is there a doctor here?' shouted the auctioneer. It didn't much matter whether there was or not. The patient had got a flying start.

Once near the exit door the sick man seemed to revive, and before anybody could ask if he was feeling better, he had slipped out, and was off down the street like a wing three-quarter with the wind behind him. What he hugged was no ball, but a bottle. And the word 'Foulenough' was already being whispered in the hall which he had left so unceremoniously.

AFTER YOU, MISS STEIN

Roland Milk, who admires so much the prose of Miss Stein, has set himself the task of trying to import her principles into poetry. He could not bring himself, at his first effort, to cast aside those fairy rhythms that have made him famous. This, then, is how he wrote:

> I see, I see the daffodils,
> The daffodils I see, I see
> Upon the hills, upon the hills,
> Upon the hills I see, I see,
> Hills upon the hills I see
> The daffodils the hills upon
> The hills upon the hills I see
> The daffodils upon upon.
> Upon upon upon upon
> Upon upon upon upon.
> See I see I see I see
> Upon the daffodils the hills.

At his second attempt he was more successful, and produced this really beautiful poem, striking alike in its economy and its restraint.

> Daffodils, daffodils,
> Daffodils, daffodils, daffodils,
> Daffodils.

He is to recite it himself through a paper funnel next Sunday night at the Harringay baths, to an audience of unemployed grouters.

Chapter 19

The Thunderbolt

WITHIN A few weeks everybody will be talking about 'Thunderbolt' Footle, the new discovery of that greatest of British boxing promoters, Scrubby Botulos.

Mr Botulos said yesterday, in an interview, 'Here, at last, is the genuine article. He's very handsome, dresses well, and has a number of good books at his lodgings. I have worked out a preliminary programme. I'm going to fix a fight with someone not too good. The Thunderbolt will win, and we shall then have no difficulty in getting him on to the films. During the making of his first film he will become more or less engaged to an actress – or, better, to a society girl. That will keep his name before the public, and there will be no need to tire him with too much fighting. The idea of calling him Thunderbolt before he has done any fighting is to get the public to realize how good he's going to be.'

Mr Botulos then distributed photographs of the new world-beater, showing his enormous muscles, which, said Mr Botulos, 'are harder than iron, and bigger too'.

I understand that a fifteen-round contest has been fixed up between 'Thunderbolt' Footle and 'Slugger' Faxafloi, the man-eater from Iceland. It will take place some time within the next year, if Footle's theatrical and film and concert engagements permit. Footle said yesterday, 'I shall not train much. I don't have to. My dancing keeps me fit. And, anyway, one blow will finish the fight. He won't know what hit him.'

It is rumoured that Footle is engaged to be married to Miss Mae West. But he said yesterday, 'We're just good pals.' Miss West said, 'Where does he get that stuff about being good?' Meanwhile the

Thunderbolt is being sued for breach of promise by a friend of his publicity manager, Joe Bulgetti.

Mr Billy ('Haunch') Venison, the boxing critic, said yesterday, 'It's difficult to say much about the Thunderbolt till we've seen him fight. He'll have to fight somebody sooner or later. That yarn about how he can smash through a six-foot wall with his bare fist doesn't impress me. It is told of every British heavyweight. I know that wall. It's a cardboard one, kept in the training quarters and photographed with a hole in it.'

'I SHALL WIN' ('Thunderbolt' Footle)

The Thunderbolt's manager, Scrubby Botulos, announced yesterday that the fight between his man and Faxafloi will have to take place very soon, because the film and cabaret people are not inclined to give good contracts to an unknown boxer. 'The pooblic,' he said, 'was not interested in a singer or a dancer until he will be have won a fight or two. What we was have got to get is that our man Footle shall have been proved to be a chimpiron.'

Footle said: 'The fight's as good as over. He won't know about it until the hospital surgeon brings him round. He won't know what hit him. I'll just give him one jab. He needn't bother to come into the ring. I'll just knock him through the ropes. You may say that I shall win easily by a knock-out in the first second of the fight.'

The boxing critic, Billy ('Haunch') Venison, said: 'It's difficult to say anything until one has seen the fighters at work. I think that Footle should win unless Faxafloi proves too much for him. The same may be said of Faxafloi, only vice, of course, versa.'

Asked by his publicity manager whether the newspapers were to be informed that he had a deadly right or a deadly left, the Thunderbolt said, 'Everything about me is deadly. I'm dynamite from head to foot. He won't know what hit him.'

Faxafloi said, 'I shall win. He'll never know what hit him. I've got a load of dynamite in each fist.'

Informed of this, Footle said, 'I shall win. I've got more dynamite in my little finger than he'll ever have in his whole body. He won't know what hit him.'

Informed of this, Faxafloi said, 'I won't have to hit him. Just a flick. I'm dynamite. He'll never know what hit him.'

Asked what his tactics would be, Footle said, 'I won't need any. Just a tap and he'll be in the doctor's hands for a year. I'm made of dynamite. He won't know what hit him.'

It was announced at Footle's headquarters today that the Thunderbolt had strained his throat while fulfilling a crooning engagement at a cabaret. But he was out in the afternoon, skipping and being photographed. Later he dislocated his thumb with a savage blow at the punchball, which bounded back, struck him on the head, and knocked him down.

'He is a real fighter,' said Scrubby Botulos. 'He doesn't seem to know the meaning of defence, he's so aggressive.'

The Thunderbolt said, 'I shall win. He won't even guess what hit him.'

'Even if he did guess he wouldn't believe it,' sneered an onlooker.

Mrs Dietrich, when asked if she would attend a film with the Thunderbolt, said, 'You can say we are just pals. I hope to meet him soon.' Joan Crawford, when asked if there was anything in the rumour of her affection for Footle, said, 'I have never met him, but we are just good pals.' Constance Bennett said, 'I've never heard of him. We are just pals, that's all.'

'Thunderbolt' Footle, Britain's new heavyweight boxer, has signed a contract to appear as Faust in Gounod's opera. A daily paper has acquired the rights of *The Story of my Fights*, which will not be published until he has done some fighting. Meanwhile, he is still training for his fight with Faxafloi, the mystery heavyweight from Iceland. Owing to the calls upon him for making gramophone records and being photographed at parties, the Thunderbolt will probably have training quarters in a large flat off Piccadilly. To-morrow he is skipping in Hyde Park for United International Films, Ltd. It is hoped that before his training is over he will appear at the first night of a new film with Mrs Dietrich.

'Thunderbolt' Footle was knocked out four times yesterday, once by each of his sparring partners. His trainer said, 'Thunderbolt wasn't really trying, and he wasn't ready, and the sun was in his eyes. You can tell what he's made of by what he said when he came to in his dressing-room. He said, "He'll never know what hit him. I'm dynamite. That's what I am. Dynamite." '

Rumour is still coupling Footle's name with that of Miss Mae West. 'You may say we're just pals,' he said yesterday.

Asked what his tactics would be in the fight with Faxafloi, he said, 'I won't need any. I shall just come out of my corner like a whirlwind on the stroke of the bell. One blow will finish it.' At last Britain seems to have a champion.

Faxafloi appears to be a grim young man. He can't croon, doesn't like dancing, and doesn't want to be an actor. 'In fact, all he can do is fight,' said his trainer.

The fifteen-round contest between 'Thunderbolt' Footle and Rink Faxafloi, the Iceland Wizard, will take place on Monday night. The hour has been changed from nine-thirty to eight-thirty, because the Thunderbolt has a cabaret engagement later in the evening. Footle said yesterday, 'I shall win. He won't know what hit him. Then I'm ready for Louis, Schmeling, Baer, Farr, one at a time or all together. I'm set for the championship, and you may say that I consider it an honour to bring glory to British boxing.'

Scrubby Botulos said, 'I'll be surprised if that Icelander even gets out of his corner to begin the fight.' And 'Haunch' Venison, the boxing critic, said, 'The fellow with the most dynamite in his fists is going to win. It's always been my experience that, in a heavyweight fight, the winner is the one that can put the other fellow down for the count. If I had to hazard a guess, I should say this fight will be no exception to that rule.'

England is talking of nothing but the forthcoming big fight tonight at Burlington House. Has Britain at last found a native champion? Will this, Footle's first fight, put him at one bound in the forefront etc., etc., etc.?

A round-by-round description of the fight will be broadcast, the running commentary being in the capable and experienced hands of Mr Guy Babblebotham and Mr Hardleigh A. Mouse. ('Slop' of the *Sporting Chance*.)

Footle took things quietly yesterday, to avoid becoming stale. He lay in bed and read Upchurch's *Pragmatism and the Endocrine Gland*, while his publicity manager wrote thousands of telegrams wishing him good luck, signed by such celebrities as Rabindranath Tagore ('Sock him, feller!'), Mae West ('May victory smile upon you!'), Gabriele d'Annunzio ('Atta Thunderbolt!'), the League Council ('Geneva is with you, cully'), the Southern Railway ('May the decenter man win'), and Rear-Admiral Sir Ewart Hodgson ('Lots Road is watching you').

Hardly had my little pen come trippingly off the paper at the end of that last sentence, when a news agency message was handed to me by my assistant under-secretary.

The fight is postponed! Not enough people have bought seats. Lack of interest is attributed to the fact that Footle has not become engaged to any actress. So, in order to lose as little time as possible, the publicity manager has got him engaged to that tiresome old-stager, Boubou Flaring. As I write this, they are being photographed together. He is saying, 'Boubou is just swell,' and she is replying, 'Thunderbolt's a great guy.' And already seats are being bought like hot cakes. So it is unlikely that the postponement will be for more than a day or two.

Tonight the British hope, Footle, will meet the Iceland Man-Eater, Faxafloi, in a fifteen-round contest at Burlington House at 9.30. The running commentary by Mr Guy Babblebotham and Mr Hard-leigh A. Mouse will be broadcast.

Footle is said to have developed a curious back-hand swing which will prove deadly. He said this morning, 'I shall will. Probably a knock-out in round one. I'm dynamite.' Faxafloi said, 'I shall just rub him into the floor with my heel.'

'Haunch' Venison, the boxing critic, said, 'If you ask me, I should say that the man who can hit hardest, stand up longest, and prove himself a winner will win the fight. If it doesn't end in a knock-out there will probably be a decision on points. A dead-heat is hardly likely. Nor is a draw without a verdict. Both men will have to box. And the result – well – wait and see.'

THE BIG FIGHT BROADCAST

If you buy a debenture or any other form of loan capital your asset cover will cooee wheeeee squunk . . . We are now taking you over to Burlington House to listen to the big fight between 'Thunderbolt' Footle and Faxafloi. . . . Mr Babblebotham and Mr Hardleigh A. Mouse are going to describe the fight for you. . . . Well, here we are. Burlington House is packed. I don't think I've ever seen such a crowd, have you, Mouse? No. Ah! You hear that cheering? Some-body's just come in. I think it's the French Ambassador, isn't it, Mouse? . . . No. I think it's Jack Hobbs . . . Oh. Right. And here's – surely it's – isn't it Lady Cabstanleigh, Mouse? . . . No. It's two bankers . . . Oh. Right. The ring is filled with famous boxers, and the referee is introducing them. I can see Louis, Schmeling, Neusel, Foord, Farr, Max Baer, J. H. Lewis, Wilde, Dempsey, Tunney, Beckett, Carpentier, Harvey, Thil . . . Hullo! What's happened? Oh, you heard that roaring. Footle has arrived, but he can't get into the ring owing to the mob of famous boxers. And here comes Faxafloi now. They'll have to clear the ring. . . .

Footle looks magnificent in his blue dressing-gown with golden dragons on it. Faxafloi is wearing a green dressing-gown with red spots. He looks very fit. I'm sure we all want to see a sporting fight, but that doesn't prevent us from wanting to see a British victory. I think they both look pretty fit, don't you, Mouse? . . . Of course they do. Why wouldn't they? . . . Er – I've just heard that Lord Towcher is somewhere among the audience. . . . Now, we'll be off soon. The gloves are on, and the referee is just making his little speech to the two men. Faxafloi looks very cool. Footle is grinning, and he is evidently the idol of the crowd. . . . There goes the bell for the first round. . . .

Footle has rushed from his corner like an express train. No wonder they call him 'Thunderbolt'. Faxafloi looks puzzled. Footle was in such a hurry to get at his man that he apparently had no time to aim a blow at him when he came within striking distance. Faxafloi has sidestepped and Footle has crashed into the ropes. Ah! He's coming back. He's certainly doing all the attacking so far. Full of spirit. Hullo! He's slipped. He's down. He's up again. He's a bit dazed, and has aimed a wild blow in the air. Faxafloi is at the other side of the ring talking to his seconds. He seems amused. Don't know why. Footle's coming for him again. What spirit! He's still doing all the attacking. If one of those blows connects! Now they're face to face. The bell just saved Faxafloi from one of those terrible swinging punches.

Round II. – Footle's changed his tactics. He's more cautious. Neither man has landed a blow so far, but if the fighting spirit counts for anything, the first round was Footle's. Hullo! Faxafloi has moved forward. He's hit Footle hard under the chin. Footle's down. One – two – three – four – five – six – seven – eight – nine – ten. Out! Faxafloi wins. The crowd is going mad. Booing, hissing, screaming. The verdict is evidently unpopular. But I must say I think Faxafloi won without a doubt. Don't you, Mouse? . . . I think so. Oh yes. But it was rotten luck on Footle . . . He's come to. Phugh! He's in a rage, kicking and scratching. Faxafloi came over to shake hands, but Footle shouted something at him, and then burst into tears. The crowd is cheering him for his plucky effort . . . We are now taking you over to Morecombe Bay Casino to hear Squelch Rongero's Band. . . .

In his dressing-room Footle said, 'I wasn't feeling well at the start. The lights were in my eyes, and I thought he was going to foul me. I'm confident that I was the better man. It wasn't his blow that knocked me out, it was the impact of my head on the floor of the ring. I'm ready for Louis or Schmeling now. I wasn't fairly beaten. I won the first round on points. I think I slipped just before he hit me in the second round. I was just going to hit him with all my might when it happened. I wasn't well, and my gloves weren't put on properly. I had him beat, then I slipped up. I don't think he hit me at all. My shoes were slippery, and the floor was dangerously slippery, too. I think I won on points.'

* * * * *

ANTHOLOGY OF HUNTINGDONSHIRE CABMEN

It can hardly be claimed for the newly published *Anthology of Huntingdonshire Cabmen* that it is, in the words of an over-enthusiastic critic, 'a masterpiece of imaginative literature'. The Anthology consists of the more striking names (with initials) from each of the three volumes. It is a factual and unemphatic work, and the compiler has skinned the cream from the lists. Here are such old favourites as Whackfast, E. W., Fodge, S., and Nurthers, P. L. The index is accurate, and the introduction by Cabman Skinner is brief and workmanlike.

SERIALS

Now that plays are being published like serials there is a chance for my new Symphony, which I am sending to one of our leading monthly reviews. I have divided it into instalments, taking care to end each instalment on an exciting note, so as to keep the reader in suspense. For instance, the second instalment ends in the middle of an almost unplayable passage for violins.

It may be objected that a symphony is meant to be heard right off the reel, in a half-hour or so, and cannot be spread over many months in this fashion. To this I reply that genuine music-lovers won't care how my new work is presented to them.

Next week I hope to reproduce the first (left-hand) half of Rembrandt's Portrait of his Mother. The second (right-hand) half will follow in due course.

Arrangements are also being made to serialize the Cavell statue – one lump of stone at a time will be on view, beginning at the top right-hand corner.

COSMO SMELLINGHAM-SMITH

It is reported that forty bottle-nosed whales are stranded on a beach in Forfarshire. One naturally jumps to the conclusion that the famous angler, Cosmo Smellingham-Smith, has been at work again. Last time I mentioned him he was, you may remember, catching goldfish in the consulting-room of a nerve specialist. But this does not mean that he will only go after small fry – he who has been known to land a crocodile using only a poisoned cherry on the end of a shooting-stick.

His method with bottle-nosed whales[1] is to tire them out. He lures them after him in a motor-boat. He himself sits in the stern, dangling over the side a selection of succulent marine monsters. This goes on

[1] See Index under 'Sausage, vanilla, stuffed with, partially'.

all day and night until the whales are worn out and sick of the whole affair. He then dashes for the nearest beach, and as the beasts lie panting on the shore administers the *coup de grâce* with an iron flail.

LETTER FROM A NARKOVER BOY

Dere Dad,
Now that I here from the mata that you are in jug again, whos going to keepe op the paymince for my plaice in the cricket teme, carenent you touch unkle Roy for a tenor, sorry you got copped over the black market agane, i wunder if yore sell is anywere nere Sudgeon's dads, he's in for seting fiar to something, we had a wip round last night at the schule conkert for all the chaps whos dads are in the jug, so I expeck im paying for yore exterer cumfurts, so what about fixing the next paymince for my plaice in the teme, eh, good hunting dad and i hope yore out soon.

> *yore loving son*
> *Tom.*

THOSE CABMEN

A camera unit is on its way to Corfu to select scenes for the *List of Huntingdonshire Cabman*. It was thought, at first, that the film would have a Huntingdon background. But, as it is a question of earning dollars, the glamour of Huntingdon is not thought powerful enough to excite American audiences.

Whether the Americans will be interested in the names of these cabmen is another matter. 'The whole idea is extremely daring, and the ballet amid the ruins of Luxor suggests that the approach to the task is an imaginative one.' So writes one of the most exasperatingly foolish of the critics.

CUCKOO

To all those who are about to hear the cuckoo, my greeting.

Of all the birds that gather in the path that spring will tread—

PRODNOSE: Oh, Lord! More fine writing!
MYSELF: Peace, pest!

Of all those birds I take my hat off highest to the brave wren, the small bird that creeps about in the hedges, and longs for the sun. He cannot feed, like a pipit or a lark, on any old seedling or twopenny berry. He needs insects, and he cannot get them. But you always know when he has found the meal he enjoys, because he sings out at the top of his voice a very pleasant song that no vagrant spy of the wireless people has ever succeeded in incorporating in Uncle Beethoven's Hour.

Therefore, rascals, to the Devil with despair.

PRODNOSE: Have you heard the cuckoo yet?
MYSELF: Yes.
PRODNOSE: Well?
MYSELF: Well?'
PRODNOSE: Is that all you have to say about it?
MYSELF: Yes.

IDYLL

I knew a child called Alma Brent,
  Completely destitute of brains,
Whose principal accomplishment
Was imitating railway trains.

When ladies called at 'Sunnyside',
Mama, to keep the party clean,
Would say, with pardonable pride,
  'Now, Alma, do the six-fifteen.'

The child would grunt and snort and puff,
  With weird contortions of the face,
And when the guests had had enough,
  She'd cease, with one last wild grimace.

One day her jovial Uncle Paul
  Cried, 'Come on, Alma! Do your worst!'
And, challenged thus before them all,
  She did the four-nineteen – and burst.

COMING SHORTLY

Volume V (Ruxton-Zoroaster) of the list of Huntingdonshire Cabmen will conclude this standard work. An introduction by Mrs

Benjamin Upchurch describes the usual alphabetical method used in compiling the list, and pays a graceful tribute to the untiring efforts of Mr E. S. Nurgin, who tracked down many crypto-cabmen to their shelters, and tactfully elicited their names from them. Unwillingness to supply their initials was a characteristic of young cabmen, a peculiarity attributed (by Dr Goltz in his *Kabmannschaft und Schriftlicke Gemeinenwürst*) to a non-co-operation in personal matters amounting almost to a Medea-complex.

TCK, TCK!

One fishmonger had a fine surgeon on his slab.

(News item.)

The biter bit. Hourly protests from Harley Street. Deputation of specialists calls at British Medical Association. Billingsgate cheers. Fishmonger mobbed in Wimpole Street. Famous physician stunned by spent mackerel. 'Lie still, sir,' cries shopkeeper. The last roes of summer. Victim's plea for anaesthetic. 'Nurse, nurse, keep his foot out of the prawns.' Tradesman accused of fishful thinking. Sets lobster on intruder. 'Red in tooth and claw,' murmurs onlooker. Watch-chain reveals error. Fish turns out to be man. Printer blamed.

EPITAPH

A glassblower lies here at rest,
Who one day burst his noble chest
While trying, in a fit of malice,
To blow a second Crystal Palace.

Chapter 20

The Case of Juliette Milton

A MRS WEBCROSS writes to me as follows:

Dear Sir,

I have seen it stated in the Cardiff Bugle *that the fairies now appearing at the foot of Knockfierna in County Limerick are the celebrated red-bearded dwarfs who have made Mr Justice Cocklecarrot's life a hell. This is not so. The twelve little gentlemen are at present my lodgers, and I have no complaint to make of them, apart from a tendency to bawl for second helpings of meat (which are not included in our board), and a readiness to flirt with my pretty boarder in the most outrageous manner. In the term 'flirting' I include ear-pinching, eye-rolling, lip-smacking, nudging, giggling, and even, upon occasion, Sudden Embracing in the passages. But my object in writing to you, sir, is to put it on record that neither I nor the late Mr Webcross has ever harboured fairies, either knowingly or unknowingly.*

Believe me, sir,

Yours respectfully,

(Mrs) Lottie Webcross.

THE TWELVE DWARFS

Dear Sir,

We, the undersigned dwarfs, desire to bestow our heartiest approval upon the wise and timely letter of our dear and revered landlady, Madame Webcross. We are not Little People in the fairytale sense of the words. We are merely small in the human sense of the word. As to flirtation, when you are as small as we are, and redhaired into the bargain, you have to take your fun where you find it. Full many a furtive kiss changes hands, or rather mouths, without Church and state rocking on their foundations, and if there is a jollier pastime for a spare moment in a corridor than the tweaking of some alluring ear, we, the undersigned dwarfs, would be glad to hear of it. Evil be to him who thinks evil, say we. Horseplay is no more out of place in a humble boarding-house than in the gilded mansions of the great, and a loving heart is just as likely to beat beneath the ready-made waistcoat of a lodger as beneath the braided and double-breasted garment of a loftier Lothario. All this we say, well knowing that one of our number, Churm Rincewind, is even at this moment encircling with adventurous right arm the provocative waist of Juliette, the sylph-like diseuse who, after bringing down two houses a night at the Old Victoria in Oldham has, bird-of-passage-like, made her temporary nest in No. 8, adjoining the linen cupboard.

> *We are, sir,*
> *The Twelve Dwarfs.*

THE PRETTY BOARDER REPLIES

Dear Sir,

As the 'pretty boarder' referred to by Mrs Webcross in her letter to you, I should like to take this opportunity of denying the statement made by a dwarf of the name of Churm Rincewind to the effect that he put his arm round my waist. All that happened was this. Mr Rincewind put a small ladder against me while I was reading a letter. He mounted the ladder and kissed the tip of my right ear. Thinking he was crazy I pushed him away, and he fell from the ladder and hurt his wrist. I understand he is claiming damages. The whole incident is too foolish to be taken seriously. One does not expect to have ladders put against one in respectable boarding-houses, nor to see a grinning face on the top rung.

> *Yours truly,*
> *Juliette Milton.*

I learn that the red-bearded dwarf, Churm Rincewind, who fell from a small folding ladder on the third-floor landing of Sea View boarding-house, Chelsea, while kissing the ear of Miss Juliette Milton, is bringing an action for damages. The case will come up for hearing shortly. The judge will be Mr Justice Cocklecarrot. Miss Milton said yesterday, 'The whole affair is too ludicrous to discuss. My solicitor tells me that there has never before been a case of a small man planting a ladder against a lady, and then bringing an action because he is pushed away and hurts his wrist.'

The nearest approach to such a case was when a man-about-town tried to throw a brass curtain-ring over the head of one of the giraffe-necked women from Burma. He mounted a ladder to get better aim.

MRS WEBCROSS GIVES EVIDENCE

The hearing began yesterday, before Mr Justice Cocklecarrot (with full jury), of the case in which Mr Churm Rincewind, a red-bearded dwarf about town, seeks to recover damages for an injury to his wrist, sustained when he fell from a ladder which he had mounted for the purpose of kissing the ear of a young lady boarder at Sea View, Chelsea (proprietress, Mrs Webcross). Mr Tinklebury Snap-driver was for the defence, Mr Graham Gooseboote for the prosecution.

MR GOOSEBOOTE: You are Hermione Webcross, proprietress of the boarding-house known as Sea View?

MRS WEBCROSS: I object, m'lud.

COCKLECARROT: What – to the boarding-house?

MRS WEBCROSS: It is not 'known as' Sea View. It *is* Sea View.

MR GOOSEBOOTE: And what sea, may one ask, does it view? The Pacific?

MRS WEBCROSS: Properly speaking, there is no view of the sea, as we overlook Delton and Mackworth's Cycle Accessories. But the name handed down by my late mother, Clara Webcross, is Sea View.

MR GOOSEBOOTE: Very well. Now, Mrs Webcross, do you encourage your male boarders to make overtures to your female boarders?

MRS WEBCROSS: Certainly not. My house is not a co-educational roadhouse.

MR GOOSEBOOTE: Then how do you explain the fact that one of your boarders, a lady, was kissed on the ear from the top rung of a small ladder in broad daylight?

MRS WEBCROSS: It was the exception that proves the rule. It might happen to anyone.

(*The court then rose for drinks.*)

JULIETTE CROSS-EXAMINED

Miss Juliette Milton, dressed in a four-piece gabardine of moiré tussore with green revers and crotted manchlets, was cross-examined yesterday by Mr Gooseboote.

MR GOOSEBOOTE: I suggest that you yourself helped to place the ladder up which your assailant climbed.

MISS MILTON: No. I can get plenty of kissing without having to act as a sort of builder's mate.

MR GOOSEBOOTE: No doubt, no doubt. Er – did you in any way extend your ear, in order to make the dwarf's pleasant task easier?

MISS MILTON: I am an actress, not a contortionist. I cannot move my ears at will.

MR GOOSEBOOTE: Not even a fraction of an inch, in order to avoid an unorthodox salutation?

COCKLECARROT: May we see this ladder?

MR SNAPDRIVER: Certainly, m'lud. It is here. It shall be passed up to you.

MR GOOSEBOOTE: With your ludship's permission, I would like to try an experiment.

COCKLECARROT: With the ladder and the lady's ear? Fire ahead. I'm sure the whole court envies you.

(*The court then rose for more drinks.*)

Mr Gooseboote was half-way up the ladder, which he had leaned against Miss Juliette Milton, and was already stooping to her ear, when a cry rang out.

RINCEWIND: M'worship, I object. Why should the learned counsel be allowed to do with impunity what I am being prosecuted for doing without impunity?

COCKLECARROT: It is in the interests of justice.

MISS MILTON (*blushing*): Not entirely, I hope.

MR GOOSEBOOTE (*beaming at her*): No, of course, not entirely. There is the human element.

COCKLECARROT: That element, Mr Gooseboote, must be strongly controlled in a court of law. The present experiment with an ear should be scientific, cold, detached. Meaning no slight to the – er – quite obvious charms of the lady.

MISS MILTON: Thank you, m'lud. You are all most kind. It is so difficult for a lonely girl—

RINCEWIND: In every reconstruction of a crime that I can remember it was the accused who was given the leading part.

COCKLECARROT: There is no question of a crime in this case. It is no crime to – er – fondle such an ear.

RINCEWIND: Then why am I here?

MR SNAPDRIVER: To claim damages, you fool, for a sprained wrist.

(The court then went rushing out for drinks.)

IN COURT

MR GOOSEBOOTE: Now, Mr Rincewind—

RINCEWIND: Sir. Yours to command.

COCKLECARROT: Please, please, Mr Rincewind.

RINCEWIND: With pleasure, m'ludship.

COCKLECARROT: Please do not speak until you are questioned.

RINCEWIND: I was under the impression that I *was* being questioned.

COCKLECARROT: Oh, very well. But try not to interrupt or to waste the time of the court. Pray proceed, Mr Gooseboote.

GOOSEBOOTE: Now, Mr Rincewind, how do you account for the fact that you fell from the ladder without Miss Milton pushing you?

RINCEWIND: Emotion.

GOOSEBOOTE: What do you mean – emotion?

RINCEWIND: It is difficult to balance on a ladder while indulging in dalliance and gallantry, as you probably know.

GOOSEBOOTE: The experience has not yet come my way.

RINCEWIND: Live in hope, cully, live in hope.

(The court then rose as one man and dashed madly for the canteen.)

MR SNAPDRIVER: I put it to you, Mr Rincewind—

RINCEWIND: Put away.

SNAPDRIVER: What?

RINCEWIND: I said 'put away'.

SNAPDRIVER: Put away what?

RINCEWIND: That's what you were going to tell us.

COCKLECARROT: Come, come. This is ludicrous. Mr Rincewind, you must endeavour to refrain from interruption.

RINCEWIND: Your wish is law, Big Chief.

COCKLECARROT: Would that it were.

RINCEWIND: Were what?

COCKLECARROT: Law.

RINCEWIND: Oh.

SNAPDRIVER: Now, I put it to you, Mr Rince—

RINCEWIND: Now we're coming to it.

SNAPDRIVER: M'lud, this is impossible.

RINCEWIND: He's losing his nerve.

COCKLECARROT: I shall have to fine you for contempt.

RINCEWIND: All the dough in the world wouldn't pay for my contempt of this court, not meaning any offence.

(*Sensation. The court is cleared.*)

SENSATIONAL DISCLOSURE

COCKLECARROT: This case seems to have got out of hand. We are here to consider the claim for damages of little Mr Rincewind, who fell from a ladder while kissing the ear of the plaintiff, Miss Juliette Milton. Mr Gooseboote, learned counsel for the defence, has repeated Mr Rincewind's experiment with success. Mr Snapdriver, learned counsel for the prosecution, now demands to follow suit. Well, if we are all going to reconstruct the case so realistically, we shall be here for weeks. But I cannot for the life of me see what these experiments, dangerously pleasant in themselves, can possibly prove. Miss Milton, did you push Mr Rincewind off the ladder?

MISS MILTON: No.

COCKLECARROT: Then you encouraged his advances?

MISS MILTON: Certainly not. He is so small. I did not see him until he kissed me.

COCKLECARROT: Do you ask me to believe that you did not notice that you had a ladder leaning against you?

MISS MILTON: Of course, I noticed it, you bl— m'lud.

COCKLECARROT: Then why did you leave it there?

MISS MILTON: Must I answer?

COCKLECARROT: Of course you must.

MISS MILTON (*shyly*): I thought it might be someone else coming up it.

(*Sensation.*)

COCKLECARROT SUMS UP

Mr Justice Cocklecarrot said: 'As it seems quite impossible to conduct in a normal manner any case in which these little gentlemen are involved, I suppose I may as well make a kind of summing-up. If the jury think that Mr Rincewind was pushed from the ladder, they will consider his claim for damages reasonable. If, however, they are satisfied that he was not pushed but fell, as it were, of his own volition, their duty is clear. One thing that has struck me as odd about the case – apart from the interludes of lunacy which we have all deplored – is the fact that Miss Milton awaited the marauder, calmly allowing a ladder to be laid against her, as though she were a wall. She must have heard the approaching steps of this little bravo, and descried his face as it was advanced menacingly towards the goal of his unlawful whim – I refer to the perilously beautiful ear of the defendant. Now, Mrs Webcross has assured us that ladder-gallantry is not part of the everyday life at her boarding establishment, yet Miss Milton expressed no surprise when she felt the ladder against her body, nor when she saw this little gentleman's moon face gazing up at her. I am puzzled; and I am bound to add that the two learned counsel have merely confused the issue by their prodigious display of idiocy and incompetence. I will end on that note. It is for the jury to make what they can of all this nonsense.'

*   *   *   *   *

SMALL BEGINNINGS

'A Taxidermist,' I read, 'must begin in a small way.' How true! Let him concentrate on stuffing wrens and chiff-chaffs and leave ostriches to the veterans. He may even get out of the bird class altogether, and work on Rhinoceroses and elephants. I knew a taxidermist once, in Chichester, who believed in beginning in the smallest way possible. He started with bacilli and worked up to midges. Some of his stuffing had to be done with the aid of a microscope, and after a few years' work on flies and water-beetles he became unbalanced. Grand ideas seized him, and he was finally arrested for trying to stuff the Severn Tunnel.

PRODNOSE: With what?
MYSELF: Sage and onions, of course.

THE YOUNG STRABISMUS

The best news today is that that enterprising firm of publishers, Graft and Goole, have arranged to publish next autumn the unabridged, unrevised, unedited and uncensored reminiscences of that famous scientist, Dr Strabismus (Whom God Preserve) of Utrecht.

The Doctor's absent-mindedness, which has endeared him to so many people, will be found to play a great part in his memoirs.

One of the best stories tells how the Doctor sent a friend and colleague who was interested in anthrax in horses to see Mr Galsworthy, under the impression that the famous novelist kept a stable of old horses.

The Strabismus family came originally from Sluys on the Belgian border. The Doctor's grandfather, who was a gardener, moved to Utrecht in 1841.

Young Jan was born in 1872, and, as though by instinct, dissected a frog while still in his cradle. At the age of eight he blew up his father's house while experimenting with dynamite, and at twelve he had invented a triangular trouser-button.

ABUSE

PRODNOSE: Do you know, I would rather be wading through wet clay than reading you?

MYSELF: Well, what is to prevent you wading through as much wet clay as you please? I don't want you hanging about here, I can assure you.

PRODNOSE: Steady, now, I am one of your readers, and you cannot afford to be rude to me.

MYSELF: You miserable, wall-eyed, sheep-faced, spavined, long-eared, lily-livered pig, I care less than nothing for you and your rotten little opinions.

PRODNOSE: Anybody can be rude.

MYSELF: Go ahead, then, wart, if you have the courage.

PRODNOSE: I will not be drawn into an undignified brawl.

MYSELF: Undignified brawl! If I had my way, you'd be dragged head-first into an inn and dipped into —'s ale, which is the worst in England, until you screamed for mercy.

PRODNOSE: What would that prove?

MYSELF: It would prove that you were the kind of fool that gets his head dipped in bad beer by better men than himself.

A CRICKET PLAY

'Cricket is not taken seriously enough by the players.' – (Evening paper.)

(Scene: The Oval)

UMPIRE: Out!

BATSMAN: Oh, please! Not that!

UMPIRE: Out, I said.

BATSMAN: Have you thought what this means?
                    (*a long pause*)
Have you visualized the aftermath; the lonely walk to the pavilion, the jeers of one's mates, the comments in the Press?

UMPIRE: I see no other course.

BATSMAN: You yourself, Umpire, have fans. You know what it is to run the gauntlet of hostile eyes, to be held up to ridicule. Little children, years hence, will tell the story of how I was given out, l.b.w., in this match, and will say, 'He was given out l.b.w. by Soames.' [1]

UMPIRE: You only make it harder for me.

BATSMAN (*quickly*): But supposing I were not really out—

UMPIRE: It would not matter. I have said you are out, and that is all that matters. After all, a man must be either in or out. Life is like that. Some are in, others are not.

BATSMAN (*with lowered head*): Very well. You are but the victim of a system, and I bear you no ill-will. Your training leads you to believe that I am out. You act according to your lights. Nevertheless (*with raised voice*), I dream of a day when no batsman will ever be out, and when umpire and batsman will work hand in hand to build a better cricket field. Good-bye, Umpire, good-bye!

(Exit to pavilion.)

[1] No relation to the wooden-headed old humbug in Mr Galsworthy's Saga. (*sic*).

THRUMS UP!

Every little mother needs a little boy to need her mother-love, and every little mother-love that a little mother gives to a little boy needs another little mother to give mother-love to another little mother. And when the faries laugh, every little mother whose mother-love is true mother-love feels that she must have a little mother-love to give to all the children in the great world of mothers.

MY SCOOP!

A Scoop! A Scoop!

The prematurely, if only partially, denied unofficial semi-confirmation of the almost official report of the tentative announcement of the quasi-engagement of a so-called athlete to the beautiful daughter, as it were, of a mother has now been pseudo-officially announced as informally denied. The belated announcement of the formal denial of the prematurely confirmed refusal of either party to say anything is to be followed by a partial report of an official refusal to deny the rumour of a confirmation.

THRUMS DOWN!

When the first little mother cried, her tears broke into a million crystal fragments, and each little fragment became a little fairy mother, and all the little babies in the world came hurrying into her mother-arms; and that was how little Never-Go-Away found himself in the heart of Motherland, where mother-love grows in the fairy Tree Tops That-Hate-To-Be-Visited. Oh, children, if only all the mothers in the world could come to Motherland the fairies would never die. If you believe in fairies, sign your little name along mother's dotted line.

ETON AND HARROW

For several hundred years he has not missed a single Eton and Harrow match. He told me yesterday that he remembered when the players were dressed in doublet and hose. 'Lord's,' he said, 'was a desolate place, haunted by highwaymen, and many a man was held up on his way to the crease and had his bat and pads stolen.'

His eyes became dreamy. 'The boys don't hit as they used to,' he said, 'and dresses are shorter than in my day, but I think our policemen are wonderful.'

In his hand was a big, heavy book by Mr Galsworthy, and he kept on going up to people's great-grandmothers and saying, 'Surely it's my old friend's great-grand-daughter?' And once he thought he recognized Queen Elizabeth. 'The woman wears devilish well,' he said. But whoever it was, she cut him.

'This is the place,' he said, in the lunch interval, 'where tanned men from the lonely outposts of Empire rub shoulders with rosy-faced bishops, and laughing eyes of slim girls bestow the guerdon of their approval upon the dark or light blue, as whim or family tradition dictates.'

When I left him he was still maundering on. 'This could not happen in any other country,' said I, pinning my country's flag into my top-hat.

THE SONG OF THE SPATS

The mention of buttons and fashion leads me to that ingenuous song which describes the feelings of a social climber, who, the moment it was known that he had bought a pair of spats, was admitted to the houses of the Rich. Anyhow, the song says:

> *Fling wide the doors once barred to me,*
> *And let me see the Paris hats,*
> *And let me join the Rich at tea,*
> *For I have bought a pair of spats.*

> *Ah, happy day, thrice happy day!*
> *I can attend the social chats,*
> *And see their monstrous Lady A.,*
> *For I have bought a pair of spats.*

> *Now shall I hear the flow of wit*
> *In all the most expensive flats,*
> *Contributing my little bit,*
> *For I have bought a pair of spats.*

Nay, *even Thelma Stalagmite,*
  And that preposterous dog she pats,
Will welcome me with sheer delight,
  For I have bought a pair of spats.

WITH GORDON TO KHARTOUM

'Bedside manna,' vouchsafed the doctor when plaster fell from the ceiling.

(Collapse of ceiling)

Towards Peace

BY ROLAND MILK

I

If the armies of the world
Dropped their guns,
From the very biggest of all
To the smallest ones,
There would be far less danger
Of a stranger
Invading someone else.

II

My suggestion is that soldiers,
And sailors too,
Should all be armed with popguns
Then they couldn't do
The damage that they do at present
And life would be more pleasant.

Field-Marshal, couldn't you have as much fun with a popgun?

Also available from Mandarin Paperbacks

W. C. SELLAR & R. J. YEATMAN

1066 and all that

A book that has itself become part of our history. The authors made the claim that 'All the History you can remember is in the Book' – and for most of us, they were probably right. But it is their own unique interpretation of events that has made the book a classic; the result is an uproarious satire upon textbook history and our confused recollections of it.

'. . . possibly the best thing of its kind ever done. Indeed . . . the *only* thing of its precise kind . . . quotation is hopeless: every sentence clamours for it.'
                                        Observer

W. C. SELLAR & R. J. YEATMAN

And now all this

By the authors of the best-selling classic *1066 and all that*

In *1066 and all that* Messrs Sellar and Yeatman set out to provide a history book to end all history books – and succeeded brilliantly. In this hilarious sequel they turn their satirical pens to geography and general knowledge with equal mastery.

FRANK MUIR and DENIS NORDEN

The Complete and Utter 'My Word' Collection

Thirty years ago Frank Muir and Denis Norden, already highly acclaimed comedy scriptwriters, began to improvise short stories on the BBC radio programme *My Word!*, each of which was designed to offer a (far-fetched) explanation for a well-known phrase or saying. It turned out that they had invented a new comic literary genre. Four volumes of their stories were published: this collection brings together the contents of all of them. Now they have returned to print with a brand new volume of verbal pyrotechnics: *You Have My Word*.

'Consistently brilliant tales'
                    TLS

TOM LEHRER

Too Many Songs
by Tom Lehrer

The most complete collection of the words and music of
the songs by the Harvard mathematician whose subversive wit delighted the 1950s and 1960s and recently
resurfaced in the triumphantly successful revue *Tomfoolery*. Contains 'Be Prepared', 'Poisoning The Pigeons
in The Park' and many other unsavoury favourites.

S. J. PERELMAN

The Most of S. J. Perelman

The Most of S. J. Perelman contains Perelman's best and funniest writing from the period 1930 to 1958. It was first published in 1959 and reissued in 1978 shortly before the author's death in 1979. For most of his writing life Perelman was one of the *New Yorker's* star wits. He also wrote screenplays for the Marx Brothers and for *Round the World in Eighty Days*.

A. P. HERBERT

Uncommon Law

A. P. Herbert, who became Sir Alan Herbert and an independent MP, was a lawyer by training who wrote for *Punch* over four decades. His most famous pieces were the series of fictitious law reports featuring the adventures of Albert Haddock written under the title 'Misleading Cases'. This volume is now being reissued in paperback – a testament to its enduring popularity.

JILLY COOPER
Angels Rush In

Over the past 21 years Jilly Cooper has written a selection of best-selling books, mixing outrageous anecdotes from the lives of her family and friends with shrewd and wicked social satire and criticism. *Men and Super Men* was followed by *Women and Super Women* and then by the devastatingly outspoken bombshell, *Class*; the poignantly evocative *The Common Years*; the indispensable *How To Survive Christmas* and the essential handbook for Nouveau-Rustics, *Turn Right at the Spotted Dog*.

All these and more provide the material for *Angels Rush In*, a rich and sparkling selection made and introduced by the author herself.

'Reading *Angels Rush In* is a bit like spending a day with a delightfully wicked neighbour. Jilly Cooper is snobbish, unfair, unashamedly sentimental and deadly accurate. Nothing is safe from her biting humour.'
                              Today

'An intelligent, waspish, entertaining read'
                              Maeve Binchy

JILLY COOPER

Super Men and Super Women

Jilly Cooper's brilliantly funny guide to the sexes

Whatever their grading, Super Man or Slob, Super Woman or Slut, Jilly submits them all to remorseless scrutiny. In public and private, home, office or bed, none escapes her beady eye – from guardsmen to gigolos, debs to divorcees, stockbrokers to sex-fiends, tarts to Tory ladies.

'Chuckles again, plus huge belly laughs, from Jilly Cooper ... brash, bawdy, witty and, in parts, nastily true ... Super Cooper'
Sunday Telegraph

A Classic paperback double volume which includes two best-sellers: *Men and Super Men* and *Women and Super Women*.

A Selected List of Humour Available from Mandarin

While every effort is made to keep prices low, it is sometimes necessary to increase prices at short notice. Mandarin Paperbacks reserves the right to show new retail prices on covers which may differ from those previously advertised in the text or elsewhere.

The prices shown below were correct at the time of going to press.

All these books are available at your bookshop or newsagent, or can be ordered direct from the publisher. Just tick the titles you want and fill in the form below.

Mandarin Paperbacks, Cash Sales Department, PO Box 11, Falmouth, Cornwall TR10 9EN.

Please send cheque or postal order, no currency, for purchase price quoted and allow the following for postage and packing:

UK	80p for the first book, 20p for each additional book ordered to a maximum charge of £2.00.
BFPO	80p for the first book, 20p for each additional book.
Overseas including Eire	£1.50 for the first book, £1.00 for the second and 30p for each additional book thereafter.

NAME (Block letters) ....

ADDRESS ....

....

....